T0418207

BOOK

OF

MAGIC

AND THE

OCCULT

A VISUAL HISTORY

NATIONAL GEOGRAPHIC
WASHINGTON, D.C.

Legends have long told of powerful magicians, such as the sorceress Circe in Greek myth, seen here in a 1910 painting by Frederick Stuart Church.

During the 15th century, when Prague's astronomical clock was installed, astronomy and astrology intermingled with each other—evinced by the clock's use of zodiac constellations.

CONTENTS

As ancient Egyptians completed embalming rituals to ensure a good afterlife, they looked to Anubis, the jackal-headed god of funerary practices.

> Corinthian aryballos (perfume vase), circa 620–590 B.C.

Magical Living

The modern age has ushered in a surge of interest in all things magic. This new affinity is an important marker of both our cultural state and our relationship with the planet. Historically, the Western world has prided itself on a rational approach, which on reflection many see not as wrong but rather as unsatisfyingly thin and cold. Magic places us back into an enchanted universe, in which human actions—protective spells, curses, ritual acts, or forms of divination—can change the state of our lives.

Of course, the universe can influence us, too: through the movement of planets and stars, or by the actions of angels, demons, human ancestors, or spirits of the land. But in living magically, we have fostered a direct relationship with the world around us, for good and for ill—and often with a moral or ethical dimension. Through that prism, we are able to glimpse the intelligence and liveliness of the planet—a place where trees communicate, animals are social and clever, and fungi enliven the soil. These elements come together to form a living, breathing planet that will care for us if we look after it.

Surprising as it may be to contemplate, most people have at some point lived in an enchanted universe. While not always benign, it is by turns a frightening, wonderful, nurturing, and surprising place. Magic helps us tackle these mysteries by posing questions, rather than finding any fixed or final answers.

Western rationalists ask of magic: Does it work and is it true? A better question might be: Does it help us live well and care for the world around us? Magic is not the opposite of science but blends into it: We now know that the efficacy of the drugs we take depends on our psychological attitude and degree of positive thinking.

This rich and inspiring book will take you on a tour of magical practices across time and space. You'll meet Ice Age artists whose wonderfully realistic cave paintings may have helped guarantee a successful hunt. You'll walk through ancient cities laid out to mirror the movement of the sun and moon so that daily life was influenced by celestial bodies. You'll discover that modern astronomy would not have been possible without the thousands of observations made by ancient astrologers, chemistry would not have come to be without alchemy, and medicine would have been impossible in the absence of the magical herbalist.

Particular cultural traditions created their own forms of magic, including the Jewish amalgam of Middle Eastern practices and the diviners and sorcerers of West Africa. For many, the dead are still members of society, such that ghosts and ancestors need to be avoided or accommodated.

People have fallen into error through magic, convinced that Atlantis sank beneath the waves or, much more destructively, that an old lady in the village was a witch. Deception can also be delightful, as enormously long traditions of stage magicians have shown.

This book illuminates all this history and more, offering up an enchanted universe. Anyone entering it will be changed by the encounter in ways impossible to predict.

—Chris Gosden, School of Archaeology,
University of Oxford

Visions of the magical and the esoteric have inspired art for millennia, including this 1914 painting of a "mystic meeting" by Italian artist Vittorio Zecchin.

What Is Magic?

Magic, as an idea and as a practice, is as old as cave paintings and as new as social media. It is an expression of a fundamental human need to reach beyond the boundaries of the everyday world and connect to a deeper reality.

Magical beliefs and magical rituals are found in every culture around the world and in every era of history, including the current moment. Modern observers might decry the beliefs as irrational, but the search for magic reflects the perfectly reasonable understanding that the universe has mysteries yet to be explained.

Western scholars once placed magic on the bottom rung of a historical ladder, in which cultures progressed tidily from magic to religion to science. Today's historians know that this condescending view ignores the fact that magic, religion, and science evolved side by side, with considerable overlap. Both magic and religion connect their believers to a sacred sphere: a world of wonder beyond the mundane.

But magic, in general, is more individualistic—less concerned with binding a community together according to a moral purpose and more interested in manipulating supernatural forces for specific ends. Religions look to a god, or gods, and employ a hierarchy of authorities, universal rituals, and formal ceremonies. Magic practitioners, though they may recognize a god, tend to labor toward private ends with a diverse array of techniques.

But the boundary between magic and religion is frequently blurred, with some religions borrowing from magic's knowledge base and some magical traditions incorporating religious themes and rituals. And much of today's science has its roots in disciplines such as astrology and alchemy.

Magic, as a concept, is broader than spells and potions; it includes the belief that some people, animals, lands, and objects are inherently powerful. In this context, it overlaps not just with religion but with mythology, legends, and folktales. Unicorns and centaurs are legendarily magical creatures—but then again, so are cats, in some traditions. The notion that mystical islands lay just over the horizon lured many an explorer into the oceans. Enchanted swords, standing stones, and gems appear not just in fiction but in historical accounts.

Magic long ago made its way into theater and popular culture. Stage magicians enthrall audiences with mystical lingo along with their sleight of hand. Novels, games, and movies capitalize on the eternal appeal of elves and magi.

Belief in magic has always been a creative force, inspiring artists to imagine the unseen. Decorated scrolls, carved amulets, illuminated bestiaries, and more are testaments to the influence of magical ideas on human culture. The unknown carver who crafted the prehistoric Lion-Man from mammoth bone and the CGI artist who builds a dragon from pixels are connected by a long and still unbroken tradition.

This book explores that tradition in its many forms—some arcane and some familiar, across time and around the world. Readers may recognize a bit of themselves in the characters in these pages, who looked at the daylight world and asked what wonders lay in the shadows. ▪

In tales of Aladdin, magic in the form of a jinni helps him woo the princess Badr al-Budur.

HISTORY OF MAGIC

Whether to honor the dead, to see the future, or to seek protection, the impulse to understand and control the world's many secret powers through magical means goes back millennia. The events here represent just a fraction of the milestones in our ever evolving magical story.

44,000 YEARS AGO
Rock art created in modern-day Indonesia reveals a hunting scene that may contain spiritual depictions of several enigmatic figures that appear to combine human and animal features.

> 40,000 YEARS AGO
Ancient humans in modern-day Germany carve a mammoth-ivory sculpture combining the features of a lion and a human. This "Lion-Man" is among Europe's oldest archaeological evidence of organized belief systems.

∧ 9600 B.C.
Construction begins on Göbekli Tepe in Turkey, considered humankind's oldest known place of worship.

30,000 YEARS AGO
The ocher-covered body of a young man is buried in a cave in modern-day Wales alongside rods of mammoth ivory, which some scholars interpret as proto-magic wands.

∨ 90,000 YEARS AGO
Ancient humans in what is now Israel are interred in a cave, providing some of the oldest known evidence of deliberate burial and setting the stage for burial-related rituals—many of which indicate strong magical beliefs.

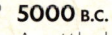

∧ 12,000 YEARS AGO
Ancient humans in present-day Jordan bury a fox skull and other remains in what is now interpreted as a possible shamanic ritual.

5000 B.C.
A cattle-herding society in what is now Egypt builds Nabta Playa, known as "Stonehenge in the Sahara" and one of the world's oldest astronomical sites.

∨ 2780 B.C.
The first steplike pyramids rise in Egypt, beginning centuries of pyramid construction.

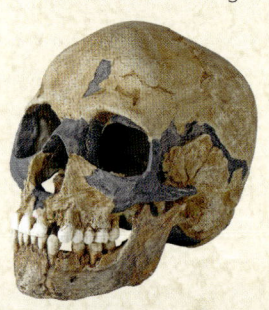

∨ 2500 B.C.
Ancient Britons begin bringing stones to the site we now call Stonehenge, beginning a multicentury construction project that yielded one of today's most iconic and spiritually significant megalith sites.

∧ 1300 B.C.
A fortune teller in China roasts a turtle shell over an intense fire until cracks form on its surface: the earliest record of China's elaborate divination ceremonies.

3RD CENTURY B.C.
A Greek papyrus mentions magi, a group of influential Persian scholars and sages who became synonymous with the Zoroastrian faith. Greek records and fascination with magi during this period lead to the word "magic."

∧ 601
Pope Gregory encourages Catholic missionaries in Britain to reconsecrate pagan temples and reframe pagan holidays as Christian celebrations.

∧ 850
Abū Ma'shar, a renowned astrologer on the court of the Abbasid Caliphate in modern-day Iraq, publishes *Kitāb al-mudkhal al-kabīr* (*The Great Introduction*), a key medieval astrological reference.

1100 B.C.
Babylonian scholar Esagil-kin-apli compiles an extensive diagnostic handbook for medical diviners, one of the earliest and most thorough references of its kind.

∨ 1300 B.C.
Egyptian priests compile the Chapters of Going Forth by Day, a collection of magical spells—now known as the Book of the Dead—meant to usher the dead into the afterlife.

1ST CENTURY A.D.
Roman natural philosopher Pliny the Elder compiles *Naturalis Historia (Natural History)*, a groundbreaking encyclopedia that describes various mythical creatures and magical practices.

∧ 6TH CENTURY B.C.
Two silver scrolls containing a Hebrew blessing are placed in a tomb outside Jerusalem—protective amulets that preserve the earliest known Torah scripture.

∧ 701
The Japanese administrative state restructures to include a special office focused on divination called the Onmyōdō: the way of yin-yang.

∧ 1256–1258
King Alfonso X commissions the Spanish translation of the Arabic astrology book *Ghayat al Hakim (The Aim of the Sage)*. The translated volume, known as the *Picatrix*, becomes an authoritative source in Europe on astrological magic.

∧ 1325
The Mexica people found Tenochtitlan, the political capital and metaphysical center of the Aztec empire.

∨ 1584
To stop what he considered to be baseless witchcraft prosecutions, Sir Reginald Scot publishes *The Discoverie of Witchcraft*, one of the first Western texts that methodically compiled the methods behind magic tricks.

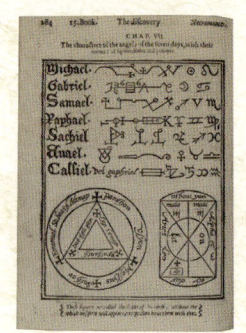

1845
French magician Jean-Eugène Robert-Houdin (1805–1871), considered the father of modern magic, opens a purpose-built magic theater in Paris.

∨ 1000
A Native American group known as the Mississippians rapidly builds out Cahokia, a nearly 4,000-acre ritual complex that becomes the largest pre-Columbian settlement north of Mexico.

1486
A Dominican friar writes *Malleus Maleficarum (Hammer of Witches)*, a tract that condemns witchcraft and lays out how to torture witches and try them in courts of law. The document helps stoke centuries of hysteria throughout Europe and North America, leading to the deaths of some 50,000 people by the end of the 18th century.

1791
Vodou priests and priestesses from across what's now Haiti gather to plot a rebellion against the colonial regime. A week later, thousands of rebels led by Toussaint-Louverture torch plantations and kill hundreds of colonizers in the Americas' largest and most successful uprising of enslaved people.

∨ 1555
The French astrologer and physician Michel de Nostredame (1503–1566) publishes *Les Prophéties (The Prophecies)*, an infamous collection of prophecies that captivated Renaissance Europe.

1896

French magician and inventor Georges Méliès releases "Le Manoir du Diable" ("The House of the Devil"), a three-minute short about a devil inhabiting a medieval castle that is considered the first horror film.

1899

A vaudeville producer begins to promote Hungarian-American magician and escapist Harry Houdini, largely on the strength of a "Metamorphosis" escape routine that Houdini performed with his wife, Bess.

1939

Russian-American immigrant Gleb Botkin forms the Church of Aphrodite, the first pagan group recognized as a religion by a modern state.

1954

British author Gerald Gardner publishes the book *Witchcraft Today*. In it, he claims to have been part of an underground witch cult that had survived centuries of persecution, sparking a new religion called Wicca.

1971

American philosopher David Spangler publishes *Revelation: The Birth of a New Age*, compiling the core tenets of New Age philosophy.

1875

Russian spiritualist Helena Blavatsky and American author Henry Steel Olcott found the Theosophical Society in an attempt to merge science, religion, and philosophy, ushering in the first large-scale occult movement.

2012

A human rights group in Tanzania estimates that from 2005 to 2011, 3,000 people in the country—largely older women and people with albinism—were killed in the face of witchcraft accusations.

1941

American magician Gloria Dea performs at Las Vegas's El Rancho Hotel—the first magic act ever presented in Las Vegas, the modern epicenter of stage magic.

1848

New York sisters Margaret, Kate, and Leah Fox tell their neighbor that ghostly raps on the walls and furniture of their room could answer questions they posed. The Fox sisters' "spirit rapping" performances help spark the Spiritualism movement.

1909

British occultists Arthur Waite and Pamela Colman-Smith publish the first modern deck of tarot cards, known today as the Rider-Waite deck.

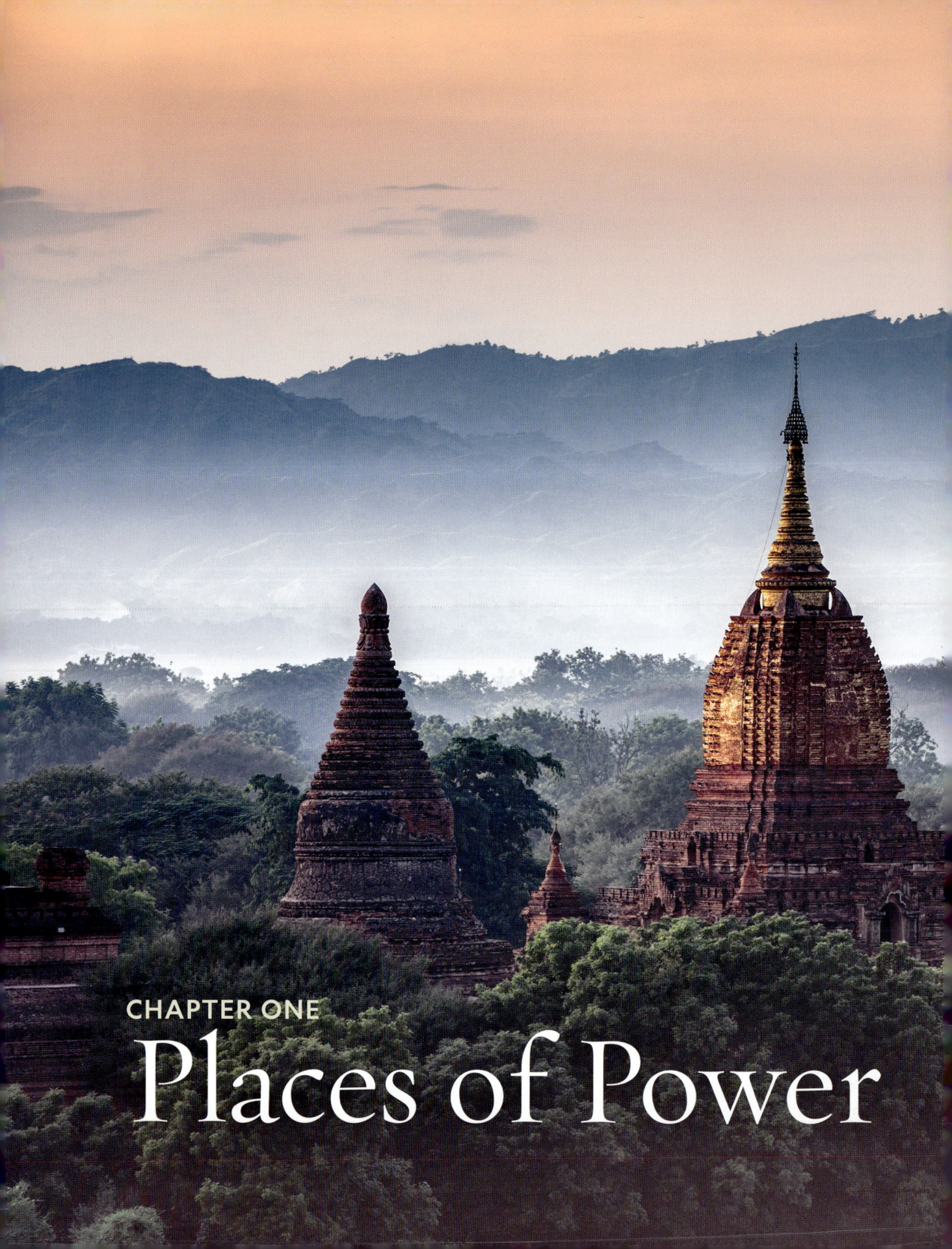

CHAPTER ONE

Places of Power

From the 11th to the 13th centuries, the temple city of Bagan (in modern-day Myanmar) was the spiritual capital of the Pagan kingdom.

The Birth of Magic

Unearthing History & Lore

Some places on Earth, both natural and built, seem possessed of a certain preternatural energy—one that suggests magical beliefs once thrived there. The signs may be subtle: bones arranged in ritualistic patterns or mysterious paintings daubed on ancient cave walls. Some evidence is more overt: monumental stones erected in intentional, if inscrutable, patterns. Such places can hold an inexplicable eeriness, engendering a sense that we're in the presence of something larger than ourselves. Even if for just a moment, they can connect us with something deeper and stranger than we're used to encountering in our everyday lives.

That moment of connection represents the calling card of magic: a break in the natural world order, or a moment that disrupts the expected. Traces of magical belief are evident everywhere, from the Neolithic proto-city Çatalhöyük—among the world's oldest large settlements, founded some 9,000 years ago in what is now Turkey—to the ritual sites of Mesoamerica, including the bloodstained temples in the 14th-century A.D. Aztec capital Tenochtitlan. In the ruins of these cities and many places in between, we can catch glimpses of the world people once knew and infer what motivated them to erect monuments, sanctify lands, and build new societies. In other words, their efforts and intentions imbued the places they left behind with a kind of magical power.

The world bears many examples of such places: some ancient, some modern, some legendary, but all historically significant. They are remarkable for the hold they maintain on our curiosity and beliefs. And together, they offer a window into humanity's fascination with all things magical: a pursuit that has spanned the length of human history. ■

∧ Limestone figurine found in Çatalhöyük

The Aztec goddess Coatlicue, both creator and destroyer. This statue was buried in Mexico City by Spanish invaders and rediscovered in 1790.

PLACES OF POWER

There's no doubt about it: certain destinations evoke an otherworldly feeling. A sacred site may radiate religious and spiritual beliefs that remind us it was built for a purpose that reaches beyond the physical realm. Or we may be drawn toward mysteries that prove some things are still inexplicable, even in the face of modern science.

From impossibly balanced stones to long-lost cities to indecipherable cave drawings, here are some of the world's most magical places.

5 HOPEWELL CEREMONIAL EARTHWORKS
Huge geometric mounds of earth along tributaries of the Ohio River showcase the Hopewell culture's mastery of astronomy, in service of building a vast complex for important rituals. (p. 48)

1 INISKIM UMAAPI MEDICINE WHEEL
Medicine wheels, sites of profound ritual importance to Indigenous groups in North America, go back millennia. The oldest dates back 5,000 years, making it as ancient as Stonehenge. (p. 52)

2 WINNEMUCCA LAKE SUBBASIN
Nevada's Winnemucca Lake subbasin contains petroglyphs carved into boulders 10,000 to 15,000 years ago. Pictures of clouds, lightning, and plants show early human efforts to understand nature's power. (p. 26)

6 TENOCHTITLAN
The Aztec, or Mexica, founded their ancient capital city around A.D. 1325. A prophecy from their patron deity, Huitzilopochtli, instructed them to settle where they saw an eagle on a cactus eating a snake. Its ruins are in modern-day Mexico City. (p. 54)

3 PUEBLO SETTLEMENTS
From A.D. 500 to 1300, the ancestral Pueblo built settlements across Colorado, Utah, Arizona, and New Mexico, including ceremonial rooms still used by the Hopi and other Pueblo peoples for rituals and meetings. (p. 51)

4 CAHOKIA MOUNDS
This ritual complex in present-day Illinois stands as the largest pre-Columbian settlement north of Mexico. Its Monks Mound symbolized a connection between earth and the heavens. (p. 48)

7 MALINALCO
Located in central Mexico's Malinalco, the ancient Aztec fortress of Cuauhtinchan, built 500 years ago, features mountain-carved temples used for elite rituals. The site is linked to the Aztec goddess Malinalxochitl. (p. 51)

8 CUSCO
The Inca capital city in southeastern Peru is centered on Coricancha, its most sacred religious site, which once contained a gold-adorned temple dedicated to the sun god Inti. (p. 52)

9 STONEHENGE

With more than 160 stones, Stonehenge, completed around 1500 B.C., is perhaps the world's most famous megalithic site. (p. 35)

10 CARNAC ALIGNMENTS

The world's largest concentration of megaliths stands on the northwestern coast of France. (p. 32)

11 LASCAUX CAVE

This cavern in France, home to more than 600 animal paintings between 16,000 and 19,000 years old, captures a snapshot of ancient humans' everyday—and possibly spiritual—relationship with wildlife. (p. 26)

12 CHAUVET–PONT D'ARC CAVE

Europe's ancient art and spiritual complexity have been preserved in these celebrated caves in France, showcasing early efforts to understand or control natural forces. (p. 22)

13 ÇATALHÖYÜK

Archaeological evidence spanning 2,000 years reveals a life rich in magical rites in one of the world's oldest known large settlements, located in south-central Turkey. (p. 28)

14 GÖBEKLI TEPE

Six millennia before Stonehenge, hunter-gatherers in what is now southeastern Turkey built a city featuring massive carved limestone pillars, once part of the world's oldest known temple. (p. 28)

15 PYRAMIDS AT GIZA

Egypt's celebrated Giza Pyramids were built by the pharaohs Khufu, Khafre, and Menkaure. Khufu's pyramid, started around 2550 B.C., was the largest and possibly the tallest for nearly 4,000 years. (p. 38)

16 NABTA PLAYA

Often called Stonehenge in the Sahara, this site in southern Egypt was built over 7,000 years ago by early cattle herders. Located where a seasonal lake once existed, it may have been an ancient astronomical observatory. (p. 32)

17 KINGDOM OF KUSH

Around 255 pyramids in modern-day Sudan are relics of the ancient Nubian kingdom of Kush. These burial sites for early African rulers hold unexplored chambers that could reveal valuable insights into ancient beliefs about religion, the afterlife, and magic. (p. 41)

18 MOUNT FUJI

In Japan, this mountain is revered as a sacred gateway to the divine, often called a "living god." It is central to Shinto belief, and more than 2,000 sects worship it and perceive ascending it as a spiritual duty. (p. 56)

19 ANGKOR WAT

This 12th-century Cambodian temple complex and the world's largest religious structure was designed to align with celestial events. (p. 56)

20 INJALAK HILL

These natural rock shelters in Australia display an 8,000-year-old painting of the spirit Yingarna, along with images of fish, wallabies, and the Tasmanian tiger. Aboriginal lore often associates caves with spirits like the Nargun, a stone beast that drags victims inside. (p. 24)

21 BUCHAN CAVES

These mystical caverns in Australia hold an ancient limestone maze carved by an underground river. The caves have been used spiritually by the Gunaikurnai people for more than 18,000 years. (p. 24)

PRESERVED IN STONE

Caves & Rock Art

Signs of behaviors that later gave rise to magic flourished throughout the earliest human settlements around the world, notably in the form of symbolic rock art. These images demonstrate an early step toward spiritual belief, rituals, and what we might even call magic. Whether to ensure luck with a hunt, honor ancestors, or explore a realm of spirits, the practice of creating images representing the vast, mysterious powers around them would have given early humans a new—and potent—means of interacting with the world.

The oldest rock art is often found on the walls of caves. A panel of images at least 44,000 years old found on the island of Sulawesi, in modern-day Indonesia, reveals a hunting scene that might contain spiritual depictions: several enigmatic figures that appear to combine human and animal features. Although debate continues over interpretation of these figures, one thing is certain: Such beings didn't exist in flesh and blood. The art reveals humans' ability to conceptualize immaterial beings—whether in this realm or in some kind of otherworld.

France's remarkably rich record of cave art has also fueled speculation over how ancient people related to animals and the magical power they potentially wielded. The Chauvet–Pont d'Arc and Lascaux Caves—located in southern France's Ardèche and Dordogne regions, respectively—preserve astonishing depictions of animal life created between 18,000 and more than 30,000 years ago.

The Cave of the Trois-Frères, in southwestern France's Ariège region, adds to the menagerie—and to early art's spiritual complexity. In the 1920s, French archaeologist and clergyman Henri Breuil made a detailed drawing to record one of the cave's paintings, a work some 13 feet (4 m) off the cave floor that covers about four square feet (0.4 sq m) of a wall of the chamber known as the Sanctuary. The figure in the painting has a humanoid torso but a horse's tail, an owl's eyes, and a deer's antlers. Over the years, it has been interpreted as a sorcerer, a shaman (Breuil's favored idea), or some kind of deity. In any case, the figure may well represent an attempt to reckon with, or even control, the spirits and forces governing the world of the wild.

Rock art correlating with ritual practice has also been found on the other side of the globe. Australian caves preserve early chapters of the great human story, with testaments to the Aboriginal peoples who have lived on the continent for more than 65,000 years. More than 100,000 rock art sites—dating back as far as 17,000 years

The Chauvet-Pont d'Arc Cave holds incredible paintings (shown here in replica) dating back more than 30,000 years.

ago—feature animals, spirits, and figures from the vast, diverse Aboriginal belief system known as Dreamtime.

In southeastern Australia, archaeological evidence suggests that Gunaikurnai people have used the Buchan Caves—a maze of ancient limestone caverns carved out by an underground river—for more than 18,000 years. Among the Gunaikurnai, shaman-like practitioners known as *mulla-mullung* were seen as having the powers to heal and curse.

Sites elsewhere in Australia chronicle interactions with spirits, shedding further light on the origins of belief. A rock monolith called Injalak Hill boasts an 8,000-year-old painting of the revered spirit Yingarna, believed to be the mother of creation who emerged from the ocean. Other colorful imagery shows fish, wallabies, evil spirits, and the now extinct Tasmanian tiger. In some Aboriginal traditions, caves may be inhabited by both good and evil spirits including the Nargun—a stone beast that drags victims into its den.

Other sites around the world demonstrate that rock art could be charged with the presence—and power—of those who came before. The Tsodilo Hills of Botswana, inhabited intermittently by humans over the past 100,000 years, contain some 400 rock art sites with more than 4,000 individual paintings. Many of the images, which are considered to be more than a thousand years old, consist of animals, simplified humans, and geometric patterns. Locals believe that these hills contain the spirits of their ancestors. ■

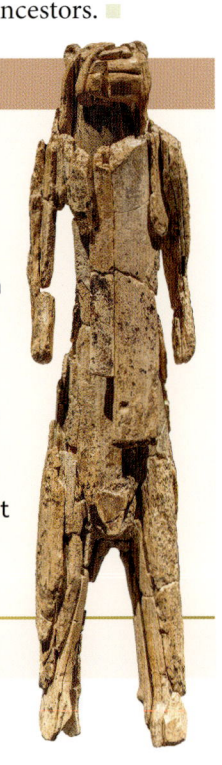

ARTIFACT SPOTLIGHT

LION-MAN

In August 1939, geologist Otto Völzing was digging in the German cave of Hohlenstein-Stadel when he came across hundreds of fragments of a sculpture carved out of mammoth ivory. Further excavations in the 1960s and the 2000s turned up more pieces. Restoration has revealed a stylized, 12.2-inch (31 cm) figurine bearing the head and upper body of a lion but the lower body of a human. Considered one of the oldest types of evidence of belief systems among Europe's ancient humans, the Lion-Man—dating to roughly 40,000 years ago—may represent the melding of the powers of three species: human, lion, and mammoth. It must have been an important figurine. A modern attempt to carve a similar piece with stone tools took more than 400 working hours.

Lion-Man's reconstruction continued as additional pieces were found.

In Aboriginal mythology, Yingarna created and provides for humankind while also holding the power to cause destruction.

ANCIENT ROCK ART

Around the world, ancient humans painted and chiseled their marks on stone to explore and reinforce connections between themselves and the vast wilds around them. Through this art, they might have been attempting to engage with—or even control—the power that animals, weather events, and spirits represented.

More than 600 paintings in France's Lascaux Cave, roughly 18,000 to 21,000 years old, offer detailed hunting scenes that showcase fine anatomical and behavioral details of prehistoric animals. Half a world away from Lascaux, the Winnemucca Lake subbasin in what's now Nevada features petroglyphs several feet across, carved deep into jagged boulders at least 10,000 to 15,000 years ago. Some of the enigmatic patterns may represent clouds and lightning, while others seem to depict plants. Illustrations of humans' early attempts to grapple with the power of nature can be found preserved on stone all over the globe.

Lascaux Cave, France

Ubirr, Australia

Winnemucca Lake, United States

Laas Geel, Somalia

Tswalu Kalahari Reserve, South Africa

Bhimbetka rock shelters, India

TEMPLES & FIGURES

Magic in Ancient Turkish Cities

Six thousand years before ancient humans erected Stonehenge, people in what is now southeastern Turkey (Türkiye) built humankind's oldest known place of worship. Göbekli Tepe, a series of towering limestone pillars arranged in circles, was constructed between 9600 and 8200 B.C. by hunter-gatherers. The stones scattered across the 22-acre (9 ha) site are 16 feet (5 m) high and weigh up to 11 tons (10 metric t) each. Some boast intricate carvings of animals; others show human forms. Other archaeological discoveries have hinted at more mysteries still lurking beneath the surface at Göbekli Tepe.

Because archaeologists initially found no signs of human settlement—fires, trash, or homes—they believed these acres of ringed towers had been an enormous religious complex for ancient mankind. But recent excavation of the site's lowest levels produced evidence of a permanent settlement nearby, leading scholars to reimagine Göbekli Tepe as a young society existing around what may have been the world's first temple.

The site of Göbekli Tepe holds at least 20 mysterious ring-shaped rock formations, and archaeologists have now identi-fied around a dozen other temple-like structures under nearby hills, leading a Turkish tourism official to call the area home to the "pyramids of southeast Turkey."

Magic may also lurk underneath two mounds, both 60 feet (18 m) tall, in another Turkish landscape. Around 7500 B.C., more than a millennium after the stones of Göbekli Tepe were erected, ancient people began to set-tle in the wetland region of Çatal-höyük, in what is now southern Turkey. Today, Çatalhöyük is considered to be among the world's earliest known cities, and archaeological evidence spanning 2,000 years suggests that the lives of its first inhabitants were suffused with magical rites. British archaeologists first uncovered Çatalhöyük in 1958, and scientists have been enthralled by the evidence of rituals and symbolism found there ever since.

To start with, hundreds of clay figurines have been uncovered in the settlements, nearly half of them animals. Although researchers aren't certain whether they served religious, spiritual, or utilitarian purposes, their crude molding has caused

∧ Small figurine from Çatalhöyük

Göbekli Tepe—the oldest known temple—features many T-shaped limestone pillars, often arranged in circles.

The sacking of Troy by the Greeks, depicted in a turn-of-the-15th-century Italian illustration

some to believe the very act of crafting them served as a ritual. One theory posits that the process of molding clay served as a magical rite that could protect a house or bless a hunt. These figures may have been thought to hold the power to grant wishes—perhaps their creators recited those hopes as the figures were shaped. Many of the figurines lack rubbing patterns or long-term wear, and their discovery in refuse piles suggests they were discarded soon after being made. Many, too, appear to have been ceremonially broken, raising the possibility of their use in a pre-hunting ritual.

In foundations of homes in Çatalhöyük, archaeologists have discovered human skulls, sculptures, and other materials purposefully embedded into the building material. Bodies lay buried under the floors of houses while inhabitants lived above. It's likely that both animals and the dead were seen as vessels for special powers that could influence the living.

Both Göbekli Tepe and Çatalhöyük were relatively unknown until recently. Not so the celebrated city of Troy, which has held a grasp on the world's imagination for millennia. The lore that encircles its legend is full of magic, myth, and deception. In Greek myth, the Trojan

queen Hecuba has a prophetic dream that her unborn child—the Trojan prince Paris—will lead to Troy's downfall. Eventually, the city's fate hinges on a kind of magic trick: the now infamous Trojan horse that allows the Greeks to smuggle soldiers into Troy and topple it. In the Euripides tragedy *Orestes*, set in the war's aftermath, the Greek demigoddess Helen—whose elopement with Paris triggered the Trojan War—inexplicably disappears during an attempt on her life. Her vanishing act, one witness conjectures, may be a sign of "magic spells or wizards' arts."

Over the years, researchers have debated the real location of Troy, with theories ranging from the Baltic states to the South China Sea. Today, its remains are believed to be in modern-day Hisarlık, Turkey, founded around 3000 B.C. and inhabited for more than 4,000 years before it mysteriously fell into ruin. ◼

ARTIFACT SPOTLIGHT

TREASURES OF TROY

At the crossroads of Europe and Asia, an epicenter of ancient trade has long anchored the roots of legend. Not far from the Aegean coastline, Hisarlık may have been the setting for the epic Greek battles of the Trojan War as described—thousands of years later—in *The Iliad*, as well as the hiding spot of the demigoddess Helen of Troy. In 1822, Scottish journalist Charles Maclaren used geology and ancient literature to pinpoint Troy's supposed location in Turkey. It took another 50 years for German archaeologist Heinrich Schliemann to begin excavations and unearth a priceless haul of some 9,000 items, including gold cups, silver bottles, bronze daggers, and an array of elaborate headdresses—indicating a tantalizing kernel of truth hiding in the legend of Troy.

Gold fibula (brooch) found in the archaeological city of Troy

STANDING STONES

Powerful Alignments

Across the world, hundreds of sites littered with towering stones known as megaliths continue to pique modern curiosity. Were they built to enable certain magic-adjacent activities like rituals, astronomy, or deity worship? Or were they utilitarian—for tracking time, or burials? Megaliths' stony surfaces shimmer with mystery.

NABTA PLAYA

An ancient society of early cattle herders built Nabta Playa, known as Stonehenge in the Sahara, more than 7,000 years ago. Although the site's stones were found in a vast expanse of sand, the area was once a seasonal lake bed. Built thousands of years before and 700 miles (1,127 km) south of Egypt's Pyramids at Giza, the narrow stone slabs that make up Nabta Playa seem to align with both due north and the direction of sunrise on the summer solstice, possibly making it one of the world's oldest astronomical observatories. The monument is now closed to visitors; a replica stands near the Nubian Museum in Aswan, Egypt.

CARNAC ALIGNMENTS

On the northwestern coast of France, Brittany holds the world's largest concentration of megaliths: the Carnac Alignments, dating back 6,500 years. Its 3,000 stones are a mix of sizes; the largest is 21 feet (6.4 m) tall. (One stone at Locmariaquer, another megalith site close to Carnac, once weighed more than 308 tons [280 metric t] before falling and breaking on the ground thousands of years ago.) They are extraordinary not just for their size and age but for their placement. The Carnac stones stretch in lines for nearly four miles (6.4 km), descending in order of size and ending in a circle. Their abundance may relate to the vast stone resources in the region or to the particular importance ancient inhabitants placed on these structures.

But what was their purpose? Legend has it that the wizard Merlin turned a pursuing army of Roman soldiers into stone, leaving them entombed in the

< Bronze Age nomads installed 1,500 enormous deer stones that still stand in central Mongolia.

Neolithic stones in France's Carnac region—the world's largest collection of megaliths

Few sites have captured the imagination and inspired spirituality like Stonehenge, completed around 1500 B.C.

Carnac structures. Today, researchers posit that the structures could have served as funerary or religious monuments, or as astronomical calendars to guide early farmers in the cycles of planting and harvesting. More recent evidence indicates the monuments were used as places of worship; under Roman rule, depictions of gods were carved into them, while Christians added crosses.

STONEHENGE

In the waning days of the Neolithic period, a group of people in Britain moved enormous boulders weighing between two and five tons (1.8–4.5 metric t) from Wales, 175 miles (282 km) away, to the Salisbury Plain. Even larger specimens, weighing between 22 and 33 tons (20–30 metric t), were sourced nearby. More than 160 stones made up the iconic circle of Stonehenge, completed around 1500 B.C. and today the most celebrated megalithic monument in the world.

Stonehenge's builders have been rumored to be Romans or Druids, but in fact, Stonehenge was built by Neolithic peoples in phases over several centuries, starting around 3000 B.C. Five centuries later, the site's largest standing stones (now known as sarsens) and smaller Welsh-sourced stones (known as bluestones) began to arrive. According to one 2012 estimate, the site's builders installed more than 30 sarsens and a double ring of at least 50 bluestones in less than 150 years,

STONEHENGE'S UNIQUE POSITIONING, WHICH ALIGNS PRECISELY WITH SUNRISE AT THE SUMMER SOLSTICE AND SUNSET AT THE WINTER SOLSTICE, HAS ENCHANTED THE MODERN WORLD.

an impressive pace for a project of this size and scope. In the centuries that followed, Stonehenge's stones were periodically rearranged, with the last major construction on the site—the digging of two rings of concentric pits—wrapping up around 1500 B.C.

The legendary rocks at Stonehenge are not alone in the region: Just 20 miles (32 km) away is Avebury, a henge more than a thousand feet (305 m) across—the largest in the world. But Stonehenge's unique positioning, which aligns precisely with sunrise at the summer solstice and sunset at the winter solstice, has enchanted the modern world. The alignment was used to keep track of the astronomical calendar, but scholars disagree on whether this was for religious or scientific purposes. Adding to the mystery, the remains of 58 people have been found buried there.

The mystique of Stonehenge is an enormous draw for tourists and modern-day worshippers alike. Druids and pagans conduct religious ceremonies at the site on solstices and equinoxes. Some researchers believe it has always been a site of pilgrimage: Nearby burial evidence shows it's possible that people traveled from as far away as the Alps to partake of the healing properties of the stones, even chipping off pieces to wear as amulets thought to cure their ailments. Special powers attributed to the stones would explain why builders went to such lengths to relocate them. A nearby wooden circle may have served in tandem with the stones to represent the temporary and the permanent—the living and the dead.

DEER STONES

In the wilderness of central Mongolia, Bronze Age nomads erected clusters of freestanding boulders starting around 1200 B.C. For 600 years, they continued to install so-called deer stones, which can rise up to about 13 feet (4 m) high, eventually installing 1,500 of them across the steppes of Eurasia. A mythical spirit deer appears on many; these decorative carvings are some of the most ornate examples of megalithic artwork.

While these stones are named for the spirit deer, it's their other carvings that enthrall archaeologists. Images of humans with open mouths indicate that the sites could have been used in shamanistic ceremonies, while evidence of horse sacrifice (perhaps to summon the deer spirit) gives clues to the ceremonies conducted as each stone was erected. Each stone may have represented a leader or warrior in the community. These figures, sometimes replete with tattoos of birds and deer, might have offered the person the protection of a spiritual guardian. ■

Druids, among Stonehenge's rumored builders, have long captivated artists. This 18th-century painting depicts a Druid-inspired masquerade.

THE GREAT PYRAMIDS

Egypt & Beyond

The first pyramid in Egypt, with a steplike appearance, rose from what is now Saqqara in 2780 B.C. Two centuries later, three pharaohs built smooth-sided pyramids as tombs 15 miles (24 km) away, in what is now Giza, creating iconic monuments that still dominate the skyline on the outskirts of Cairo. Some 4,500 years ago, Egyptian rulers filled these massive structures with the necessities and luxuries they'd need to traverse the afterlife. Paired with magical spells and rituals, these goods would ensure they'd be well supplied.

The Pyramids at Giza represent three generations of pharaohs. The largest and oldest belonged to Khufu, a king from the 4th dynasty who began construction of his tomb in 2550 B.C. The completed pyramid covered 13 acres (5 ha) and rose 481 feet (147 m), making it likely the tallest structure in the world for nearly 4,000 years. The second largest pyramid belonged to Khufu's son, Khafre, and the smallest served as the resting place of Menkaure, Khufu's grandson.

Few sites have been as carefully mapped, studied, and scrutinized as the Pyramids at Giza. As technology advances, scientists continue to discover new chambers and passages within the mammoth structures. Even so, the details of their design and construction remain a mystery: How did builders raise the heavy stone building blocks to such heights? How did engineers align the structures almost precisely to Earth's cardinal points?

For centuries, conspiracies have filled in these answers with magical solutions—from alien civilizations to divine intervention—that have tended to downplay ancient Egyptians' engineering ingenuity. But steadily, archaeologists are answering some of these enduring questions. In one stunning discovery, an international team concluded that to build the Great Pyramid, engineers ferried more than 2.3 million blocks of granite and limestone, most of them weighing over two tons, from quarries via a series of canals leading to a now-lost Nile tributary that flowed near Giza.

In the 19th century, the world fell under the spell of a new craze—Egyptology—and theories about the mysterious qualities of the pyramids began to emerge. One claimed that all pyramids, from Egypt to

< Ivory statuette of Khufu

The Great Pyramid of Khufu
is the last remaining ancient
wonder of the world.

In Meroë, Sudan, ancient funerary pyramids are evidence of the powerful kingdom of Kush, which rose to prominence in the eighth century B.C.

AROUND 255 PYRAMIDS—
TWICE AS MANY AS HAVE BEEN
FOUND IN MODERN EGYPT—STAND
IN THE DESERT AS A VESTIGE OF
THE ANCIENT LAND OF NUBIA.

South America, were built by the same group of people, originating from the mythical island of Atlantis. Edgar Cayce, a popular American clairvoyant and a spiritual founder of the New Age movement (see page 286), was among this theory's proponents. Conjectures that the pyramids are evidence of a highly advanced lost civilization—or even the work of aliens—persist today.

In recent decades, 20th-century theories that the pyramids aligned with certain stars have been disproven, but speculation about the connection between the pyramids and the cosmos survives. Ancient Egyptians were careful stargazers, and it's possible that some stars were used to orient the pyramids' builders. This may explain why the base of the Great Pyramid is aligned almost precisely with due north and due south.

"Pyramidology" is an umbrella term that surfaced in the 1850s for ideas that the pyramids hide secret messages, particularly in their measurements. In one influential 1859 book, London publisher John Taylor claimed that the biblical Noah had directed the pyramids' construction. He further claimed that the pyramids' measurements—if converted into units slightly bigger than the British inch—precisely encoded the size of Earth and the length of a year.

A later hypothesis posited that the pyramids were conduits of energy, serving as an ancient plant that powered the region. The idea of pyramid energy was embraced by followers of New Age beliefs, along with the idea of "pyramid power," which suggests the structures possess a mysterious ability to preserve mummies and even sharpen razor blades.

In Sudan, another set of pyramids may hold its own mysteries. Around 255 pyramids—twice as many as have been found in modern Egypt, though much smaller and steeper—stand in the desert as a vestige of the ancient land of Nubia. The rulers of the kingdom of Kush, one of Africa's earliest civilizations, rest in chambers underneath these pyramids, many of which have yet to be explored. These spaces may contain priceless insights into the beliefs of the world's earliest civilizations about religion and the afterlife, as well as how magical ideas seeped into their lives.

MYTHICAL MAPS

Legendary Islands of the Atlantic

From antiquity through the 15th and 16th centuries' age of exploration, mythmakers and European travelers spread tales of mystical isles that contained long-sought treasures or civilizations. Some of these legendary realms made it onto early nautical charts, becoming "phantom islands" that eluded centuries' worth of sailors. Some of these places had connections to real locations, while others have proved to be nothing more than myth.

HY-BRASIL

In Irish myth, the fog-shrouded island of Hy-Brasil, first mapped between 1325 and 1330, was said to magically appear once every seven years, only to disappear upon any adventurer's approach. As cartographers deferred to their predecessors, Hy-Brasil ended up appearing in some 300 different charts through the 1800s. Some have speculated that tales of this mystical place correspond with Porcupine Bank, a shallow seabed in that region.

ANTILLIA

Many of the maps used by 15th-century Spanish and Portuguese explorers contained a mysterious landmass: a large rectangular island some 850 nautical leagues (around 2,900 mi/4,700 km) west of Portugal, known as Antillia. According to legends of the time, as the Umayyad Caliphate conquered Iberia in the early eighth century A.D., a group of Visigothic Christians fled the Muslim conquest by setting sail. These Christians landed at Antillia and built seven cities, each led by one of seven bishops—creating a prosperous, if elusive, island utopia. Though sailors never did find Antillia, the phantom island's name has persisted: As Europeans colonized the Americas, the Caribbean Sea's major archipelago became known as the Antilles.

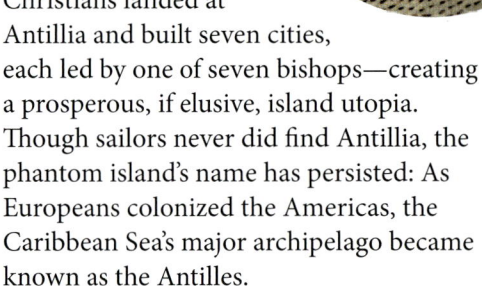

ST. BRENDAN'S ISLAND

Legends of far-off western lands beyond familiar waters entranced European audiences centuries before the age of exploration. One ninth-century tale centers on St. Brendan the Navigator, a sixth-century Irish abbot who set sail with a crew of 14 monks to find the Promised Land of the Saints, a heavenly island paradise. Over seven years, St. Brendan and his crew discovered a series of islands, some inhabited

> Map from *Theatrum Orbis Terrarum,* published in 1570, considered the first modern atlas

by fantastical creatures such as giant sheep, and a fish or whale so massive that St. Brendan and his crew mistook it for a landmass. After their odyssey, the sailors found the promised land before returning home to Ireland. Starting in the late 1200s, mapmakers speculated on the location of St. Brendan's island paradise, placing it anywhere from present-day Madeira to the Azores and Faroe Islands.

THE ISLE OF DEMONS

Starting in the early 1500s, maps of North America began to include a large, ominous island off the coast of modern-day Newfoundland. When boats passed the fog-shrouded island, it reportedly hummed with a strange, unnerving murmur that sounded like human voices.

Cartographic depictions of a huge "Isle of Demons" had disappeared by the 1700s. However, a smaller island went by that name in the early days of French-occupied North America. In 1542, French colonizer Jean-François de La Rocque de Roberval set sail for the New World with settlers including a likely relative named Marguerite de La Rocque de Roberval. As punishment for having an affair with a fellow passenger, Marguerite, her lover, and her servant were marooned on the Isle of Demons. Of the group, only Marguerite survived; she lived there for nearly two years before being rescued by fishermen.

Based in part on Marguerite's account, contemporary scholars have suggested that the real Isle of Demons could be Quirpon Island, off the coast of Newfoundland, or Harrington Harbour, an island in the Gulf of St. Lawrence. The unearthly noises? Most likely seabirds hidden in fog, possibly including the now extinct great auks.

ATLANTIS

No mythical island looms larger than Atlantis, the mighty maritime kingdom said to have been swallowed by the sea in a day and a night. Its first mentions date to the fourth century B.C., in Plato's *Timaeus* and *Critias;* Plato asserts that the "lost isle" existed 9,000 years prior to his own time, "beyond the Pillars of Heracles"—usually understood to mean west of the Strait of Gibraltar. Atlantis was said to have been sent to the depths of the ocean by floods and violent earthquakes when its denizens fell out of favor with the gods after attempting to invade ancient Athens.

In antiquity, some interpreted Plato's tale as authentic history; today, classical scholars treat Atlantis as a myth of Plato's invention, told in part to illustrate Plato's theories of the ideal state, represented by ancient Athens. That said, it's possible that he found inspiration in ancient stories of natural disasters. Between 1600 and 1500 B.C.—more than a thousand years before Plato—a volcano erupted on the Aegean

M. Canaria.

Is: S. Brandano.

Insula Fortunata:

Cabo de No:

In this 17th-century engraving, St. Brendan conducts a Mass on the back of an enormous fish or whale.

The tale of Atlantis helped inspire this haunting 20th-century painting, in which mermaids hoist the remains of sailors swallowed by the waves.

island of Thira, also known as Santorini. The eruption unleashed tsunamis that devastated settlements belonging to the Minoan civilization, perhaps giving rise to the idea of an entire kingdom swept into the depths of the sea.

The story of Atlantis has inspired many fictional islands with idealized cultures in works such as Thomas More's 16th-century treatise *Utopia*. The idea of Atlantis as a real place saw a resurgence in the late 19th century; Ignatius Donnelly's 1882 book *Atlantis: The Antediluvian World* posited that Atlanteans were global seafarers who helped seed all major ancient civilizations. Donnelly's ideas were panned by archaeologists, but early 20th-century occultists including the Theosophists (see page 184) imagined Atlantis as a lost beacon of spiritual perfection. In the 1930s, Nazi ideologues built on these notions to advance the outrageous claim that Atlantis myths recounted a long-lost "Aryan homeland."

IN LEGEND

THE SUNKEN ISLAND OF LEMURIA

In a short 1864 essay, a British zoologist offered an unusual theory about the global distribution of lemurs. Because they were scattered between Africa and Asia, there must have once been a land bridge connecting the two continents; that bridge, he posited, now sat at the bottom of the Indian Ocean. He gave it a name: Lemuria. Like Atlantis, this lost land spurred myths and theories, notably by the occult Theosophical movement, which claimed Lemuria was the home of the mythical "Third Root-Race," a people who once ruled over great civilizations. In the 1960s, scientists agreed that continental drift was the cause for such biodiversity phenomena. Still, the lure of Lemuria continues to draw believers.

This 19th-century illustration imagines what the "lost" continent of Lemuria might have looked like.

FROM THE EARTH

Sacred Spaces of the Americas

With ingenuity and spiritual devotion, Indigenous peoples across the Americas have carried earth and carved stone to build homes and cities with exacting ritual purposes in mind, creating legacies that modern Indigenous groups maintain today.

HOPEWELL CEREMONIAL EARTHWORKS

Eight massive squares, circles, and octagons, made by hand from the earth itself, are spread along the tributaries of the Ohio River. These soil monuments likely served as pilgrimage centers for people who sought connections with the cosmos. Known collectively as the Hopewell Ceremonial Earthworks, they were built between 100 B.C. and A.D. 400 by Hopewell peoples. Many of the mounds were laid out with the same standard unit of measure of 1,054 feet (321 m), revealing a mastery of geometric principles.

One of these structures, the Octagon Earthworks, showcases the Hopewell culture's astronomical skill. The site's main axis almost perfectly aligns with the maximum northern moonrise at the earthworks' latitude, viewable only for a few months every 18.6 years. The walls of the site's octagonal enclosure point toward other notable lunar alignments, such as the maximum northern sunset and the minimum northern moonrise.

CAHOKIA

Centuries after Hopewell's earthworks were laid down, another earthen monument rose from the ground in present-day Illinois. Known today as Cahokia, this ritual complex was the largest pre-Columbian settlement in the Americas north of Mexico.

Cahokia was occupied from roughly A.D. 700 to 1350 by a group known as the Mississippians. Starting around 1000, they rapidly laid out a nearly 4,000-acre (1,619 ha) "pilgrimage city" featuring four central plazas aligned with the cardinal directions. At the city's heart stood Monks Mound, an earthwork nearly 100 feet (30.5 m) tall with a base covering nearly 15 acres (6 ha)—the tallest such structure in the Western Hemisphere. At Cahokia's peak, around 1100, archaeologists estimate that it housed between 10,000 and 20,000 people—at least as many as London at the time. But by 1350, the city was largely abandoned for reasons that remain unknown.

< Coyote-shaped tobacco pipe, Hopewell culture

An 1848 illustration of Hopewell Ceremonial Earthworks in Marietta, Ohio

Cliff Palace, a 13th-century ancient Pueblo dwelling built in what's now Colorado, has 150 individual rooms and more than 20 kivas.

PUEBLO KIVAS

Between A.D. 500 and 1300, the ancient Pueblo people built settlements across what is now Colorado, Utah, Arizona, and New Mexico. Some of these settlements' buildings included large, circular structures that were forerunners to the ceremonial rooms known today as kivas, which symbolize the primordial underworld from which Pueblo people believe they emerged. Today, the Hopi and other modern Pueblo peoples use these semisubterranean, elaborately painted chambers for both private rituals and casual meetings.

MALINALCO

Some cave-like spaces were also built high among the clouds. In what is now central Mexico, the town of Malinalco has commanded a view of the surrounding landscape for more than 500 years. The site is associated with the Aztec goddess Malinalxochitl, who, according to legend, was abandoned there by her brother, the sun and war god Huitzilopochtli, because she had practiced witchcraft.

Malinalco's most imposing feature is the archaeological site of Cuauhtinchan, an Aztec fortress city built at the turn of the 16th century in mountain slopes more than 400 feet (122 m) above the modern town. Three of the site's temples were carved into the mountain rock itself, an unusual practice in the Americas. Many Mesoamerican religions hold underground caves as places of emergence, the wombs through which humans were created.

One of these temples is thought to have hosted important rituals for elite Aztec military units, the *cuauhtli* (eagle warriors) and *ocelotl* (jaguar warriors). Initiates would have climbed up 13 stairs—possibly representing the 13 heavens in Aztec belief—and walked through a doorway styled as a serpent's mouth to enter a cave-like shrine within the mountain. Once inside, the initiates likely perforated themselves with thorns, obsidian razors, and eagle or jaguar claws—acts of self-sacrifice that yielded blood offerings for the gods.

∧ Wooden drum, Malinalco

NASCA LINES

The land outside the modern city of Nasca, Peru, preserves monuments to Andean ingenuity and spirituality. Across more than 190 square miles (492 sq km), more than 2,000 gigantic geoglyphs are etched into the ground itself, ranging from straight lines to recognizable creatures such as birds, spiders, monkeys, and even humanoid shapes. These features are thought to have been made between 500 B.C. and A.D. 500 by the region's Nasca people. The glyphs' purpose remains unknown, but they might have served as roadways, ceremonial labyrinths, stages for performances or important rites, or aquifer markers. Regardless, they were clearly monuments of great significance to their creators and still inspire observers of all stripes today, including New Age spiritual seekers.

This spider geoglyph outside Nasca, Peru, spans approximately 150 feet (46 m).

SACRED LANDMARKS

Indigenous peoples throughout North America have also treated natural landmarks as sacred. The Winnemem Wintu, who live in what's now Northern California, trace their origin to a spring on the mountain they call Buliyum Puyuuk (also known as Mount Shasta). Tribes including the Lakota consider a striking butte in modern-day Wyoming to be highly sacred: a place for praying to the Great Spirit and conducting important ceremonies. Often referred to as Bear Lodge or Bear's House among Indigenous peoples, this butte is officially known as Devils Tower, a name tracing back to an 1875 military expedition that surveyed the area while looking into reports of local gold discoveries.

HUACAS

For millennia, Indigenous Andean people in Bolivia and Peru created sacred places and shrines called huacas, which ranged from natural caves and springs to carved rock features and temples. Many huacas were thought to connect the three realms of Andean cosmology: the underworld, the earth, and the sky. The sites were considered living entities full of ancestral wisdom, echoing Andean creation myths of the first humans emerging from the land.

As the Inca consolidated power in the Peruvian Andes during the early 15th century A.D., they incorporated huacas into the Inca state religion. Cusco, the Inca capital, was surrounded by more than 328 huacas, all falling along pathways that originated from a single point: Coricancha, the most important Inca religious complex. Coricancha contained the most sacred huaca of all, a gold-decorated temple dedicated to the sun god Inti. Some of these huacas survive today. ■

SPELLBINDING SYMBOL

MEDICINE WHEELS

Many Native American tribes find spiritual significance in symbols or hallowed spaces known as sacred circles or medicine wheels, whose four quadrants may represent different stages of life, seasons of the year, or aspects of reality. When built as structures, medicine wheels typically consist of a central stone cairn surrounded by at least one outer circle, with the two connected by spokes. The oldest, known as Iniskim Umaapi, has existed in modern-day Alberta, Canada, for 5,000 years—making it as old as Stonehenge and among the world's oldest religious monuments. Medicine wheels across North America are regularly used by Indigenous peoples for ceremonies, prayer, and vision quests; the Siksika (Blackfoot), for example, still use Iniskim Umaapi.

The Blackfoot Confederacy built Calgary's Nose Hill Siksikaitsitapi Medicine Wheel in 2015.

A Catholic convent now stands on the foundations of the main temple of Coricancha.

TENOCHTITLAN
Gods & Temples

In 1519, when Spanish colonizers arrived in what is now Mexico, they encountered a bustling metropolis of more than 250,000 people, far exceeding the size of Europe's cities at that time. This city, known as Tenochtitlan, was the capital city of the Aztec empire and the center of Aztec religious life. Its very existence sprouted from myth and prophecy.

The Aztec (who called themselves Mexica) founded the city in approximately A.D. 1325 in accordance with a prophecy laid down by Huitzilopochtli, the god of the sun and war, and their patron deity. According to legend, Huitzilopochtli told the Mexica to settle on the spot where an eagle could be seen perched on a cactus and eating a snake. The Mexica saw this very sign on an island on Lake Texcoco and built Tenochtitlan there. To grow the

RITES & RITUALS

TEOTIHUACAN

Teotihuacan, an enormous pre-Aztec complex some 30 miles (48 km) to the northeast of present-day Mexico City, is a testament to the vast ritual enterprises of ancient Mesoamerica. Built between the first and sixth centuries A.D., the ceremonial center is aligned almost precisely north-south and features several pyramids that served as ritual landmarks. The city center's northern end is capped with the Pyramid of the Moon; to the south stands the Pyramid of the Feathered Serpent, where the bodies of more than 200 people sacrificed during its construction have been found. To the east sits the far larger Pyramid of the Sun, Teotihuacan's biggest building and the world's third largest pyramid. In 1971, archaeologists discovered a tunnel underneath the Pyramid of the Sun that ended in a cloverleaf of four chambers. These spaces, looted long ago, seem to have held burials or offerings of great importance: Archaeologists found remnants of 17 different dividing walls that once guarded them.

Funeral mask, decorated with turquoise stones and red shells, Teotihuacan

island beyond its natural extent, the Mexica reclaimed land and grew food on *chinampas*, artificial islands made of vegetation, dirt, and mud.

Tenochtitlan was seen as an indomitable "giver of life," a place that sat at the center of the 13 heavens and nine hells of Aztec belief. At the heart of Tenochtitlan stood the Huei Teocalli, the religious and metaphysical center of Aztec life. This structure, also known as the Templo Mayor (Main Temple), stood 90 feet (27 m) tall and consisted of two temples, built atop two stepped pyramids that symbolized sacred mountains. The pyramid on the left symbolized Tonacatepetl, a mountain protected by Tlaloc, the god of rain and fertility. The pyramid on the right symbolized Coatepec, the hill where Huitzilopochtli was said to have been born.

The complex was embellished with intricate sculptures and colorful murals, as well as the blood of sacrificial victims, which left scarlet trails down the Templo Mayor's otherwise gleaming white staircase. These sacrifices—performed by cutting open a victim's chest and removing their heart with a ceremonial knife—were thought to nourish the gods and continually repay them for creating both humans and the world. In the Toxhiuhmolpilia (New Fire Ceremony), a ritual that took place only once every 52 years, a brave warrior was sacrificed at the Templo Mayor to ensure the rebirth of the sun. If the ritual failed, the world as the Aztec knew it would end.

Over nearly two centuries, the Templo Mayor was rebuilt seven times, largely to showcase the Aztec Empire's growing political might. After Spanish colonizers destroyed the temple and the rest of Tenochtitlan in 1521, they built what is now central Mexico City atop it.

∧ This map of Tenochtitlan originally appeared as a woodcut in a letter from explorer Hernán Cortés.

SPIRITS OF NATURE

Sacred Spaces of Asia

It's not uncommon for humans to assign spiritual power to natural spaces. Mountains often hold a sacred allure, and in Japan, Mount Fuji has reigned as the pillar of spiritual belief for at least 2,000 years. It is considered the stairway to heaven, home to ancestors and deities, and a portal to the world beyond this one. One eighth-century poem described the volcano as a "living god," and that's how it continues to be treated today.

According to the dominant Shinto faith, natural landscapes are filled with spirits called *kami*. More than 2,000 religious sects have shrines in the mountain's shadow, including one called Fujiko that specifically worships the mountain and considers climbing it a religious imperative.

Across Myanmar, the distinctive sprawling banyan tree serves as a hub for worship and appeasement of the *nats*, spirits thought to reside in every aspect of nature from rocks to waterfalls. Trees across the country hold colorful shrines dedicated to them— some so old that the trees' roots have grown around them.

Few of Asia's sacred sites inspire more wonder than Angkor Wat. The 12th-century Cambodian complex spans 400 acres (162 ha) and is considered the largest religious structure in the world. Like the pyramids of Egypt, Angkor Wat has inspired rumors about its alignment with the cosmos and messages that might be embedded in its measurements. In fact, the temples were built to align with certain astronomical events. The western entrance perfectly frames the rising sun during the equinoxes and solstices; inside the temples is a passage where devotees could view the twice-annual zenith, when the sun passes overhead without casting a shadow. The complex's engineers may have seen the sun connecting with the temple as an alignment between mankind and the heavens, and the spellbinding effect it provided would have allowed the kings who ruled the Khmer Empire starting in the ninth century to show off their celestial allies. Future kings likely boasted of this connection, allowing them to align their reign with their predecessors' and confirm that power was a divine right.

Other sacred Asian sites are far less traversed than celebrated destinations like Angkor Wat. Whalebone Alley, located on

< Bronze deity, Cambodia, 12th century

Japan's most important spiritual site, Mount Fuji, is worshipped by more than 2,000 different religious sects.

an uninhabited Siberian island in the Bering Sea, may have once offered Indigenous groups a unique pathway into mystical belief. For 601 yards (550 m), dozens of whale bones protrude from the ground in parallel lines. The bones, ranging from whale jaws to ribs, are around 600 years old. A stone road leads to a boulder-filled area with a central hearth.

Soviet archaeologists who discovered the site in 1976 believed it to be a sanctuary for a "secret male union" of whale hunters; today's theory is that the area was once a shrine for local Inuit groups. Flint and artifacts date to the first millennium B.C., meaning the area was inhabited for more than 2,000 years—until its residents moved onto the mainland in the 1900s.

A virgin cradles a unicorn in a 17th-century fresco. Legends claimed that only a maiden could tame the animal.

CHAPTER TWO

Mythical Creatures

Imaginary Beasts

Agents of Power & Chaos

"It has a triple row of teeth, which fit into each other like those of a comb, the face and ears of a man, and azure eyes, is of the color of blood, has the body of the lion, and a tail ending in a sting, like that of the scorpion. Its voice resembles the union of the sound of the flute and the trumpet; it is of excessive swiftness, and is particularly fond of human flesh."

This intimidating beast is the manticore, as described by Roman naturalist Pliny the Elder in the first century A.D. It is just one among thousands of fanciful creatures that populate the myths, legends, folktales, and everyday accounts of cultures around the world. Like other aspects of magical belief, stories of fantastical animals reflect the human need to see into the beyond, to cross the boundary between the visible and invisible worlds. Magical creatures may be thought to embody visiting spirits, human or otherwise. They can be imagined as shape-shifters, changing from human to animal and back again. Often, they are envisioned as hybrids like the manticore, exhibiting the fiercest aspects of frightening real-life animals, such as serpents, birds of prey, or hunting cats. Animals have been thought to be accomplices to witchcraft; tales of their deeds have illustrated lessons in cultures throughout human history. They may be considered agents of chaos or bearers of powerful gifts.

Did people really believe in these beasts? Not all, but many did, couched in in the context of faith, tradition, or scholarship. Greeks and Romans had seen gigantic fossil skulls that fit no living beast. Travelers in the ancient and medieval worlds described giraffes, rhinos, and camels along with griffins and dragons. To them, unicorns were no more improbable than elephants. ■

∧ A crouching porcelain manticore dates from the 18th century.

Huge but gentle, a Persian simurgh carries off three elephants in its beak and claws.

FIERCE GUARDIANS

Mythical Creatures of Mesopotamia

In the fertile lands around the Tigris and Euphrates Rivers, where the first great cities arose around 6,000 years ago, gods, demons, and magical beasts were a recognized part of daily life. The farmers and shopkeepers of Babylon and Nimrud understood that gods lived atop the cities' ziggurats (stepped temples). They knew that supernatural forces—good, evil, sometimes both—visited households and guarded palaces.

These forces frequently took the form of animals or human-animal hybrids, mirroring the power of the dangerous creatures that surrounded Mesopotamians every day: lions, serpents, scorpions, and bulls. Mesopotamian rulers adopted these animals' images to project strength. Reliefs depicted kings slaying lions in hand-to-paw combat. Hundreds of bulls, dragons, and lions paced the tilework of Babylon's Processional Way.

EPIC GUARDIANS

The Mesopotamian epic *Enuma Elish*, at least 3,000 years old, tells how the goddess Tiamat created monsters—dragons, scorpion men, fish men, bull men, and more—to go to war for her. Tiamat's monsters became a part of Mesopotamian culture, living on in story and art. Many represented protection. The *lamassu*, for instance, was an intimidating guardian deity shown in massive sculptures watching over entrances in Assyria. With a lion's body, eagle's wings, and human head (typically square-bearded in Assyrian fashion), it embodied strength, freedom, and intelligence. An Assyrian ruler noted that lamassu, "because of their appearance, turn back an evil person, guard the steps, and secure the path of the king who fashioned them." Ugallu, the lion-headed, eagle-footed storm demon, was also a protector, appearing on many Mesopotamian amulets and reliefs.

Scorpion men and women, frightening as they might have seemed, were also sentinels. They are featured in the epic poem *Gilgamesh*, where they defend the mountain of sunrise. "At its gate the Scorpions stand guard," the epic relates, "half man and half dragon; their glory is terrifying, their stare strikes death into men, their shimmering halo sweeps the mountains

⋀ This ancient Persian lion's-head ornament symbolized power.

Enormous *lamassu* guard the Gate of All Nations in Persepolis in Iran.

that guard the rising sun." Luckily for the hero Gilgamesh, they allow him to proceed on his quest. Mesopotamian cylinder seals show scorpion men battling griffins (lion/eagle hybrids).

The Babylonian dragon, the *mushussu*, could serve as a bodyguard as well. It appears in Mesopotamian art as early as 2100 B.C. Its name means "furious snake," and like its Mesopotamian counterparts, it is a gallimaufry of predatory features, mixing the forelegs of a lion, the hind legs of an eagle, the scales of a reptile, the head of a snake, and a scorpion's sting. The mushussu can be seen in art striding jauntily across the walls of Babylon's Ishtar Gate, seemingly daring anyone to confront it.

DEMON BEASTS

Evil spirits, thought to be responsible for nightmares, illness, or death, also visited in the form of animal hybrids, according to Mesopotamians of the second millennium B.C. and afterward. One such spirit was the

---

THE EPIC OF GILGAMESH

The *Epic of Gilgamesh*, dating to about 2100 B.C., tells a story that is heroic yet deeply human. The poem, inscribed on tablets found in Nineveh and elsewhere in the Middle East, may be linked to a real king of Uruk who ruled in the third millennium B.C. However, the Gilgamesh of legend was much larger than life: a semidivine adventurer who fights and then befriends the wild man Enkidu, kills the Bull of Heaven, and then loses Enkidu to the bitter reality of death. Gilgamesh is shocked to realize that he, too, may die. The story may not be over; new bits of the larger text are still being discovered.

A portion of the tablet inscribed with the *Epic of Gilgamesh*

hideous Lamashtu, daughter of the sky god Anu. The epics recount that she was exiled because of her evil deeds. With the head of a lion or bird of prey, the ears of a donkey, long hair, sharp teeth, and eagle's claws, Lamashtu was said to invade houses and attack pregnant women, children, and babies. An incantation describes her predations: "She intercepts the running youth, she disposes of the hurrying son … she utterly smashes the tiny ones."

To guard against Lamashtu, Assyrians might call on an equally fearful entity, the wind demon Pazuzu. His thin human body, propelled by two sets of wings, sported a scorpion's tail and a horned animal head. With an amulet of Pazuzu to guard them, women in labor could fend off Lamashtu's assaults.

Mesopotamia's magical creatures were powerful precisely because they straddled the border between this world and the one beyond. Neither human nor animal, they linked the present to the mythical past. In this, they foreshadowed marvelous beasts that would appear in later cultures around the world, from dragons to gorgons to unicorns.

∧ Snake-headed and scorpion-tailed, a *mushussu* walks across Babylon's Ishtar Gate.

THE ETERNAL DRAGON

Serpents of Legend

Of all legendary creatures, the dragon surely reigns as the most visceral and universal. Tales and depictions of monstrous serpents, sometimes winged, occasionally fire-breathing, date back more than 3,000 years to Mesopotamia's mushussu (see page 64).

Scholars have proposed diverse theories about the dragon's origin in the human imagination. It may have stemmed from the discovery of dinosaur fossils by ancient excavators. Or perhaps it reflects a deep-rooted fear of dangerous predators, such as snakes and predatory birds, burned into the human brain as an evolutionary defense.

Whatever its roots, the dragon has an astonishing reach in world culture. In its most basic definition—a huge, predatory serpent—it appears in myths and legends from Australia and New Zealand to China, Korea, and Japan, from ancient Assyria and Egypt to North America and Europe. The enormous Rainbow Serpent, with its daggerlike teeth, dates back at least 6,000 years in Australian art. Greek myths tell of Typhon, son of the gods Gaea and Tartarus, who has a hundred snakelike heads and "blares fire" from his eyes and mouths. The Cherokee Uktena, a giant, crested snake, was said to live in remote pools and mountains. The divine Quetzalcoatl, of Aztec lore, was a feathered serpent with powers over life and death. Most familiar to us today are the dragons of two disparate cultures: ancient China and medieval Europe.

CHINESE DRAGONS

Nowhere is the dragon more important than in Chinese culture; archaeologists have unearthed dragon figures from tombs more than 6,400 years old. In China, the dragon is considered powerful but beneficent, a companion to kings and heroes. Sinuous, scaled, and horned, it incorporates the features of multiple animals. In the words of Han dynasty writer Wang Fu, "The dragon's horns resemble those of a stag, his head that of a camel, his eyes those of a demon, his neck that of a snake, his belly that of a clam, his scales those of a carp, his claws those of an eagle, his soles

< Head of Quetzalcoatl from the Pyramid of the Feathered Serpent, Teotihuacan

Chinese dragons, as shown here on a silk tapestry, were sinuous and horned.

St. George dispatches a winged dragon in this 15th-century painting.

those of a tiger, his ears those of a cow." Some accounts portray dragons holding valuable pearls below their jaws.

Unlike many of their Western counterparts, Chinese dragons rarely breathe fire, and they are associated with the positive benefits of rain and clouds, lakes and rivers. According to one Qing dynasty account, a lethargic dragon could be prompted to end a drought by throwing tiger bones in its pool. The dragon and the tiger would then fight and stir up a storm.

In many tales, dragons befriend or even marry humans, breeding powerful children. They are particularly associated with the Chinese imperial family; until the abdication of the last emperor in 1912, rulers sat upon a richly decorated dragon throne in the Forbidden City. While emperors reigned, commoners were banned from displaying dragons on any ordinary article of clothing.

EUROPEAN DRAGONS

Dragons have deep roots in Western cultures as well. Greek historian Herodotus confidently stated that winged serpents lived in Arabia, guarding frankincense crops. Hipparchus placed a dragon in the sky as the constellation Draco. And in Arthurian legend, Merlin the magician convinces King Vortigern to dig beneath the unstable foundations of his tower to discover two fire-breathing dragons.

Medieval Christian allegories often employed dragons as symbols of sin and greed, murderous beasts sitting atop hoards of gold and jewels. Probably the best known of these creatures was the unfortunate reptile who confronted England's patron saint, St. George. According to legend, the dragon was demanding human sacrifices from a king in Libya, and one day the lot fell to the king's daughter. George, coming across the scene, slew the dragon in exchange for a promise by the Libyan ruler to baptize his people.

DRAGONS AROUND THE WORLD

Fire-breathers or venom-spitters; four-legged, two-legged, or legless; small enough to fit in a teacup or enormous enough to spawn earthquakes: Dragons may be the most malleable of magical creatures. These fantastical interpretations of snakes are slender, fanged, scaly cousins to mythical sea serpents and recur across many cultures. Some scholars consider the Egyptian deity Apep to be an early version of the dragon theme; an enormous serpent, Apep was a chaotic force who waged constant war on the sun god Re. Chinese dragons were also serpentine, though they typically had four legs with five-clawed feet. Dragons could sometimes turn into humans and vice versa. The Norse dragon Fafnir, venomous though not fire-breathing, began its life as a dwarf but became a dragon to guard its treasure hoard.

Winged dragons more commonly appear in medieval cultures. According to the Renaissance Italian naturalist Ulisse Aldrovandi, "winged dragons flying through Africa beat enormous animals such as bulls to death with their tails." Wyverns, often seen in heraldry, were a kind of two-legged dragon with a barbed tail. And thanks to the unforgettable Smaug, one of the villains in J. R. R. Tolkien's *The Hobbit*, a large, winged, fire-breathing, treasure-clutching monster is today's dragon of choice.

∧ VIETNAMESE EWER
This 15th-century Vietnamese ewer was filled through the dragon's tail.

∧ CLOSE HELMET
A winged dragon adorns a French close helmet, 1630.

PECTORAL ORNAMENT >
This double-headed serpent, an Aztec pectoral ornament, was probably worn during ceremonies.

< DRINKING VESSEL
A dragon's body forms the bowl of a wooden Norwegian drinking vessel.

< COAT OF ARMS

The coat of arms of Milan's Visconti family features a man-eating, dragon-headed serpent.

TANIWHA >

This Maori jade ornament is in the form of a coiled *taniwha*, a serpentine sea monster.

< MING VASE

A maned dragon flies through clouds on a Ming dynasty vase.

< MUSHUSSU

A *mushussu* looms over a temple on a Babylonian carving from the 12th century B.C.

< KOREAN EWER

Dragon and turtle merge in a Three Kingdoms–era Korean ewer.

THERIANTHROPES

Enduring Creatures of Greece & Rome

Classical Greek culture was a wellspring of magical creatures. The centaurs, gorgons, harpies, sphinxes, and other entities of Greek myth and literature took hold in the collective consciousness of other lands and lived on in Roman and medieval European stories, as well as modern popular culture.

Many of these beasts were therianthropes: human-animal hybrids. Such figures can be seen in the earliest human artwork (see page 22) and appear on tombs and avenues in ancient Assyria and Egypt (see page 62). In the hands of the great classical writers, who absorbed some of their stories during Middle Eastern travels, they took on new lives and complicated histories.

CENTAURS

Centaurs are perhaps the most recognizable example of the human-animal amal-

gam. In modern depictions they're often shown as benevolent teachers, but in ancient Greek stories, most centaurs were brutish. According to legend, the first centaurs descended from Ixion, the thuggish king of Thessaly, whose son Centaurus mated with the wild mares of Thessaly's Mount Pelion. Typically, but not always, male, these offspring had human torsos atop equine bodies.

Centaurs were the frat boys of Greek legend, dedicated to alcohol, fighting, and lust. The centaur Nessus, for instance, met his end for assaulting Deianeira, Heracles's wife, as he carried her across a river. A few did transcend their bestial natures. Perhaps the most famous is Chiron, healer and tutor to heroes including Achilles. The Greek poet Hesiod attributes various wise sayings to the centaur, including, "Decide no suit until you have heard both sides speak." It is Chiron (or in some accounts, another wise centaur, Pholus) who the gods place in the heavens as the constellation Centaurus.

HARPIES & GORGONS

Like other legendary monsters, harpies and Gorgons borrowed features from predatory birds and venomous snakes. But

< Hybrid creatures glare from an Italian column.

The centaur Chiron schools Achilles in an 18th-century painting.

The painter Caravaggio used his own face as a model for this portrait of the beheaded gorgon Medusa.

they weren't always villains. According to Hesiod, the original harpies were two female spirits, descended from the ocean, who embodied storm winds. Named Aello (Storm-swift) and Ocypetes (Swift-flier), "on their swift wings [they] keep pace with the blasts of the winds and the birds; for quick as time they dart along." In later tales, their birdlike beaks are employed for vengeance, tormenting the impious King Phineus by snatching food from his hands before he can eat. By Roman times, legend had evolved to focus on three harpies, and they had become fully hideous (a fact not lost on modern commentators, who have noted the sexist implications of the word today). According to Virgil's *Aeneid:* "bird-bodied, girl-faced things they are; abominable their droppings, their hands are talons, their faces haggard with hunger insatiable."

Similarly dreadful, the Gorgons were a trio of snake-haired women—Medusa, Stheno, and Euryale—who lived in the far reaches of the ocean. In some descriptions, they also have wings and claws. Medusa's appearance was so terrifying that to look on her was to turn to stone.

Of the three, only Medusa was mortal, and it was she whom the hero Perseus was able to slay as she slept. In some stories, the unfortunate Medusa became a Gorgon through no fault of her own: The angry goddess Athena transformed her from an ordinary woman after she'd slept with Poseidon in one of Athena's temples. Perseus was able to defeat her because he "looked at her ghastly head reflected in the bright bronze of his shield" as a way to avoid her petrifying gaze. After the hero killed the Gorgon, from her neck sprang Poseidon's sons, the man Chrysaor and the winged horse Pegasus. Medusa's gruesome countenance lived on for centuries as the gorgoneion motif in Greek art and weaponry, decorating temples, dishware, and shields.

> ACCORDING TO HESIOD, THE ORIGINAL HARPIES WERE TWO FEMALE SPIRITS, DESCENDED FROM THE OCEAN, WHO EMBODIED STORM WINDS.

THE MINOTAUR

Not a race of creatures but a unique human-animal hybrid, the Minotaur is sometimes said to represent the animalistic impulses hidden in the maze of the human heart. According to Greek myth, the Minotaur was the child of Pasiphae (wife of Crete's King Minos) and a snow-white bull. With the body of a man and the head of a bull, the brutish creature was imprisoned in the center of a labyrinth. Every nine years, it demanded a sacrifice of seven young men and seven maidens. Greek hero Theseus was able to kill it with the aid of Minos's (human) daughter Ariadne before escaping the labyrinth and eventually ruling the city of Athens.

Greek oil flask in the shape of the Minotaur

MEDIEVAL BEASTS

Griffins, Basilisks & Unicorns

Europeans of the Middle Ages have bequeathed a marvelous array of legendary beasts, immortalized in scholarly texts and on the pages of illuminated manuscripts, to world history. The era seems to have been particularly rich for lovers of animal lore; after all, everyday citizens lived amid farm animals and their predators. Clerics immersed themselves in classical texts, which combined stories of dragons and unicorns with travelers' tales of equally exotic antelopes and giraffes. The church then employed these creatures to deliver moral lessons.

GRIFFINS

Griffins were said to combine the physical features of hunting beasts with a dragon's lust for treasure. The medieval encyclopedia *Hortus Sanitatus (The Garden of Health)* describes them this way: "The grype [griffin] is both bird and beast and it hath wings and feathers and four feet and the whole body like the lion, and the head and forefeet and wings be like the eagle." Medieval writers made much of griffins' size and strength. According to Sir John Mandeville, "One griffon [*sic*] there will bear, flying to his nest, a great horse ... or two oxen yoked together." But they were known for more than their ferocity. Medieval English scholar Alexander Neckam observes that "griffons [*sic*] are said to constantly dig up gold, and to delight in the inspection of this metal. Because there is no scope for gain, they are not said to be charged with the crime of covetousness."

BASILISKS

According to classical Roman legend, basilisks were snakes—but not just any snakes: Their glance could kill, and their very presence scorched the earth and polluted

< An antelope with its horns entangled in a bush

> A griffin raises a taloned foot in this medieval Sicilian mosaic.

Red-eyed basilisks flank the Basel coat of arms.

the winds. According to many medieval writers, however, the basilisk had an unlikely nemesis. "According to reports, the weasel kills this serpent," the German philosopher Albertus Magnus observes. "When local inhabitants find themselves overwhelmed by a multitude of basilisks, they let loose weasels into the serpents' dens; the serpent tries to escape, but in the end the weasel slays it." He adds dryly, "If this account is true it seems to be well-nigh miraculous."

UNICORNS

The unicorn—a deer- or horselike creature with a single horn—appears in stories across many cultures. Early writers often merged the reported traits of rhinos, onagers, and other real animals to describe the beast. In his *Natural History*, Pliny the Elder writes that in India, there is "a very fierce animal called the monoceros, which has the head of the stag, the feet of the elephant, and the tail of the boar, while the rest of the body is like that of the horse; it makes a deep lowing noise, and has a single black horn, which projects from the middle of its forehead, two cubits in length." Roman writer Aelian reports the unicorn's ability to counteract poison: "From these horns they make drinking-vessels, and if anyone puts a deadly poison in them and a man drinks, the plot will do him no harm."

By the Middle Ages, the unicorn had come into its own as a symbol of mystery and Christ-like faith in Europe. Though fierce, according to medieval sources, the unicorn could be tamed by the ministrations of a maiden. "It has such strength," writes Isidore of Seville, "that it can be captured by no hunter's ability, but ... if a virgin girl is set before a unicorn, as the beast approaches, she may open her lap and it will lay its head there with all ferocity put aside, and thus lulled and disarmed it may be captured." It was a scene portrayed over and over again in art and tapestry: hunters slaying a recumbent unicorn, often to the shock and sorrow of the maiden.

> ### "FROM THESE HORNS THEY MAKE DRINKING-VESSELS, AND IF ANYONE PUTS A DEADLY POISON IN THEM AND A MAN DRINKS, THE PLOT WILL DO HIM NO HARM."
>
> —Aelian

^ A 15th-century German handwashing vessel in the form of a unicorn

UNICORN IN THE GARDEN

Possibly the best known Western image of a unicorn is "The Unicorn Rests in a Garden." It is one of seven woven wall hangings that make up the Unicorn Tapestries, now in the Met Cloisters in New York. Woven by unknown artists in the Netherlands around 1500, the hangings depict a unicorn hunt in loving detail and may be an allegory of the pursuit of love and marriage. The resting unicorn, which occupies its own tapestry, is a rare scene of a unicorn alone and at peace. Confined but content, it has pomegranate juice (a symbol of fertility) dripping down its chest.

"The Unicorn Rests in a Garden"

MEDIEVAL BESTIARIES

Some of the loveliest and most engaging medieval texts were bestiaries: accounts of real and legendary beasts whose attributes were often allegories of Christian faith. Gospels, psalters, and herbals were also widespread in the Middle Ages, but bestiaries were particularly popular from 1100 to 1300, and they are among the most heavily illustrated of that era's codices.

Many bestiary creatures would have been familiar to their European readers: roosters, hedgehogs, snails, and rabbits, for example. Some, such as giraffes, elephants, and hyenas, were known mainly from travelers' tales. Still others were magical beasts or human-animal blends of legend and fable, including unicorns, dragons, phoenixes, manticores, and mermaids. Some curious bestiary creatures have faded into obscurity: The serra was a gigantic, winged fish that enjoyed racing against ships; the wodewose, a hairy wild man, lurked in the forest.

Bestiaries, like other illuminated manuscripts, were created with enormous care and technical artistry. The pages were typically vellum, animal skin scraped and dried. Scribes hand-lettered the text, while illuminators painted the decorations after sketching them lightly on the page. Gold powder or gold leaf lent brilliance to the page before the illuminators applied the handmade paint. Finally, the artists inked in outlines and highlights.

GRIFFIN >
A griffin and its struggling rider form the letter *s*.

∨ DRAGON & ELEPHANT
A dragon entangles an elephant's feet.

∧ RARE CREATURES
Four rare creatures fill a page from a 13th-century bestiary: a man without knowledge of fire, a man on a crocodile, a centaur, and a man-beast hybrid, Sanrus.

PROPERTIES OF ANIMALS >
This folio on "The Properties of Animals" included beasts real and imaginary.

LION MEETS BEAR
A lion and bear meet in the Ashmole Bestiary.

WEASEL VS. BASILISK
A weasel takes down a basilisk in the Aberdeen Bestiary.

SIREN & CENTAUR
A siren, representing vanity, preens in front of an intrigued centaur.

SEA CREATURES
A literal sea horse swims among other real and imaginary sea creatures.

YŌKAI

Danger & Luck in Japan

With origins in animism, folklore, Chinese tales, and more, Japan's mystical creatures are a spooky, shape-shifting lot. They belong to the diverse collection of beings known as *yōkai*, a group that encompasses monsters, ghosts, spirits, demons, animals, insects, and even uncanny household objects. Some appear in tales going back to the eighth century, but stories of these ambiguous beings flourished in the Tokugawa period, from the 17th to the 19th century and into today's culture, where they star in anime and film.

Before the term "yōkai" became popular, such a creature was known as *bake-mono*, or "changing thing." These entities were said to be found at crossroads, at the water's edge, or in the twilight, emphasizing their in-between natures, existing in two worlds and yet native to neither.

KITSUNE

Kitsune, magical foxes, exemplify this dual nature, appearing as heroes in some tales and tricksters in others. These shape-shifters had long lives and gained power and a new tail for every century they spent on Earth. Nine-tailed kitsune were considered particularly potent visionaries. Helpful kitsune are associated with the rice god Inari, probably because foxes

---

ARTIFACT SPOTLIGHT

CRANE & TURTLE

In Japanese tradition, the crane and the turtle are symbols of longevity. According to one proverb, "Cranes live for one thousand years, and turtles for ten thousand." Accordingly, the animals appear on scrolls, textiles, and carvings to convey health and good luck to the owner. It may seem ironic that they would also appear on weapons, such as an arrowhead (*yanone*) crafted during the 16th century's samurai era. However, this kind of carved weaponry was designed for beauty, not slaughter, and it was probably meant to be an offering at a shrine.

A crane faces a turtle on a samurai arrowhead.

eat the rats and mice that gnaw away at the rice harvest. Less helpful kitsune are deceivers, using their powers to enter women's bodies and seduce men, though an alert observer can spot them by the fox shadow they cast even in human form.

TANUKI

Tanuki are real animals, also known as raccoon dogs. (They are not in fact raccoons, but mammals related to dogs and foxes.) Their counterparts in Japanese lore are also called tanuki, or sometimes *bake-danuki*, monster raccoons. Like kitsune, they are believed to morph into human shape. The eighth-century Japanese text *Nihon Shoki* describes them changing into human form and singing in springtime. Japanese art portrays them as jolly, potbellied creatures, sometimes carrying a bottle of sake. They are often shown with oversize testicles: symbols of prosperity big enough to be slung over the shoulder like backpacks.

KAPPA

Equally tricky but more dangerous are *kappa*, scaly water creatures with tortoise shells and peculiar bowl-like heads that hold their liquid life force. Cause the kappa to spill this liquid, and the creature loses power and may be forced to obey you. Sometimes kappa are pranksters, but they are also known to lure travelers beneath the water to drown them. They can be placated, though, by throwing a cucumber into the water.

^ A cat demon, or *nekomata*, plays the shamisen next to a *kitsune*, or magical fox, on an Edo-period scroll.

ANIMAL SPIRITS

Power & Trickery in the Americas

Hundreds of Indigenous nations span North America, with histories going back thousands of years. Their traditional myths vary widely, but themes of hidden power within the natural world emerge across cultures. For many Native American peoples, the winds or the mountains might at times appear as humans or animals, and the smallest stones could hold meaning.

As in other cultures, the legendary creatures that appear in Native American histories personify the strength of dangerous animals seen every day—eagles, bears, and snakes—as well as the smarts of crafty beasts that sometimes outwit humans, such as coyotes and ravens. They can shift their forms between animal and human and may display the characteristics of both, as it suits them.

COYOTE

Clever and powerful, foolish and funny, the Coyote figure appears in many Native American legends, particularly in the southwestern United States. (In Navajo tradition, Coyote stories may only be told in the winter.) Coyote is both a generative force and a chaotic one. In some accounts, he is a creator spirit. In one Crow tale, for example, Old Man Coyote makes the world and all its beings, including people, adding and revising as he goes along. But in a Caddo story, he runs in terror from an imaginary foe that turns out to be a turkey feather stuck in his teeth. Coyote's trickster nature often gets him in trouble, as when he talks nighthawks into breaking up a boulder that is chasing him but is then crushed when the angry birds build the stone back up again and it rolls onto him.

RAVEN

In Pacific Northwest cultures, Raven takes many of the same roles as Coyote: He is creator and hero, trickster and dupe. A Salish tale explains how Raven turned black: Disguised as a white owl, he stole the sun, moon, stars, and fire from a shaman who had hidden them beneath the sea and

∧ Beaver effigy pot from the Mississippian culture, about A.D. 1000

Petroglyphs of a rattlesnake and a coyote, common characters in Indigenous lore, climb a rock face in New Mexico's Petroglyph National Monument.

THE UNDERWATER PANTHER
HAS A LYNXLIKE FACE BUT THE BODY
AND LONG TAIL OF A SERPENT.

them two painted monsters which at first made us afraid, and upon which the boldest savages dare not long rest their eyes. They are as large as a calf: they have horns on their heads like those of a deer, a horrible look, red eyes, a beard like a tiger's, a face somewhat like a man's, a body covered with scales, and so long a tail that it winds all around the body, passing above the head and going back between the legs, ending in a fish's tail."

The terrifying images, sketched by later travelers but now lost to erosion, may have depicted the legendary underwater panther, or *mishepishu*. As a symbol of the perils of open water, it bears a family resemblance to the Japanese *kappa*, to sea serpents, and to other treacherous creatures that seek to drown travelers, with a lynxlike face and the long tail of a serpent. The mishepishu is a powerful figure in the lore of the Ojibwe, Cree, and other Indigenous peoples around the Great Lakes. Some stories tell of humans cutting valuable copper from its horns or tail—if it didn't drown them in a whirlpool first. ▪

released them into the world to help humanity, even though the heat from the sun burned his feathers and shriveled his feet. In an Aleut story, Raven is little more than a hapless suitor, marrying one woman after another only to have them leave him because he smells of fish. As a clan or family symbol, Raven appears on totem poles and in other art in the Pacific Northwest.

UNDERWATER PANTHER

"While skirting some rocks," wrote explorer Jacques Marquette in 1673 while traveling the Mississippi River near what is today Alton, Illinois, "we saw upon one of

---

IN LEGEND

THE THUNDERBIRD

Just as the water panther personifies the dangers of lakes, the thunderbird embodies the threats of the sky. In some stories, the two creatures are enemies. The thunderbird features in Indigenous lore ranging from the Algonquian peoples of the East to the Ojibwe of the Great Lakes and into the Northwest. In most accounts, thunder rolls from the beating of the huge bird's wings and lightning flashes from its beak. In one Tillamook tale, the thunderbird is hefty enough to pick up a whale. According to the Shawnee people, it can take on human form, although its propensity to speak backward gives away its identity.

A thunderbird radiates power on a Hunkpapa Lakota shield cover.

This two-sided Haida carving of a raven and a crouching figure is crafted from walrus ivory with a shell inlay.

ANIMAL FAMILIARS
Companions & Accomplices

Animals don't need to take on fantastical shapes to be credited with fantastical powers. Cultures from Africa to the Americas feature shamans and witches who change themselves into ordinary creatures to work their magic or who employ possessed animals to carry out their schemes. Hyenas, crocodiles, owls, bats, wild cats, and toads have aided witches in accounts from Sudan to Uganda. The Nez Perce of the American Northwest told of evil rattlesnakes or badgers that encouraged human magicians. These sinister assistants in everyday forms are known as animal familiars.

Some of the best known accounts of animal familiars come to us from European witch trials (see page 164). From the late Middle Ages through the early 18th century, church authorities linked suspected witches to a wide variety of animal sidekicks. Demons (and even Satan himself) were said to inhabit the creatures and aid the witches in their spells and curses. According to transcripts of medieval European witch trials, larger beasts, such as hogs, carried the witches by night to satanic Sabbath gatherings (see page 167).

The purported familiars were typically ordinary animals that could live unremarked in or near any household. British witch trial documents often cited cats, dogs, pigs, or goats, but familiars were not always of the domestic variety. Toads were among the accused, as were snails, snakes, calves, polecats, and even butterflies and wasps.

< An early 20th-century French carving depicts a witch and her feline familiar.

AS WITCH-HUNTING FADED AWAY, SO TOO DID MOST ACCOUNTS OF DEMONIC ANIMALS.

Investigators charged Gwen ferch Ellis, executed as a witch in 16th-century Wales, with harboring an unusually large and ugly fly as her devilish accomplice.

Englishwoman Mary Hockett, interviewed in 1645 by the notorious witch-finder Matthew Hopkins (see page 169), admitted to owning three mouse familiars named Littleman, Prettyman, and Daynty. Hopkins believed that the very names of such animals might point to guilt. He noted that one accused witch's "imps" (probably cats) were named Pyewacket, Grizzel, and Greedigut, "which no mortall could invent."

Witch-hunters often claimed that witches fed their familiars with their own breast milk or blood as part of their demonic pact. This notion hardened into a belief that witches possessed an extra teat through which they nursed the animals. Searching for such a witch's mark, which might appear even on men, became a standard part of a witch-hunter's checklist.

As witch-hunting faded away in the late 18th century, so too did most accounts of demonic animals. Some of today's Wiccans (see page 292) still recognize the existence of familiars, now seen as benign links between this world and the spiritual realm.

An owl, a cat, and rats accompany a witch's daughter in this 19th-century painting.

NESSIE & BIGFOOT

The Search for Cryptids

According to believers, folkloric creatures still shamble through forests and surface in Scottish lochs. Reputed modern-day monsters such as Bigfoot, the chupacabra, and the Loch Ness Monster are known as cryptids: storied animals that have not been proven to exist. Cryptids don't necessarily trace their roots to ancient mythology and religion, but they occupy the same space in the human psyche. They also support an industry of cryptid books, films, and tourist destinations, from California's Bigfoot Discovery Museum to Australia's Yowie Trail.

LOCH NESS MONSTER

"Feeling the water above disturbed," writes an early biographer of sixth-century St. Columba, "[the monster] suddenly swam up to the surface, and with gaping mouth and with great roaring rushed towards the man swimming in the middle of the stream." The saint raised his hand, the biography continues, and, with the sign of the cross, drove away the water beast of Loch Ness.

This seventh-century biography is the first written account of one of history's most beloved cryptids, the Loch Ness Monster. Often described as a dark, long-necked, humpbacked animal, Nessie is the best known purported inhabitant of a murky Scottish lake almost 800 feet (244 m) deep. It is most familiar from a grainy black-and-white photo published in 1934 showing a plesiosaur-like neck rising from the lake. In 1994, the photo was revealed to be a hoax: The Nessie of the image was a toy submarine with a plastic and wooden head.

The revelation did little to quench public enthusiasm for Nessie, who has garnered more than a thousand sightings over the years. Nor has scientific research quelled belief. In 2018, a team led by geneticist Neil Gemmell of the University of Otago conducted a DNA study of the loch to identify its inhabitants. The team found traces of more than 3,000 species, including humans—but no Nessie. The lake does hold many eels, the scientists noted, though none known to science is the size of the legendary water beast.

BIGFOOT

Reports of wandering, hairy, humanlike cryptids are not new—see, for instance, medieval stories of the wodewose (see page 80). The Nepalese claim the yeti and the Indonesians the Orang Pendek, while in Australia, the apelike Yowie appears in Aboriginal stories. Bigfoot is the American version of this archetypal figure.

Nessie threatens boaters in a 20th-century illustration.

The famous, or notorious, still image of a gorilla-like figure from Roger Paterson and Bob Gimlin's 1967 footage of what they said was Bigfoot

The Salish people of the Pacific Northwest tell stories of the *se'sxac,* or Sasquatch, but the creature became famous as Bigfoot in 1958. That October, the *Humboldt Times* of Northern California reported that a road crew had found enormous footprints in the soil east of Eureka. A plaster cast of the prints was 16 inches (41 cm) long and 7 inches (18 cm) wide (roughly a size 26 in men's shoes). Bigfoot stories proliferated. In 1967, two men filmed a distant, gorilla-like figure walking on two legs into the woods near the location of the original footprint. Since then, Bigfoot sightings have been reported in every state except Hawaii—and have continued despite legitimate repudiations.

In 2002, the widow of one member of the road crew who discovered the original footprint confessed that the plaster cast was a fake. Geneticists at the University of Oxford have examined purported Bigfoot hair samples and found them to be shed by deer, black bears, raccoons, and other ordinary mammals. Black bears can and sometimes do walk upright on their hind legs, Bigfoot-style.

> ## THE SALISH PEOPLE OF THE PACIFIC NORTHWEST TELL STORIES OF THE *SE'SXAC,* OR SASQUATCH, BUT THE CREATURE BECAME FAMOUS AS BIGFOOT IN 1958.

Rational argument and scientific evidence have not dissuaded the legions of cryptid believers. It's tough to prove a negative: to show once and for all that creatures like Bigfoot and Nessie don't exist. People who search for legendary creatures generally do so for psychological, not scientific, reasons. They value intuition over cold evidence. They want to see what the culture has told them they will see. They want to believe that there is more to life than the finite and mortal—that the world still has wonders to be found. ◼

IN LEGEND

SEA MONSTERS

Nessie belongs to the ancient and widespread family of legendary sea monsters. In the Bible, the leviathan appears several times as a huge sea serpent and enemy of Israel. In Norse mythology, the Midgard Serpent lives in the ocean and wraps Earth in its coils. Its Scandinavian relative, the kraken, drags ships into the depths with squidlike tentacles. Even hardheaded New England scientists have documented sightings of such creatures. An 1817 report of a committee of the Linnean Society of New England describes a large marine animal, a serpent "of immense size," spotted by observers off the coast of Cape Ann, Massachusetts.

The kraken as a giant octopus, in an 1802 illustration

CHAPTER THREE
The Arts of Divination

What Is Divination?

Signs & Symbols

A soaring bird's path through the sky. The spots on an animal's liver. Jumbles of thrown sticks, dice, or bones. For thousands of years, people have sought to find deeper meaning in these and other omens, mining them for otherworldly insights into what has passed and what is yet to come.

Such practices, collectively known as divination, abound across human cultures. In ancient Mesopotamia more than 5,000 years ago, medical practitioners searched for omens during their walks to visit the sick, hoping to shed light on their patients' ailments. Astrologers in the Renaissance looked to the heavens for signs of war or disease. And today, people still seek answers and solace in tarot readings.

Since divination's earliest days, its practitioners have taken on many roles. They've counseled kings and advised generals. They've helped everyday people understand recent misfortune and plan understand recent misfortune and plan

for an uncertain future. They've been royal staff and street-corner buskers, religious figures, con artists, and everything in between.

For divination to find such universal purchase, historians point to what they call "omen-mindedness": the human instinct to discern signs of agency in the surrounding environment. In a world suffused with belief in the natural and supernatural, an otherwise mundane occurrence can easily be imbued with meaning and design.

Though the tools of divination have varied over time, one fundamental belief has remained the same: that the answers to our questions lie hidden just out of view. Whether they read runes, entrails, or wisps of smoke, people past and present have attempted to tap into and interpret a range of vast, inscrutable sources of knowledge. ■

∧ Stoneware figurine of a Taoist priest holding a rooster, Song dynasty (960–1279)

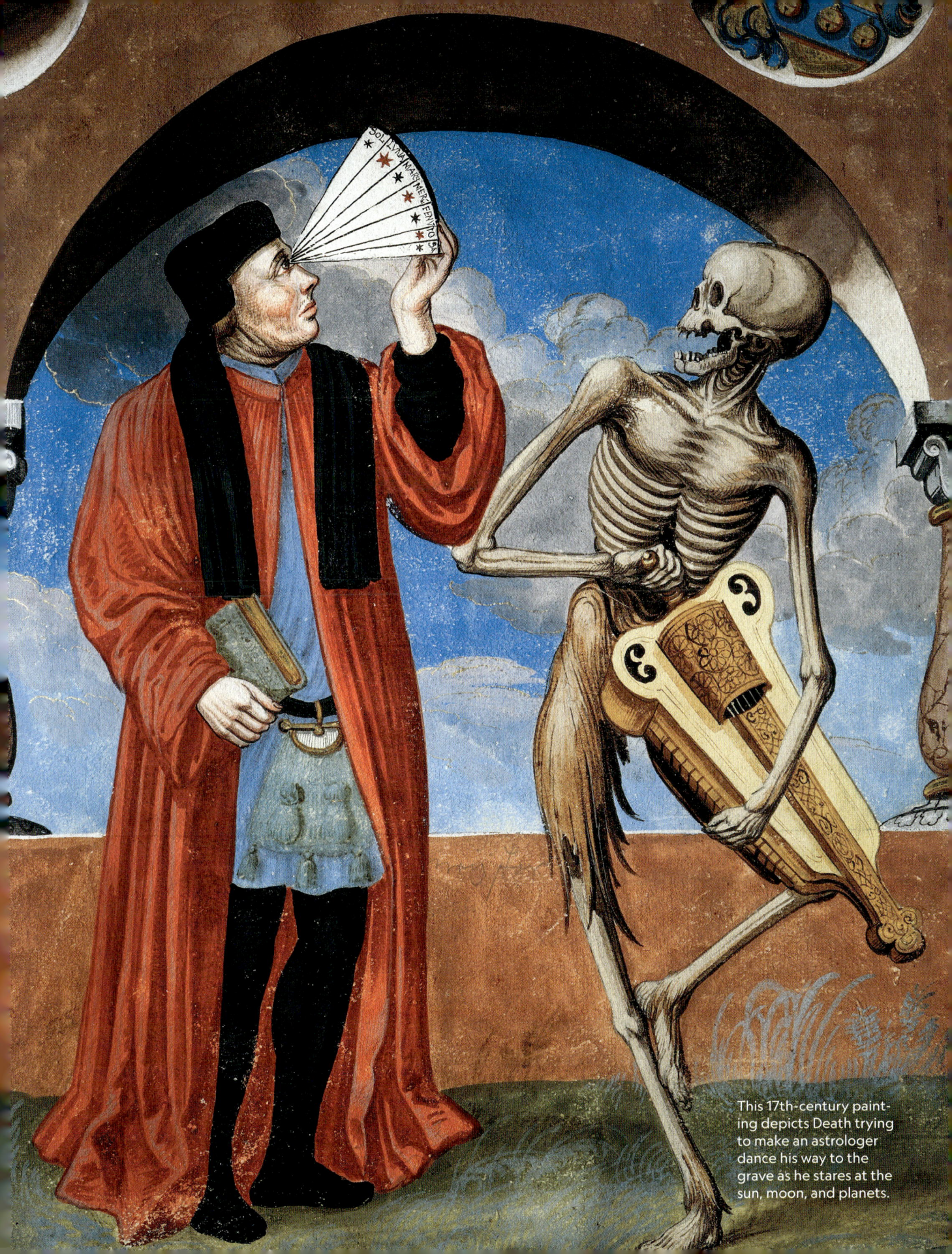

This 17th-century painting depicts Death trying to make an astrologer dance his way to the grave as he stares at the sun, moon, and planets.

READING THE OMENS

Augurs, Seers & Oracles

The earliest definitive records of divination date from around 3000 B.C., documenting the practice among ancient civilizations of Mesopotamia in what is now Iraq. By the time of Babylonia—the region's reigning state from 1894 to 539 B.C.—scholars in Mesopotamia had laid the foundations of Western astronomy by carefully observing the locations of celestial bodies and using them to make astrological predictions. The Enūma Anu Enlil, a major astrological reference from this period, relates the positions of the moon and stars to events on Earth.

In addition to reading the stars, Mesopotamians believed they could ritually induce their gods to give them peeks into a predetermined future. Ceremonies conducted by a ritual specialist known as a *bārû* relied heavily on extispicy, a form of divination that interprets signs found within the structure of an animal's entrails (see page 140).

Ancient Greek artifacts and literature reveal a bulging divinatory toolkit. Homer's *Iliad*, dated to the seventh or eighth century B.C., alludes to the good omen of a bird landing on one's right hand. The Euripides play *Electra*, written between 421 and 416 B.C., includes a scene in which a calf is killed for extispicy. The Greek diviner Artemidorus Daldianus, writing in the second century A.D., specialized in interpreting dreams. Some laymen dabbled in cleromancy, tossing objects like dice or bones and interpreting their landing positions to gain insight on future events.

By the Hellenistic age—323 to 30 B.C.—anonymous Greek authors who wrote on magic falsely attributed these practices to ancient Persian magicians, to legitimize them by appealing to what historian Arnaldo Momigliano has called the "alien wisdom" of faraway cultures. In fact, the word "magician" comes from the Greek form of *magus*, a priest of the Persian-founded Zoroastrian faith (see page 142).

In the Greeks' conception of the cosmos, the gods had designed a natural world in which certain kinds of events would be preceded by corresponding signs. The gods, in turn, relied on human agents to identify these signs and give them voice. Oracles generated the most prestigious and most reliable signs of all, in the form of their prophetic utterances.

< Terra-cotta hydria (water jar) depicting Ajax and Achilles throwing dice, sixth century B.C.

Painting of "idol-worshippers" (possibly Buddhists) from a 16th-century Persian Falnama, a book of divination ritually opened to random pages

The man on the right in this sixth-century B.C. Etruscan mural is carrying a *lituus*, a hooked staff that served as an augur's wand.

None were as widely reputed—or sought out—as the oracles at Delphi (see sidebar), who were said to channel the voice of the Greek sun god Apollo.

Greek intellectuals debated the mechanism behind the oracles' prophecies. Some theorized that Apollo moved an oracle's soul like the wind, allowing prophecy to emerge. Others argued that the prophecies were mediated by demons, guardian spirits that bridged the gap between god and oracle.

Ancient Romans had far less use for human oracles; their method of divination consisted mainly of a practice known as augury. Specialists known as augurs searched for signs throughout the natural world. Drawing on the traditions of Italy's Etruscan culture, Roman historians kept a careful record of *prodigia*: unusual events that sometimes portended a soured relationship with the gods, such as pestilence, a lightning strike on a temple, or the appearance of a talking cow (such as the one reported in A.D. 169 by the Roman historian Livy). In response to prodigia, high-ranking Roman officials conducted

ANCIENT ROMANS HAD LITTLE USE FOR HUMAN ORACLES. ROMAN DIVINATION CONSISTED MAINLY OF A PRACTICE KNOWN AS AUGURY.

∧ Ravens and crows were seen as divine messengers.

PROFILE

ORACLE AT DELPHI

For more than a thousand years, ancient Greeks visited a religious shrine on Mount Parnassus that they considered the center of the world: Delphi. In its heyday, women oracles stood in the middle of the temple there and channeled Apollo, making declarations and predictions for the future. In the 1990s, geologists found cracks in the limestone and springs near the temple that bore traces of ethylene and methane, gases that produce feelings of euphoria. Could the oracles' visions have come from breathing in these fumes? At a minimum, the vapors may have served as a psychological trigger for an oracle's delivery of a momentous prophecy.

An 1891 painting of a Pythia, the high priestess of Delphi

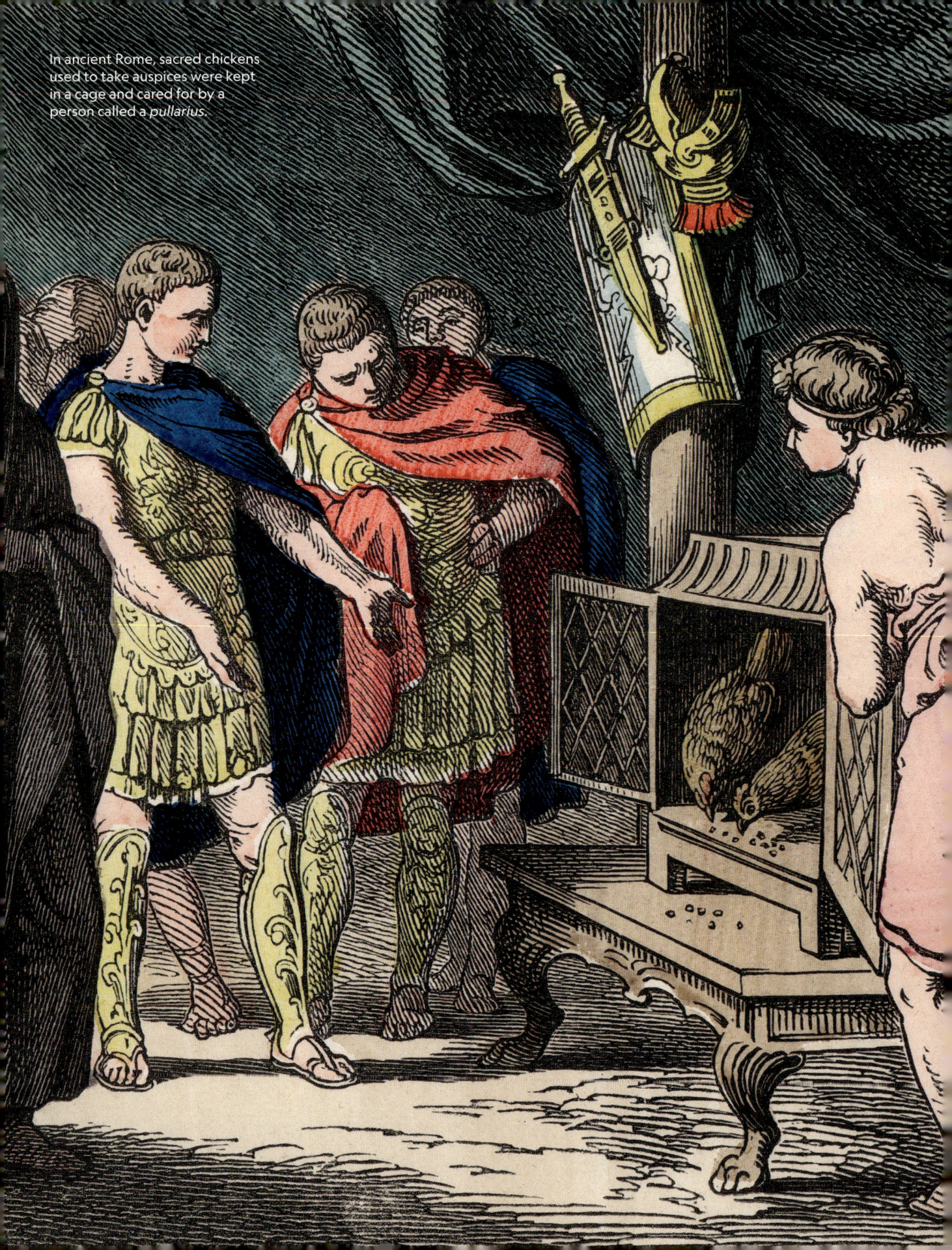

In ancient Rome, sacred chickens used to take auspices were kept in a cage and cared for by a person called a *pullarius*.

ceremonies known as expiations to restore divine peace.

Roman augury focused most of all on the behavior of birds (auspices), which were seen as divine messengers. A raven flying to one's right signaled good fortune, while one flying on the left boded ill. (Exactly why these interpretations took hold was a mystery even to the first-century B.C. Roman politician Cicero, a skeptic philosopher who was himself an augur.) The best signs of all were eagles and vultures: symbols of the will of Jupiter, the Roman king of the gods.

Rome's preoccupation with augury traced to its mythological dawn, with auspices settling a disagreement between legendary twins Romulus and Remus about where to build a new city in 753 B.C. Six vultures flew above Remus's head, but 12 flew above Romulus's, leading Romulus to claim the gods' favor. The brothers' dispute ended famously in fratricide with Remus's death; Romulus became the new city's first king.

In the centuries that followed, augury permeated Roman public life, taken as seriously as the pervasive belief that the gods cared for their human supplicants. Rome's augurs took auspices before practically all major public events—including battles—in attempts to discern Jupiter's will.

In 249 B.C., during the First Punic War between Rome and Carthage, the Roman consul Publius Claudius Pulcher led a fleet of at least 123 ships against the Carthaginian port of Drepana, in modern-day Sicily.

Before attacking, Pulcher sought the gods' input via sacred chickens used to take auspices during military expeditions. When the chickens were placed in front of feed, they did not peck: an omen to wait. Impatient, Pulcher proceeded with the attack and had the chickens thrown overboard.

The result was a disaster, with all but 30 Roman ships lost. Pulcher narrowly avoided a treason conviction and was forced to pay a hefty fine. In his work *De Natura Deorum (On the Nature of the Gods)*, Cicero listed Pulcher's recklessness and subsequent misfortune as one reason "to acknowledge the divine power."

ARTIFACT SPOTLIGHT

CRYSTAL BALLS

Crystal balls belong to the ancient divinatory tradition of scrying, or discerning signs within reflective materials such as crystals, pools of water, or mirrors. In the first century A.D., Roman philosopher Pliny the Elder mentioned magic done with "water" or "balls," possible references to scrying tools. He also described the Druids—priests of Celtic peoples in the British Isles and northern France—using glassy "serpents' eggs" as talismans. Centuries later, crystal orbs held potency and value. In the late fifth century A.D., the Merovingian king Childeric I was buried with a polished crystal sphere. Though decried by the Catholic Church, scrying with crystals saw renewed attention in Europe during the Renaissance as educated elites experimented with mysticism.

A modern glass crystal ball on a metal base

CIVIL DIVINATION

Official Fortune Tellers in Asia

Around 1300 B.C., a fortune teller in China roasted a turtle shell over an intense fire until cracks formed on its surface—cracks that might reveal answers to questions about the future, identify good and bad omens, or even aid ruling powers in decision-making.

This shell is the earliest record of China's elaborate divination ceremonies and the fortune-telling specialists who worked for its government institutions. As China's societies became organized in increasingly complex ways—with new writing systems, walled towns, and emerging social hierarchies—they were guided by various methods of prophecy: pyromancy, or interpreting of flames; plastromancy, or reading of turtle shells; and scapulimancy, the analysis of cracks that form when animal scapulae bones are heated to predict the future.

During the Shang dynasty (1600–1050 B.C.), the emperor gained the title of chief diviner and, along with his court, used the practice to maintain control over the valley around the Yellow River. As a formalized system, divination could ensure influence over political and social structures. Modern archaeologists have found tens of thousands of turtle shells in the area, as well the scapulae of other animals, including deer, pigs, and sheep, known collectively as "oracle bones." These artifacts contain some of the oldest known examples of Chinese writing: questions for deities scratched into the bones.

As the Western Zhou dynasty gained power in 1046 B.C., the practice of counting yarrow sticks became increasingly popular. This form of divination, known as *gua yao*, incorporated more complex mathematical and numerological beliefs to make decisions, analyze the present, and glimpse the future. Gua yao, more easily accessible for the masses than bones, soon became widely used.

Through the centuries, magical belief embedded even deeper into China's political structure. Starting around the sixth century B.C., the Imperial Divination Office employed *jugon* specialists, who could exorcise evil spirits with swords and magic spells, while the Department of the Grand Astrologer was in charge of astronomy.

Chinese belief in divination, along with China's religious and philosophical beliefs, seeped into surrounding regions. Scholars of philosophy, medicine, and divination visited Japan, sparking an interest in magical concepts there that would last for more than a thousand years.

A restructuring of the Japanese administrative state in A.D. 701 included the formation of a special office called the

Some 3,000 years ago in China's Henan Province, the bottom of a turtle shell was used to divine the outcome of a military campaign.

This 17th-century woodcut depicts Abe no Seimei (right), an influential 10th-century *onmyōji*. After Seimei's death, he grew into a Merlin-like figure within Japanese legend.

Onmyōdō: the way of yin-yang (a much older Chinese philosophy loosely translated as opposite but interconnected forces), which was also known as the bureau of divination. Officials called *onmyōji* made calendars, took astronomical observations, kept time, and divined the future. As the onmyōji's duties evolved, they incorporated concepts borrowed from Chinese tradition, including Confucianism, Taoism, and folk belief.

The government limited the types of divination religious figures were allowed to practice, stating in the law governing religious entities that "monks and nuns are forbidden from divining good fortune or calamity from mysterious phenomena, thereby deluding the emperor and the people." This helped officials maintain such powers for themselves, and over time, those who practiced such magic came to enjoy the status of religious figures. The onmyōji quelled evil spirits, mollified curses, selected days for official royal events, chose locations for new temples, and decided whether omens—for example, bad weather or rats in the palace—were positive or negative. In the 10th century, when Emperor Ichijō moved into a new palace, the nation's most famous diviner, Abe no Seimei, performed a ritual to guarantee the emperor's safety.

As the onmyōji's practice flourished, their responsibilities changed and grew. Before long, diviners no longer worked only for the government; they were also employed by nobility. By the Middle Ages, the onmyōji counseled regular citizens and were organized under the auspices of a single noble family—the house of Tsuchimikado—which carefully guarded their monopoly on divination, licensing practitioners throughout Japan. The Tsuchimikados retained their grasp on divination across various governments until, in the 1800s, a military dictatorship was overturned and imperial rule was reestablished. The emperor banned numerous types of religious practitioners, eliminating the entire system of social power, and calling it "completely baseless." The last onmyōji from the Tsuchimikado family was relieved of his duties in 1870, ending the government's role in divination.

< Yarrow plant

I CHING

For some 3,000 years, the *I Ching (Book of Changes)* has stood as a monumental work of divination and Chinese philosophy, heralded as a book that can explain everything. For one, the *I Ching* is a divinatory text, meant to be used by throwing yarrow stalks to randomly generate numbers that correspond with 64 symbols called hexagrams. Each hexagram is paired with a "judgment" and six statements symbolically linked to the hexagram itself. The *I Ching* is also a philosophical work, whose commentaries frame the interconnections among the *I Ching*'s many symbols as mirroring the relationships that bind the natural world together. As a result, careful contemplation of the text's many judgments and statements could provide oracular answers and help readers contribute to a greater cosmic harmony.

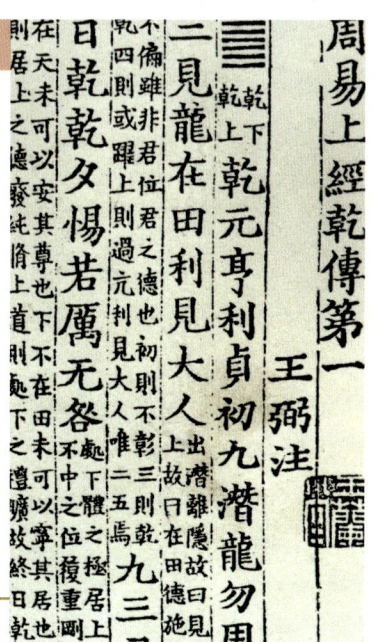

A page from a 10th-century *I Ching*, describing the *qián* (force) hexagram

THE CHINESE ZODIAC

For more than two millennia, the Chinese zodiac has cycled through a 12-year series of animal symbols. According to Chinese folklore, the order was established during a footrace of the animals organized by the Jade Emperor, the ruler of heaven.

This cycle forms part of China's traditional lunisolar calendar. Each animal pairs with each of five elements—metal, water, wood, fire, and earth—once every 60 years. Chinese astrology holds that people embody the traits of their birth year's animal, with specifics modified by the paired element. A person's zodiac sign (essential traits detailed below) can suggest relationships with other signs, affecting love life, friendships, and career.

MONKEY >
Flexible, quick-witted, social; sharp intellect; has a mercurial streak

v DOG
Loyal, reliable, friendly; has strong intuition

TIGER >
Fearless, iron-willed, impulsive; moves through the world with a strong sense of justice

< RAT
Charming, quick-witted, and talkative; thrives in social settings yet tends to keep secrets

< OX
Patient and unpretentious, strong sense of responsibility; can show flashes of stubbornness

< HORSE
Tenacious, enthusiastic, shrewd; moves quickly and speaks with authority

∨ ROOSTER
Ambitious, observant, charismatic; has a knack for organization and punctuality

∧ RABBIT
Quiet, thoughtful, polite, tenderhearted; values friendship highly

< PIG
Decisive, easygoing, forgiving; takes care of loved ones and enjoys life

SNAKE >
Quick thinking, intelligent, adaptable; stays calm in challenging situations

∧ GOAT
Compassionate, honest, peace-loving; easily moved by the suffering of others

DRAGON ∧
Energetic, driven, independent; leads with confidence

STARS & SAND

The Islamic Golden Age

In the centuries following the death of the prophet Muhammad in A.D. 632, magic and divination formed a complex relationship with the growing religion of Islam. Ancient practices from Arabia and Persia persisted, while new methods blossomed amid one of the medieval world's great periods of intellectual growth: the Islamic golden age.

By the ninth century, under the rule of the Islamic Abbasid Caliphate, Baghdad had become one of the world's largest cities, as well as a global center for philosophy and science. For two centuries, Abbasid scholars translated myriad ancient texts from Greece, India, and Persia into Arabic. The works of Aristotle and the books of second-century A.D. Egyptian astronomer Claudius Ptolemy supercharged Islamic intellectual life. Astronomy flourished as Muslim observers built on and improved ancient astronomers' observations. (Many modern star names, such as Aldebaran in the constellation Taurus, derive from Arabic.)

Astrology's star also rose during this time. The ninth-century A.D. astrologer Abū Ma'shar, also known as Albumazar, gained renown in the Abbasid court. His book *Kitāb al-mudkhal al-kabīr (The Great Introduction)*, written in approximately 850, later served as a key astrological reference for medieval Europeans. Astrology would also become the subject of theological controversy, fielding attacks that asserted only Allah (God) could know the future. But from royal courts to street corners, astrology—*'ilm al nujum*, the science of the stars—was practiced in different ways, to different ends.

The most basic astrological predictions in this period relied on naked-eye phenomena like the rise and fall of lunar mansions, groups of stars located at points where the moon's orbit crossed the sun's apparent path. Comets and meteors were treated as important omens. Astrologers commonly engaged in *masa'il wa ihtiyarat* (interrogations and elections), predictions that dealt with solving thefts or determining the best times to perform

∧ Iranian bowl depicting the sun and personifications of the moon and planets, circa early 13th century

In this 15th-century illustration, astronomers use quadrants and astrolabes atop Greece's Mount Athos while men with sticks scratch inscriptions into the dirt.

specific tasks. Detailed horoscopes based on a child's time of birth or conception offered insights into the young one's fate. Astrologers drew up charts for the city of Baghdad and other locations.

The next most common form of divination took its users from the heavens to the earth. In the technique known as *'ilm al raml* (the science of the sand), called geomancy in Europe by the 12th century, a diviner scratched 16 lines of dots, each of a random length, into dirt or sand. The lines were used to generate four figures that, in turn, yielded a "tableau" interpreted for answers. The practice was widespread enough that in the mid-13th century, a metalworker in Syria crafted a geomantic instrument, with spinning, dot-covered dials taking the place of dirt or sand.

Some forms of divination relied on the Arabic Abjad numerical system, which assigned each letter or word a specific value. Added together, the value of each letter of the opening line of the Quran—

"In the name of Allah, the most merciful, the most compassionate"—equals 786. By the same measure, "Allah" becomes 66. Magical significance was inferred from these sums in a divinatory practice known as *'ilm al huruf* (the science of letters).

Islamic riffs on onomancy (divination based on people's names) promised to predict the outcomes of war. As described in the *Muqaddimah*, an influential 14th-century Islamic history of the world, diviners could calculate the numerical values of two warring kings' names, divide each value by nine, and then compare the two remainders to predict the winner of a battle. An alternate version of this procedure, *hisab an-nim* (calculation by nine), suggested whether a given statement was true or false.

Other, more casual divinatory practices within Islamic cultures have persisted to this day. In present-day Iran, diviners use trained birds to select cards containing verses written by Hafez, a renowned 14th-century Persian poet. The message within the card's beautifully written verses can provide guidance to the reader. This form of bibliomancy (book divination), known as *fal-e Hafez*, has been around for centuries. ∎

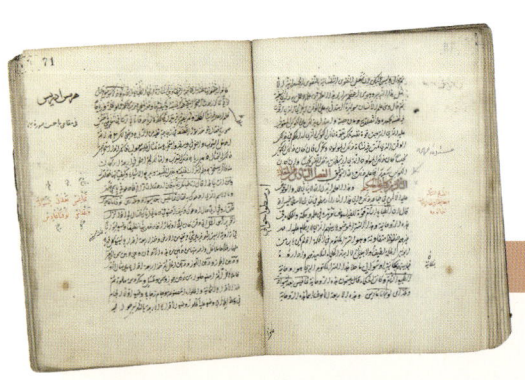

PICATRIX

In medieval and early Renaissance Europe, the *Picatrix* served as the authoritative source on astrological magic. Originally composed in Arabic, most likely by the 10th-century Moorish scholar Maslama b. Qasim al Qurtubi, it was published in the mid-11th century as *Ghayat al-Hakim (The Aim of the Sage)*.

A magical melting pot, the *Picatrix* recorded rituals and superstitions from across the ancient world, placed within a loosely unifying framework of cosmic interdependence. King Alfonso X—the monarch of Castile, León, and Galicia, in what is now Spain—had the book translated into Spanish sometime between 1256 and 1258. It was then published in Latin and eventually spread throughout the libraries of Europe.

Arabic copy of *Ghayat al-Hakim (The Aim of the Sage)*, 16th century

MEDIEVAL MAGIC

Divination & Astrology in Europe

Unlike the augurs of Rome or the *bārû* of Mesopotamia, diviners during Europe's medieval period—roughly A.D. 450 to 1500—weren't concentrated within a specific social group or class. Everyone from clergy to laymen, rich and poor alike, was exposed to magical rites and rituals, including some that fell under the umbrella of divination.

Texts published during this era attest to diverse divinatory practices. One 15th-century leechbook, a medical reference text for surgeons and barbers, advised people to avoid timing major life events with 32 "evil days" throughout the year; a wedding on one of these days, for example, would end with the bride's untimely demise. A treatise on brontomancy (thunder divination) held that thunder in January portended the deaths of many men and sheep, while thunder on a Tuesday suggested a bumper crop. According to one Irish text on birthdays, people born on Saturdays were fated to lives of mayhem, murder, and bowel disease. Numerous folk practices promised insight into one's overall luck and circumstances. In some parts of Europe, good fortune came from witnessing a hare elude hunting dogs, or in finding a horseshoe. People sometimes posed questions to themselves and then walked through crowded streets, seeking answers in words overheard from passersby. Upcoming changes in the weather could be gleaned by the number of times a raven cawed.

Starting in the 1500s, during the early Renaissance, writers began to extol the efficacy of dowsing: the use of divining rods to find lost objects or locate underground water and minerals. Once tea arrived in Europe in the mid-16th century, some diviners began practicing tasseomancy (tea-leaf reading), adapting earlier divinatory practices that found meaning—for example, the cause of an illness, or omens of good or ill fortune—within the specific shapes that formed from splatters of melted wax or lead.

Divination's regular appearances in medieval life proved a thorn in the side of the Catholic Church, which accused diviners of heeding the conjectures of demons. According to one 10th-century German

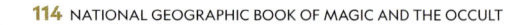

> A 16th-century clockwork celestial globe, likely crafted for Holy Roman Emperor Rudolf II, a prolific patron of alchemy, astrology, and astronomy

In this 19th-century painting, a fortune teller reads a young woman's fortune in the tea leaves at the bottom of a cup.

The zodiac signs and the constellations of the northern sky in a 16th-century Italian fresco. During the Renaissance, astrology and astronomy made strides together.

book of Catholic canon law, a woman casting divination was to be punished with penance—perhaps requiring fasts, giving alms, or going on pilgrimages—lasting from 40 days to a year, depending on her offense. Those who employed diviners were to be excommunicated unless they did penance for at least a year and a half. Despite these directives, however, monks had already gained broad exposure to astrology through their translation of Arabic texts into Latin, a practice that had existed since the 12th century. This gave medieval Europe access to the many ancient Greek works translated by Arabic authors.

Medieval astrologers also had access to so-called prognostic tables that promised to divine the future. *The Tabula Salomonis (Table of Salomon)*, published repeatedly between A.D. 1000 and 1300, used the moon's placement within the zodiac on any given day to reveal the hidden meaning behind a series of unexpected "incidents." An uncontrolled eye twitch on June 1, when the moon was in Cancer, foretold the death of a king. If mice gnawed on your

clothing on November 30, when the moon was in Scorpio, you'd soon lose money.

During this period, astrology readily intermixed with observational astronomy, without today's distinctions between magic and science. Johannes Kepler, a 17th-century astronomer famous for his laws of planetary motion, was an avid astrologer, casting more than 800 horoscopes over the course of his life. Kepler also had to contend with Europe's witch-hunting craze (see chapter 4); in 1615, his mother, Katharina, stood accused of witchcraft. Kepler led her defense in a 1620 trial that ended in her acquittal.

PROFILE

NOSTRADAMUS

Michel de Nostredame (1503–1566) was an influential French astrologer and physician whose prophecies were widely read in Renaissance Europe. A devout Catholic and voracious bookworm, he began as a physician, treating several plague outbreaks in the 1540s. Around 1547, he began writing prophecies as four-line verses known as quatrains. A collection published in 1555 as *Les Prophéties (The Prophecies)* transformed Nostredame into the celebrated "Nostradamus." Catherine de Médicis, the queen consort of King Henry II of France, commissioned him to cast her children's horoscopes.

Even today, some claim that Nostradamus's prophecies—942 in all—predicted real-world events, such as the French Revolution and the lead-up to World War II. However, he wrote cryptically about constants in an ever changing world—war, pestilence, civil and religious unrest—that may simply reflect our timeless struggles.

This 19th-century engraving of an astrologer is believed to depict Nostradamus with the French queen Catherine de Médicis.

WESTERN ZODIAC

Created in Babylonia and refined in Egypt and Greece, the Western zodiac calendar is both a testament to cross-cultural exchange and an enduring source of magical inspiration. The zodiac is a belt of the night sky that lies along the ecliptic, the sun's apparent path through the heavens. By the time of the Renaissance, astrologers had divided this belt into 12 equal parts, each represented by one of 12 constellations along it. Believing in links between earthly events and celestial alignments, astrologers track the sun, moon, and planets against the zodiac calendar; these bodies' locations during a person's birth are thought to relate to their essence of being.

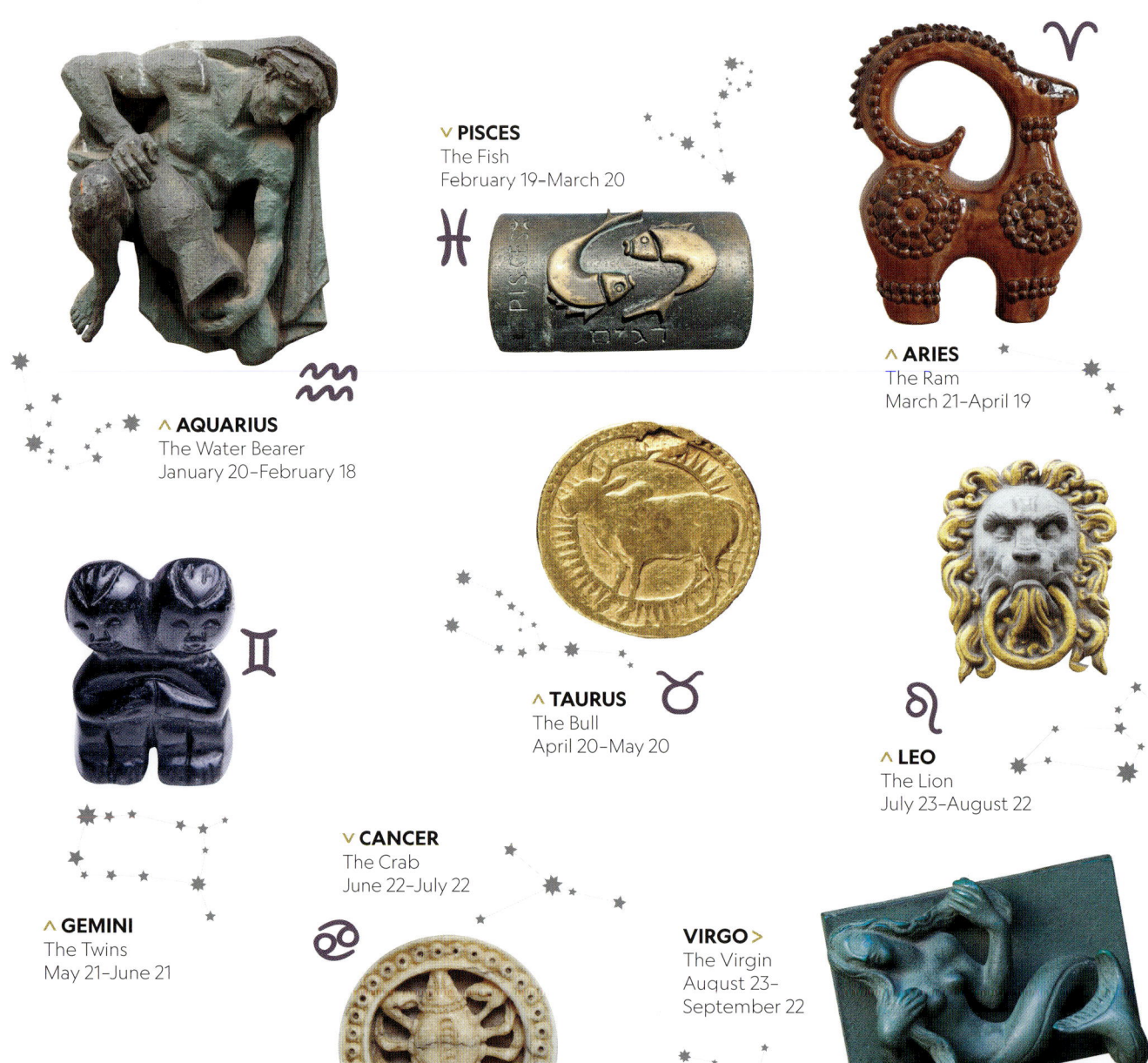

∨ PISCES
The Fish
February 19–March 20

∧ ARIES
The Ram
March 21–April 19

∧ AQUARIUS
The Water Bearer
January 20–February 18

∧ TAURUS
The Bull
April 20–May 20

∧ LEO
The Lion
July 23–August 22

∧ GEMINI
The Twins
May 21–June 21

∨ CANCER
The Crab
June 22–July 22

VIRGO >
The Virgin
August 23–
September 22

∧ **LIBRA**
The Balance
September 23–October 23

∨ **CAPRICORN**
The Goat
December 22–January 19

∧ **SAGITTARIUS**
The Archer
November 22–December 21

‹ **SCORPIO**
The Scorpion
October 24–November 21

EMPOWERING TRADITIONS

Spirituality in the New World Colonies

After being forcibly brought to the Americas, enslaved Africans maintained the rich belief systems that connected them to the cultures of their homelands. These traditions would eventually help some to shake off the bonds of slavery by emboldening rebellions and helping organize uprisings.

Across the Caribbean, several religions based in African traditions—Santeria in Cuba, obeah in Jamaica, vodou in Haiti—have much in common. All involve the concept of Obeye, supernatural forces that can be harnessed for personal use, and sometimes disguised their beliefs under the guise of Christianity. On the surface, enslaved people appeared to be worshipping Catholic saints, but in reality they had secretly reassigned the saints to represent African gods. By blending their beliefs with those of their oppressors, enslaved people could maintain their ancestral identities and traditions. This subtle yet empowering collective action subverted the otherwise complete control of slavery.

In Jamaica, faith in obeah helped fuel an underground resistance. In 1760, a small rebellion led by an alleged obeah priest ushered in the first of many laws attempting to outlaw the religion.

RITES & RITUALS

IFA DIVINATION

In Yoruba communities across West Africa, the Americas, and the Caribbean, important life moments call for a type of divination named after Ifa, the deity of wisdom. A carved wooden divination board depicts beliefs in time and cosmology. A diviner uses palm nuts or seed shells to tell whether someone's forces are balanced, in harmony with the universe, and in sync with their destiny. A priest then interprets the signs by consulting a text called *odu*, whose 256 chapters contain hundreds of poetic teachings. These spells represent the language, beliefs, and formulas of a group who struggled to maintain their identity and existence after being sold into slavery in the Americas.

Tapping this tray, known as an *opon Ifa,* allows a Yoruba diviner to invoke the god of fate.

Slaveholders forbade possession of "any poisonous drugs, pounded glass, parrot's beaks, dog's teeth, alligator's teeth, or other materials notoriously used in the practice of obeah or witchcraft." But obeah had already been absorbed into the existing populations' traditions, allowing enslaved people to keep a tenuous hold on their own culture.

Vodou—once the religion of the royal family of Dahomey in present-day Benin—thrived on the island that is now Haiti. It espouses belief in an almighty god whose will is dispatched to *lwas*, or spirit deities. Spanish and later French colonial officials tried to suppress the religion, which they saw as a threat to their control, and sentenced its practitioners to brutal punishments. Still, people masked their beliefs behind Catholic saints and confined rituals to social gatherings on Sunday evenings.

On the evening of August 14, 1791, vodou priests and priestesses from across the island gathered to plot a rebellion against the colonial regime. A week later, thousands of rebels led by Toussaint-Louverture torched plantations and killed hundreds of colonizers. It was the largest uprising of enslaved people in the Americas, as well as the most successful: In 1804, Haiti became the first nation founded by its own formerly enslaved populace.

Colonial regimes across the region felt the shock waves of the Haitian revolution. White slaveholders in the United States demonized so-called "voodoo," which came with Haitian refugees to New Orleans, by equating it with superstition, witchcraft, and black magic.

Long after slavery ended, racism and power dynamics fueled fears that Afro-Caribbean belief systems held subversive power, which in turn fueled laws against these religions. Practitioners of Santeria in Cuba continuously suffered persecution and attempts at government control. In Haiti, vodou wouldn't be recognized as an official religion until 2003.

∧ Vodou beliefs traveled from Africa to Haiti, where worshippers performed rites despite brutal colonial oppression.

IN THE CARDS

Tarot, From Game to Oracle

Long before fortune tellers dealt tarot cards to reveal their audiences' futures, tarot was a simple game. The first deck appeared in Italy in the 1440s. It contained 56 ornately illustrated cards of standard Italian suits—cups, swords, batons, and coins—as well as one fool card and 21 additional esoteric cards called *tarocchi*, which depicted figures and concepts such as the sun, moon, death, and justice. Across Italy and France, aristocrats played variants of a game in which the tarocchi trumped the standard suits. Thus, the 78-card tarot deck was born.

In the 1700s, Jean-Baptiste Alliette began developing mystical interpretations of the tarot cards. In his book *Manière de se Récréer avec le Jeu de Cartes Nommées Tarots (Way to Recreate Yourself With the Deck of Cards Called Tarots)*, the French occultist—also known as Etteilla—outlined the tarot's use in fortune-telling. In 1788, he founded La Société des Interprètes de Thot, a group that helped develop the spiritual aspects of tarot, including its use in fortune-telling and its connection to astrology. The special deck it published is believed to have been the first used in divination.

In the century that followed, organizations that studied and practiced occult beliefs flourished in Europe, and tarot decks circulated widely in Italy and France. But the cards were hard to come by in England, even as a late Victorian-era fascination with the occult revived interest in them. English occultist S. L. MacGregor Mathers was among the first to merge basic tarot teachings with cards in English. He attributed the origins of these concepts to Rabbi Akiva, a second-century mystic and author of *The Book of Formation*, which outlines the principles of Jewish mysticism known as kabbalah.

In the late 1800s, British scholar Arthur Edward Waite envisioned tarot cards as a way of transmitting the secret knowledge held by the Hermetic Order of the Golden Dawn, a mystical group Mathers helped found (see page 125). Waite, a Freemason, translator of alchemy and occultism, and member and founder of multiple mystical groups, was among the first scholars to formally study Western occult beliefs. Adding his own analysis to Mathers's, Waite changed the names of cards and sketched out a new design for each. He and

< A 19th-century tarot deck from France

In this 19th-century French painting, a fortune teller uses playing cards, which along with tarot grew in popularity for divination in the 1700s and 1800s.

Long before tarot was used to divine fortunes, it was a popular card game. This Italian set was painted by Renaissance artist Bonifacio Bembo.

his collaborator, Pamela Colman-Smith, published the first modern deck of tarot cards in 1909. He wrote of the cards' abstract nature in a small book that accompanied the deck: "The true Tarot is symbolism; it speaks no other language and offers no other signs."

In the following decades, tarot crept into the mainstream, transforming from occult into popular concept. The decks inspired artists such as Salvador Dalí and, later, Niki de Saint Phalle, who installed 22 concrete tarot-inspired sculptures in the hills of Tuscany to create Il Giardino del Tarocchi.

Today, Colman-Smith and Waite's creation, known more commonly as the Rider-Waite deck (for the Rider publishing house), is incredibly popular and sold alongside sets with historic and pop-culture motifs. Tarot is used in psychotherapy, by yoga studios, and in online consultations for topics spanning from finance to romance.

According to U.S. Games Systems, which has sold tarot decks since the 1960s, tarot's popularity often peaks during times of uncertainty and fear; the 2008 financial crisis sparked one such surge in sales.

TAROT'S POPULARITY OFTEN PEAKS DURING TIMES OF UNCERTAINTY AND FEAR.

During the first year of the COVID-19 pandemic, sales tripled.

Some institutions have taken notice, both encouraging and preserving tarot's moment in the zeitgeist. In recent years, the Massachusetts Institute of Technology libraries have added tarot cards as part of a collection of unbound books, while fashion houses like Christian Dior have based clothing lines on the deck's enchanting characters.

Not everyone agrees with the power or value of tarot: In 2018, Pope Francis condemned using tarot cards for fortune-telling as "idolatrous." But in an era when spirituality and self-reflection have become mainstream, tarot is more popular than ever, with a multimillion-dollar global market. ◾

HERMETIC ORDER OF THE GOLDEN DAWN

The Hermetic Order of the Golden Dawn, founded by British Freemasons in the late 19th century, grounded itself in Renaissance forms of alchemy, astrology, tarot, and other magical beliefs. Fascinated by the era's Egyptomania (see page 254), the group's founders infused the order with ancient beliefs; its main text combined manuscripts, spells, and conjuring. Though membership remained small, it had an outsize reach among the creative classes. Members included the Irish poet W. B. Yeats and Aleister Crowley, who would become a counterculture icon in the 20th century (see page 185). The ancient magical texts its members transcribed and republished would later inspire new magical movements, including Wicca (see page 292).

Each member of the Golden Dawn's inner order made their own Rosy Cross, a potent artifact symbolizing the spirit, planets, and elements.

MAJOR ARCANA

Tarot readers use the deck's 22 major arcana (the numbered or named cards) and its 56 minor arcana (the suit cards) to divine the past, present, and future. To make the modern tarot deck, Arthur Waite and Pamela Colman-Smith drew inspiration from French books, antique Italian tarot decks, Jewish kabbalah, and possibly even their own friends, some of whom bore an uncanny resemblance to the figures depicted on the cards.

˅ THE SUN
The promise of optimism, vitality, and success

< THE FOOL
The fool, the first figure of the major arcana, is the story's main character, who must experience the journey laid out by the cards. Tarot decks are shuffled and dealt at random; the cards' order and placement during a reading determines their significance. A card's meaning may change if it's dealt upside down or after another card. To answer a question, a tarot reader might draw one card or a series to outline the past, present, and future. The cards of the major arcana represent the most important decisions that face each person in their life; their lessons are considered long term, while the minor arcana represent daily life.

˅ THE EMPRESS
A symbol of maternity, creation, and new life

˅ THE LOVERS
Deep connections, unconditional love, and balance

˅ THE HERMIT
A search for wisdom, inner guidance, and solitude

˅ THE HANGED MAN
Letting go, reflecting, sacrifice, and surrender

˅ THE MAGICIAN
Power, manifestation of desire, and trickery

˅ THE EMPEROR
Stability, leadership, and a system bound by rules

˅ THE HIEROPHANT
A formal set of beliefs; a spiritual or faithful path

JUSTICE
A fair decision, balance, and truthfulness

TEMPERANCE
A sign of clear vision, goals, and higher learning

THE HIGH PRIESTESS
Wisdom, spirituality, and trusting your instincts

^ MINOR ARCANA
These cards interpret the short-term emotions and everyday decisions we face.

THE WHEEL OF FORTUNE
Coming change, new life cycles, and luck

STRENGTH
Determination to control emotions and have patience

THE STAR
An optimism for healing and inspiring calm

THE DEVIL
The negative constraints and influences holding back life

THE CHARIOT
Ability to overcome obstacles through willpower and focus

DEATH
Deep transformation, moving on from current situations

JUDGMENT
The resolution to make decisions and achieve personal growth

THE WORLD
Fulfillment of a journey, either spiritual or physical

THE MOON
Illusion, deception, and anxiety obscuring the truth

THE TOWER
Unexpected change, chaos, and necessary destruction

DARK FORCES

Co-opting the Occult

In the early 20th century, numerous occult movements popped up in Germany and Austria, catering to an era of supernatural and spiritual experimentation. Tarot readers, astrologers, and fortune tellers peddled their esoteric wares on the city streets of Berlin and Vienna; their clients may also have dabbled in the popular trends of the time, including a resurgent interest in Nordic mythology and paganism.

A growing nationalist movement at the close of the Habsburg Empire called for a "Greater Germany," and its followers embraced theories that ancient races and secret societies validated their identity—and belonging. Among the curious was a young Adolf Hitler, who became enchanted by Ariosophy, a racist occult philosophy of a lost Aryan civilization that could only be resurrected by weeding out Jews and other "racially inferior" groups.

As Germany tried to recover from World War I, superstitions and occult beliefs became increasingly prevalent, along with theories that the world was under the control of secret conspiracies of the Freemasons and Jews. The Thule Society, which may have counted future Nazis as members, adopted the swastika as its

PROFILE

ERIK JAN HANUSSEN

On the night of February 26, 1933, a popular clairvoyant named Erik Jan Hanussen held a séance in his Berlin headquarters, the opulent Palace of the Occult, allegedly predicting a fire at a "great house." The next day, the Reichstag was engulfed in flames, and the Nazis consolidated their power under martial law. For years, Hanussen had cozied up to the Nazi regime and even personally counseled Hitler. He was known as "Hitler's clairvoyant"—but secretly, he was Jewish. One month after the séance, Hanussen was assassinated by Nazi storm troopers, possibly over whispers about his religion, the power he was gaining, or the debts he held from gambling-addicted officers. Perhaps, considering his foretelling of the Reichstag fire, he simply knew too much.

A 1948 German magazine covering Hanussen asks: "Genius? Clairvoyant? Charlatan?"

symbol, and the Völkisch movement glorified a mythical unified Germanic race. These fringe groups often fed into the Nazi party. In 1932, one journalist described Hitler's supporters as "Theosophists, the Anthroposophists, the miracle rabbis … the death rays, the three thousand magicians who live in Berlin alone … the diviners … the astrologers … the many sects, political and medical miracle makers."

Eventually, Hitler's regime aimed to distance itself from the realm of superstition and, when it suited their needs, relabeled occult beliefs as scientific knowledge. Nazi officials might persecute occult practitioners who promoted folk beliefs and other mystical ideas independent from Nazi doctrine but would protect them for promoting Nazi-aligned "scientific occultism"—particularly if their powers were used to promote racist beliefs, create propaganda, or develop military strategy. Paradoxically, the Nazi doctrine situated itself in the fields of pseudoscience, investigating phenomena beyond human perception, while railing against popular occult beliefs like fortune-telling.

Rudolf Hess, Hitler's deputy, was enthralled by astrology, and his eventual downfall—in which he used his interpretation of the stars to launch an attempted peace deal with Britain—led to a 1941 Gestapo roundup of hundreds of astrologers, clairvoyants, and occultists. Meanwhile, magicians received special dispensation and were welcome to join the Reich Magicians' Association. At one point, top Nazi officials recruited dozens of occultists to gather military intelligence and produce propaganda.

Fascination with the occult didn't cease when Germany was defeated in 1945. After the war, German society continued to seek out popular occult figures, including faith healers and clairvoyants. On the fringes, mystical Nazi ideology has continued to fuel neo-Nazi movements in countries from Norway to the United States, some of which even perform magical rites at former Nazi Party headquarters.

∧ A séance in German director Fritz Lang's 1922 film *Dr. Mabuse, der Spieler (Dr. Mabuse, the Gambler)* reflects the period's occult fascination.

MODERN DIVINATION

Moving Into the Mainstream

By the early 1890s, astrology had taken hold of London, and the practice quickly spread to the United States. According to an 1894 article in Utah's *Salt Lake Herald*, "No hostess is considered a success … unless she provides an astrologer as one of the attractions" at gatherings in well-to-do homes. The going rate was $2 for a quick reading, while an elaborate horoscope could cost $100—around $3,500 today.

Before long, newspapers began publishing regular columns about zodiac signs, the positions of the sun, and the birthday of the reader. In newspaper headlines through the 1920s, psychics predicted the end of World War I, the births of future leaders, and outbreaks of plagues.

At different times, fortune-telling was in turn embraced and banned by governments across the world. In England, astrologers could be prosecuted under the 1824

> Palmistry entrenched itself in the United States by the mid-20th century, with fortune tellers like this New Jersey palmist working for loyal clients and passersby.

ARTIFACT SPOTLIGHT

ANCIENT ASTROLOGY

In the late 1800s, German linguists found a trove of Hellenistic astrological fragments from libraries in Europe and published a 12-volume set called *Catalogus Codicum Astrologorum Graecorum (Catalog of the Codices of the Greek Astrologers)*. In the 1990s, a group of astrologers created an initiative, dubbed Project Hindsight, that translated these texts from ancient Greek to illuminate the primitive techniques of astral interpretation. One major distinction between ancient and modern readings of the stars, they found, was that while astrology is now often used as a guide for making life decisions, Hellenistic astrology was not. In fact, many ancient scholars believed that humans had little free will, with fate already predetermining the major arc of their lives, and astrology was intended to prepare followers for life's unexpected twists.

A 17th-century Dutch depiction of Greek astrologer Claudius Ptolemy's geocentric universe

PALMIST

Hand
writing
Analysis
$1.00

Readings by MRS. JOANNA

PHRENOLOGY

HAND
Writing
ANALYSIS
$1.00

ONE
WIN
CHOICE
ON YOUR
NUMBER

TOYS

Vagrancy Act. In the 1940s, California lawmakers introduced bills that would have required a license to practice astrology; for a time, practicing or advertising astrology as a business became a misdemeanor in Los Angeles. In response, astrologers published articles and organized associations to gain scientific recognition.

Among those who would make fortune-telling a household occurrence was New York astrologer Evangeline Adams, who ushered in modern astrology and made the practice respectable for business elites. In her 10th-floor office in Carnegie Hall, she consulted with notables like J. P. Morgan, Charles Schwab, and two different heads of the New York Stock Exchange, even though fortune-telling was at the

time banned in New York as a form of disorderly conduct. In 1914, however, a magistrate noted Adams had "raised astrology to the dignity of an exact science." No longer was the practice confined to the realms of street psychics and palm readers.

As industrialization, mortgage-backed securities, insurance, and other new financial risks entered American society, some turned to predictions to cope with economic uncertainty. By the end of Adams's life, she had advised an estimated 100,000 clients and reached more than 1.3 million listeners on her triweekly WABC radio program—all while printing a monthly "forecast" of the world. Adams has been credited with predicting the stock market crash of 1929 and the outbreak of World War II.

ᐯ Astrologer Joan Quigley, seen here in 1990, advised First Lady Nancy Reagan and reportedly helped set President Ronald Reagan's schedule.

Astrology's 20th-century rise captivated society's most respectable academics. Psychologist Carl Jung called it "the science of antiquity" and studied its influence over the human psyche, believing that the stars could help illuminate the characters of individuals. In 1966, a British psychiatrist created the short-lived Premonitions Bureau, which collected normal people's predictions to test whether disasters could be anticipated—and therefore prevented— by visions and dreams.

In the 1960s, once marginal ideas and lifestyles entered mainstream America, with popular figures like the Beatles championing New Age ideas (see page 334). Divination was practiced from Woodstock to the dark-paneled meeting rooms of Washington, D.C.

In 1967, Ronald Reagan scheduled his swearing-in as governor of California for the strange time of 12:10 a.m., purportedly to assure that the placement of Jupiter— planet of kings and prosperity—was at its most powerful. It was an open secret that the Reagans put their trust in the zodiac to make important decisions. In the White House, President Reagan and his wife, Nancy, regularly consulted Jeane Dixon, the "Seeress of Washington," who had predicted John F. Kennedy's death, and astrologer Joan Quigley, whom Nancy sought out after her husband survived an assassination attempt in March 1981. Quigley boasted that she had advised on nearly every aspect of the president's schedule, as well as important diplomatic decisions during the Cold War. Reagan's chief of staff later said that "the president's schedule—and therefore his life and the most important business of the American nation—was largely under the control of the first lady's astrologer." Nancy denied this while admitting that astrological cues had been "a factor."

Today, those seeking guidance in the stars merely need to look down at their phones. Websites and apps comparing birth charts with potential friends and partners have proliferated, and one can even arrange a psychic reading or tarot consultation over a video call. ■

RITES & RITUALS

ORIGINS OF PALMISTRY

What can your hands reveal about your past—or your future? Fortune tellers practicing palmistry (also known as chiromancy) read lines, creases, and spots in search of signs. The practice's origins are murky, though they may have roots in India. Forms of palm-reading have been practiced around the world, including in Mesopotamia, Persia, China, and Tibet. Chiromancy appears in the writings of Greek philosopher Aristotle (who believed in it) and Roman philosopher Pliny the Elder (who didn't). Palmistry saw an uptick in European popularity during the Renaissance, but the practice didn't have its current cachet in the West until the 19th century, when new books by French military captain Casimir d'Arpentigny and eccentric English polymath Edward Heron-Allen, who once read Oscar Wilde's palm, contributed to a renewal of interest.

A palmistry map of the hand, circa 1890

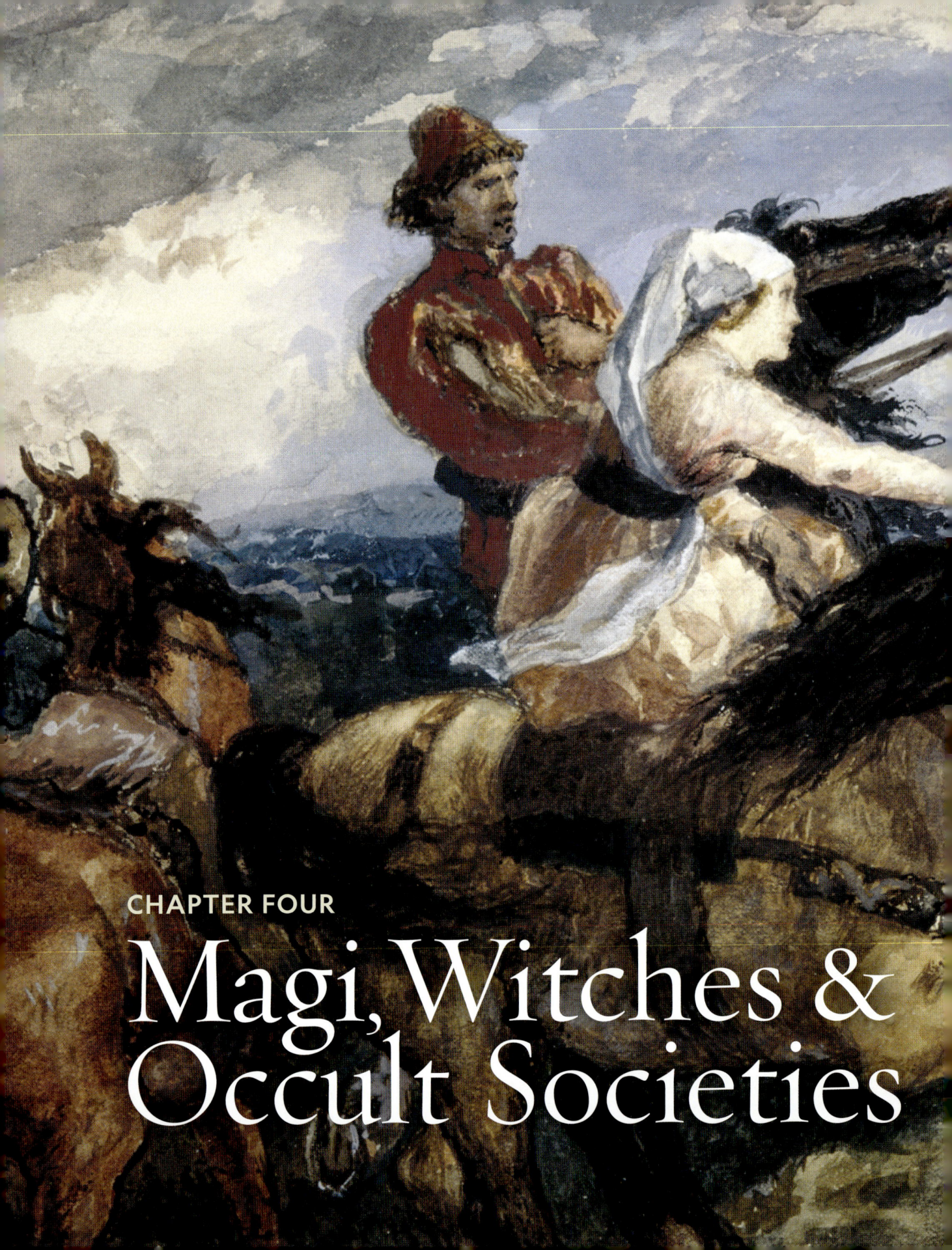

CHAPTER FOUR

Magi, Witches & Occult Societies

The supposed threat posed by witches, like the one depicted in this 1888 painting by John Gilbert, inspired, terrified, and transformed the world.

Working Magic

Practice & Punishment

Long before magic had a name, our earliest ancestors understood that some among them could bridge the spiritual and physical worlds. These magic workers would become known, through the centuries, as shamans, magi, healers, sorcerers, and witches.

Over time, magic has seeped into nearly every aspect of the social order. Those with talents for astrology, healing, and alchemy once served as consultants for royalty and nobility. John Dee, adviser to Queen Elizabeth I of England, provided counsel using a "magic mirror." The early emperors of the Mughal Empire, in what is now India, structured their entire lives around the astrological rhythms of the cosmos.

For millennia, magic was an important part of spiritual and religious beliefs. But its reputation would take a dark turn at the end of the Middle Ages, when it became pitted against organized religion. For four bloody centuries, witch hunts across Europe—and occasionally in the Americas—killed an estimated 50,000 people. Today, false accusations of witchcraft continue to fuel persecution, often of women, across Asia, Africa, and the Middle East.

Still, our collective desire to unlock the mysteries of the world around us has never diminished. And there have always been those who have offered answers—sometimes through mystery cults, secret societies, or occult organizations, but more often through individuals who claim to possess, or control, magic powers.

Over the centuries, magical traditions survived the transatlantic slave trade, witch hunts, and religious oppression, sometimes serving as sustenance through history's darkest hours. And magic workers have survived by offering an irresistible product: answers to life's most impossible questions. ■

∧ Shaman figure, Democratic Republic of the Congo

Swiss painter Karl Bodmer painted a shrine of the Mandan Native American people in the 1830s: Poles covered in hides and feathers represent the sun and the moon.

THE FIRST MAGICIANS

Shamanism Around the Globe

Thousands of years before the physical sciences captured our curiosity, prehistoric ideas of the world blended the natural, physical, and spiritual realms into a potent brew: animism. In this belief system, the world abounds in conscious entities with souls that must be controlled and appeased. Humans hope to influence this omnipresent power for their own benefit through properly delivered prayers, offerings, and rituals that might help them navigate an inhospitable world.

Shamans were specialists in these rituals, connecting to the spirit realm to negotiate on behalf of their communities. Imbued with religious and spiritual power, a shaman traveled, often through ritual trance, between worlds to seek assistance and information. Though their practices varied widely, it was thought that a spirit animal often transported the shaman into the alternate realm. Objects known as sacra aided in the journey.

Though we don't know when the Tungusic people of Siberia first introduced the word "shaman" to describe an intermediary between humans and the spirit world, the region has long been considered the

---

HILAZON TACHTIT

In 2008, archaeologists unveiled a 12,000-year-old burial of an approximately 45-year-old woman at Hilazon Tachtit, in northern Israel. Many large stones had been placed atop her head, pelvis, and arms during burial. Buried with her were more than 50 complete tortoise shells, the forearm of a wild boar, the partial wing of an eagle, the tail of an aurochs, the pelvis of a leopard, and two marten skulls. Archaeologists also found a fragment of a carved basalt bowl and a complete human foot that did not belong to the buried woman. The wide array of animal remains may indicate that the woman had an intimate connection with animal spirits, and the elaborate nature of her burial suggests that she held a special place in her community—very possibly as a shaman.

Tortoise shell found among the Hilazon Tachtit funerary offerings

een Schaman ofte Duyvel-priester.
in 't Tungoesen Clant

birthplace of the practice. And because of its place on the pathways of human migration, Siberia is thought to be the source of shamanism's spread across the Western Hemisphere.

Early shamans of Siberia and other steppe cultures operated at a time of great uncertainty and social change. In the final days of the Pleistocene epoch, more than 11,700 years ago, Earth's climate was warming in fits and starts. As modern human civilizations formed around 4000 B.C., cultural behaviors changed, too, with foraging giving way to farming. Ritual specialists could have been in high demand to help navigate these changes, binding together newly formed societies with traditions and customs that could help them weather an uncertain world.

At one time, shamans—who could also serve as medicine men, psychics, or prophets—were so prevalent that shamanism is sometimes referred to as the first profession. And while their practices have relatively opaque origins, we do have some insight into their ritual tool kits. A site more than 12,000 years old in modern-day Utah preserves evidence of humans using tobacco around the hearth—evidence of prehistoric use of intoxicating substances that may have been part of spiritual practices. In Jordan, a similarly dated site has produced a fox skull and other buried remains that scientists speculate could be remnants of a shamanic ritual. Siberian rock art going back more than 4,000 years depicts figures holding drums: critical tools for chanting and entering a shamanic trance. Headdresses, carved staffs, and bird feathers have been found in suspected shaman ritual sites around the world.

Evidence of early human belief in shamans, dating back at least 12,000 years, exists in nearly all documented hunter-gatherer cultures, from Greenland to India. The emerging global belief in shamanism would serve as the foundation for spiritual and religious tradition.

∧ Published in 1692 by Dutch explorer Nicolaas Witsen, this engraving is the earliest known European depiction of a shaman among North Asia's Evenki people.

MAGICAL PRIESTS AT COURT

Advisers, Healers & Exorcists

During the neo-Assyrian and neo-Babylonian empires (883–539 B.C.), in what is now Iraq, magic intermingled with religion and pervaded everyday life. Expert magic practitioners advised kings and rendered services ranging from the medical to the divinatory.

Professional healers and exorcists known as *āšipu* performed purification rituals for the king and the palace, and they played an important role in diagnosing and providing prognoses for especially complex and serious illnesses. Their approach often took a divinatory bent, with āšipu using rituals and incantations to determine which past offense to the gods had caused the illness. To aid them in their work, āšipu kept a close lookout for divinatory signs, both while walking toward the houses of ill patients and on the patients' bodies themselves.

Āšipu trained extensively for their roles using diagnostic handbooks. According to one such book, attributed to the 11th-century B.C. Babylonian scholar Esagil-kin-apli, if a patient came down with a terrible headache and could no longer hear, they had been struck by a god's hand and would soon die. In the Babylonians' system of magic and medicine, āšipu coexisted with other practitioners known as *asû*, who specialized in everyday care such as providing medicine or setting broken bones.

To peer into the future, Babylonians relied heavily on extispicy, the form of divination in which an expert looks for signs within an animal's entrails. Answering a king's questions—and empowering him to avoid pending misfortune—required the services of a *bārû*. Like āšipu, bārû trained extensively for their roles and were considered members of the urban elite.

Bārû ritually sacrificed a goat or sheep in offering to the two deities associated with extispicy: Šamaš, the god of the sun

∧ Model of an animal's liver inscribed with divinatory text, 13th century B.C., Assyria

and justice, and Adad, the god of the weather. Once it was assimilated with the divine, the animal's body could manifest the gods' knowledge of future events. The bārû closely examined the liver and intestines, with the organs' color, texture, and structure revealing the gods' answer to the client's question.

Mesopotamia's magical experts strove to protect people from *kišpū*—evil and aggressive witchcraft. *Kaššāpu* (warlocks)

and *kaššāptu* (witches) might have the power to render a person unable to defend themselves in legal judgments, make them a social outcast, or bring deadly omens on their head. Anti-witchcraft rituals promised to reverse these curses and ruin the sorcerers who cast them. The most thorough of these rituals, the *maqlû* (burning), required all-night chanting of nearly a hundred incantations while incinerating figurines that represented the offender.

∧ The inscription crossing this stone panel, which features a ninth-century B.C. Assyrian king (left), most likely gave divine protection to a palace.

MAGI
Keepers of Wisdom & Knowledge

In ancient Iran, starting around the third century B.C., a group of scholars and sages known as magi wielded incredible power over generations of Persian kings. The magi were fortune tellers, shamans, astronomers, dream interpreters, and guides on par with religious leaders; their powers were recognized as far afield as ancient Greece and Rome.

Although it's likely that they predated the religion itself, magi would come to be synonymous with priests of the Zoroastrian faith—today considered the world's oldest form of monotheism. Based on the teachings of Zoroaster, a Persian religious reformer and prophet who lived around the second millennium B.C., its practices revolve around a never-ending battle between good and evil spirits. As Zoroastrian priests, the magi introduced and

PROFILE

KARTĒR

When the high priest Kartēr was appointed by the Persian king Ardashir I in the third century A.D., he immediately set about reinstating the ancient Zoroastrian faith. As the *magaput*, or chief of the magi, he oversaw fire rituals—ranging from coming-of-age ceremonies to burial rites—and issued decrees about the uses of bathhouses, the slaughter of animals for meat, and the burial of the dead. Kartēr persecuted practitioners of other religions, from Judaism and Buddhism to different sects of Zoroastrianism, and served under four kings who reigned for a combined 52 years. Today, his legacy is inscribed in reliefs and inscriptions at ancient sites in modern Iran, where he appears with a tall round hat, a large necklace, and a hand raised with a pointed finger.

A relief depiction of Kartēr, at Iran's Naqsh-e Rajab archaeological site

❮ This French reliquary, circa 1200, depicts the Gospel of Matthew's description of three magi journeying to visit Jesus.

formalized fire rituals, still featured prominently in the religion today. They also retained incredible power: marching with armies, performing sacrifices, interpreting the dreams of kings, and guarding important tombs.

In a text known as the Avesta, compiled from third- to seventh-century manuscripts, the magi were described as early pioneers of medical sciences, known in particular for teaching medicine and astrology. Other texts document the magi's rituals, including sacrificial offerings of crushed plants and wolf's blood presented with spells to ward off misfortune and evil.

Much of what's known about the magi comes from ancient Greek records. In a papyrus from around 300 B.C., the work of the magi is described as incantations, sacrifices, and offerings. By the fifth century B.C., magi appeared in Greek plays and treatises as characters able to cure the sick and raise the dead. Plato and Socrates were linked to magi teachers, and the philosopher Democritus, said to have been taught by magi priests, described their use of a special herb to "conjure up the gods."

According to the Greek historian Herodotus, magi were dream interpreters, sacrifice overseers, alcohol purveyors, and killers of vermin; his vivid descriptions render them as wise foreigners who presided over sacrifices in honor of the sun, moon, and other powerful entities of the earth. (He deems one particularly chilling account of a magi horse sacrifice during a military campaign *pharmakeusantes*, or sorcery.)

Magi would be enshrined into history around 5 B.C., when they read of the birth of Jesus in the stars, according to the Gospel of Matthew. Three magi—also known as three wise men—traveled to Jerusalem to meet the newborn baby, describing themselves as priests from the East.

In time, this order of mysterious priests would become a global prototype for sorcerers, magicians, and medicine men. The term came to be used for other magicians, particularly those from Babylonia. But while the Persian magi retained their reputation as keepers of wisdom and knowledge, magicians from other parts of the world were often treated with far less reverence.

WU & WITCHCRAFT

The Emperor's Magicians

As far back as the Shang dynasty (circa 1600–1046 B.C.), oracular bones contained inscriptions of *wu,* a term used throughout Chinese history to connote shamans or practitioners of magic (its exact original meaning remains debated). Use of the word in Chinese literature blossomed beginning in the fifth century B.C. In royal writings, wu are described as ritual experts who variously summoned rain, communicated with spirits, collected magical and medicinal herbs, and tended to the welfare of the emperor and his court.

On some occasions, wu were associated with the darker arts of witchcraft. Accusations of the practice arose multiple times during the reign of Emperor Wu, also known as Wudi, of the Han dynasty. In 130 B.C., 10 years into Wudi's reign, his wife, Empress Chen Jiao, was accused of using witchcraft to harm the monarch's favorite concubine. Chen Jiao was deposed as empress, and 300 people said to be involved in the plot were executed.

In 91 B.C., near the end of Wudi's life, a power struggle between the families of two of his consorts led to a blizzard of dubious witchcraft accusations, including some aimed at his heir apparent. Paranoid and highly superstitious, Wudi approved large-scale witch hunts that ultimately led to the deaths of tens of thousands—including many of his male heirs.

Through this period, multitalented scholars known as *fang shih* also began to rise to prominence. Known as "masters of methods" or "masters of recipes," they acted as experts in a variety of disciplines, including astrology, medicine, and music. During the Han dynasty (206 B.C.–A.D. 220) and earlier Qin dynasty (221–207 B.C.), emperors became patrons to fang shih alchemists who attempted to make elixirs of immortality.

< Emperor Wu of the Han dynasty, as depicted by 18th-century Japanese artist Komatsuya Hyakki

< Mount Penglai, imagined here by 18th-century Chinese artist Yuan Yao, is a legendary island that multiple Chinese emperors tried and failed to find.

Among the most prominent was Li Shaojun, a fang shih in Wudi's employ and the earliest known alchemist mentioned by name in ancient Chinese literature. According to the *Shiji*, a major history of early Chinese dynasties, Li strongly implied that he was centuries old. He also advised Wudi on a convoluted strategy for immortality: Use spirits to turn cinnabar into gold, make life-extending eating and drinking vessels out of that gold, and then live long enough to perform important sacrifices on Mount Penglai, a legendary island in Chinese lore. Wudi sent out expeditions to search for Mount Penglai, with little to show for it.

Wudi's quest for eternal life would remain an imperial obsession. No fewer than six different emperors of the Tang dynasty (A.D. 618–907) died of poisoning after drinking potions meant to grant them immortality.

MYTHS & CULTS

Witches & Sorcerers in Classical Cultures

The mythology of ancient Greece and Rome abounds with characters from whom magic flows: witches, sorcerers, and gods of all stripes. The Greek goddess Hecate, a powerful deity born of the titans of night and destruction, governed magic and spells. According to myth, Hecate witnessed Hades' abduction of Persephone to the underworld, then helped in the search for her; thus, she is thought of as a watchful eye, warding off evil spirits. In magical papyri created between the second century B.C. and the fifth century A.D., Hecate regularly appeared in spells that invoked the dead.

Greek legends also contain stories of powerful sorcerers. In Homer's *Odyssey*, the sorceress Circe uses spells and enchanted food to transform human men into swine, wolves, and lions. After imprisoning the men for a year, she returns them to human form, lets them feast on her island, and outfits them for their voyage. Upon leaving Circe's island, Odysseus himself dabbles in dark magic, sacrificing a black ram to summon a ghost.

Medea was another powerful magician, often depicted as a priestess of Hecate. According to the myth, the lovestruck sorceress helps the young prince Jason steal the Golden Fleece, a potent and revered symbol of kingly authority, from her father. She does so in part by giving Jason an ointment that protects him from some of the fleece's guardians, two fire-breathing bulls. Jason and Medea then marry, but later, when Jason abandons her to remarry, she murders their children, as well as Jason's new wife—by sending her an enchanted robe that burns her alive.

In the real world, the religious lives of ancient Greeks and Romans swirled with secrecy in the form of so-called mystery cults. These groups promised commoners access to religious experiences beyond what they could obtain through public rituals, ensuring a privileged afterlife.

< This fifth-century B.C. Greek vase shows two of Odysseus' men transformed into beasts—the work of the sorceress Circe.

An embodiment of female vengeance, the sorceress Medea has inspired many works of art over the centuries, including this iconic 1868 painting by Frederick Sandys.

ANCIENT GREEKS AND ROMANS DEVELOPED CULTS DEVOTED TO EGYPTIAN DEITIES.

Members of these sects forged social bonds through shared ceremonies, meals, and rites.

The best known cult was the Eleusinian Mysteries, which honored Demeter, Greek goddess of agriculture and the harvest. The group's annual initiation ritual was an elaborate—and highly secretive—nine-day festival that retold the legend of Demeter and her search for her daughter, Persephone, through events that included a simulated nighttime descent into the underworld.

The cult of Dionysus, dedicated to the Greek god of wine (known in Rome as Bacchus), met regularly for secret events that entailed all manner of revelry: drinking, feasting, singing, dancing, and eating raw meat. Their events, called Bacchanalia, enjoyed backing from wealthy Roman patrons. But these groups also attracted scrutiny. In 186 B.C., the Roman Senate banned Bacchic cult activities, possibly because of the cult's growing power and influence—and the threat that it therefore posed to traditional Roman powers.

Ancient Greeks and Romans also developed cults devoted to Egyptian deities—notably Isis, wife of Osiris, a powerful healer and magician and protector of crops. Because of her association with

THE CULT OF MITHRAS

In the second and third centuries A.D., one of the Roman Empire's most pervasive mystery cults centered on Mithras, a sun god inspired by the pre-Zoroastrian Persian deity Mithra. Adherents of the religion organized themselves in a seven-rung hierarchy and worshipped in small groups within caves that symbolized the universe. Entering and departing the sacred spaces symbolized the soul's fleeting stay in the mortal realm. Many of these caves featured reliefs of Mithras sacrificially killing a bull, the deity's central myth. The Cult of Mithras was especially popular among Roman military officers, bureaucrats, and freed slaves, and it enjoyed state support into the early fourth century. However, after the Roman emperor Constantine adopted Christianity in 312, support for Mithras quickly evaporated. By the end of the fifth century, the religion had vanished.

Roman stela (relief) of Mithras sacrificing a bull, second to third century A.D.

PYTHAGORAS AS MAGICIAN

In modern culture, the Greek philosopher and mathematician Pythagoras (570–circa 490 B.C.) is probably best known for the geometric theorem named for him (although ironically, it predated his birth by more than a thousand years, having been independently discovered in ancient Babylon and Egypt). Still, in his own time, Pythagoras had a magical air about him, infused through the work of a religious order called the Brotherhood of Pythagoreans. He and his followers believed in an immortal soul that could transmigrate into different kinds of animals. They also placed great symbolic significance in numbers and maintained that mathematics described the universe at its deepest levels, from music to astronomy. One of the Pythagoreans' most important symbols was the *tetraktys*, a triangle formed from 10 dots. The number 10 was considered the perfect number, as it was the sum of 1, 2, 3, and 4: a mystical sign of unity.

fertility and agriculture, Greek observers compared Isis to Demeter and regularly worshipped the two together. The cult spread rapidly from the third century B.C. onward, but in 53 B.C., the Roman Senate ordered the destruction of private temples to Isis and other Egyptian deities. By A.D. 65, the Isis cult had been reinstated and its temple rebuilt.

Rome's openness to—and suspicion of—foreign gods extended to the deities of Asia. One of the most influential of these was the Great Mother of the Gods, also known as Magna Mater or Cybele. In 204 B.C., during the invasion of Hannibal, Roman oracles declared that foreign invaders would retreat if Cybele was brought to Rome from Pergamon (modern-day Turkey). Rome's elite orchestrated the delivery of the goddess's icon—a hunk of black meteoric iron—built her a temple, and initiated games in her honor. The cult of Cybele grew wildly popular, with annual parades that carried her statue through the streets. Her most devoted male followers, a priesthood known as the Galli, castrated themselves and dressed in women's clothing in her honor.

> Mural found in a temple to Isis in Herculaneum, a Roman town destroyed in A.D. 79 by the eruption of Mount Vesuvius

MAGIC IN THE BIBLE

Miracles & Belief

In religious texts, the line between magic and miracle is often blurred; an act may appear magical, but the results are called miracles. In Judaism, magic is explicitly outlawed by the Torah: "You shall not … practice divination or soothsaying." However, Jewish history is filled with tales of supernatural events, spells to ward off evil, healing rituals for the sick, and spirit conjuring. Ancient followers of Judaism practiced magical routines and demon exorcism, and some religious texts, including the Babylonian Talmud, were sprinkled with magical spells and recipes.

One of the most mystical figures in Judaism is King Solomon, said to control demons and variously depicted as magician, astrologer, and exorcist. Solomon possessed a ring—sometimes described as a seal—that was a gift from the archangel Michael and allowed him to summon and control demons.

In archaeological excavations across the Middle East and in Rome, a rich tradition of Jewish magic has emerged. In a tomb outside Jerusalem, excavators found two tiny silver scrolls containing an ancient Hebrew blessing, likely from around the sixth century B.C., that was intended to protect its wearer. The fragments are the earliest known Torah scripture.

In the Judaean Desert, archaeologists have found evidence that ancient Jews believed in demonic possession and exorcism, a practice that appears in the Dead Sea Scrolls. The scrolls contain spells to vanquish demons and demon-caused illnesses, perform magic, and practice divination.

In modern Syria and Rome, protective Jewish amulets ranging from the fourth to seventh centuries—some in Greek letters and others possibly made for Christian clients—have emerged from the earth. In present-day Iraq and Iran, some 2,000 clay bowls were inscribed in numerous dialects of Aramaic with spells against demons, witchcraft, and the evil eye.

The Cairo Geniza, a groundbreaking trove of Jewish texts discovered in Egypt at the end of the 19th century, contained more than a thousand fragments of magical texts, including: the Pishra de-Rabbi Hanina ben Dosa, a spell to remove all witchcraft; spells for the end of the Sabbath; and spells that promise economic gain, agricultural success, love, and memory

< Marble statue of King Solomon by 14th-century Florentine sculptor Andrea Pisano

This 19th-century Jewish amulet, featuring a hamsa (protective hand symbol) and an angel depicted as a bird, confers protection to a birthing mother

enhancement for the aim of studying. Some of these fragments helped reconstruct the Sefer ha-Razim, the Book of Mysteries, which contains magical recipes and may have modified concepts from Greek and Egyptian influences. Jewish scholars likely contributed to the spread of magic across the ancient world, particularly the Greco-Roman empires.

For many years, scholars believed that magic was an external force Jewish religion was forced to contend with, despite it breaking the faith's core tenets. Today, it's understood that magic was foundational to Jewish literature and history, and widely practiced not only by commoners but by the elite.

This widespread magical practice would seep into the emerging Christian faith. Early Christians believed that the biblical King Solomon was the original magician. His epic Talmudic poem, the *Song of Songs*, was used as a magical guide that would inspire spells and exorcisms in many future grimoires, or books of spells (see page 210), into the Middle Ages. The miracles performed by Jesus Christ—from healing the sick to turning water into wine—informed the beliefs of Christians for millennia. And as in Judaism, exorcisms and the expulsion of demons were commonly practiced by early Christians. These practices led, in turn, to both Jews and Christians being accused of practicing magic or sorcery—often to be feared, but at other times respected, by greater society.

As time went on, Christians embraced the same type of charms and spells as their Jewish counterparts, writing down or reciting biblical passages to ensure everything from curing toothaches to protecting against witchcraft.

Christianity would evolve into a contentious relationship with magic—at times embracing it in the rites and rituals of the faith, at others banning it by church decree. Over time, magic would come to be seen as heretical by the church, but some remaining practices—the use of the cross as protection and the veneration of relics—still echo early Jewish magical beliefs. ■

> A 12th-century mosaic in Sicily shows the biblical tale of Jesus healing two blind men he encounters outside Jericho.

IN LEGEND

THE WITCH OF ENDOR

According to the Old Testament, after banishing sorcerers from Israel, King Saul decided to visit a witch in Endor, located in modern-day northern Israel, who had a connection to the other world. When the king met the woman, he promised her protection from his own decree if she would conjure the spirit of the prophet Samuel. The witch possessed a talisman to summon the dead, and with it she called upon Samuel's ghost. Through her, the spirit prophesied that King Saul and his three sons would die the next day while fighting the Philistines, which indeed they did. The story of the witch of Endor would go on to inspire music, artwork, literature, and even the 19th-century Spiritualism movement (see page 260).

The Witch of Endor in a detail from a 19th-century painting by Dmitry Nikiforovich Martynov

MYSTERIOUS PRIESTS

Druids, Celts & the Origins of Arthur

Very little is known about the Druids, the priestly social class of Celtic peoples who lived in what is now Ireland, Britain, and France. The Celts left no written records of them, so historians have been forced to rely on outsider accounts to understand the rituals of these mysterious priests. The oldest Greek and Roman sources date to the first century B.C.

Julius Caesar, who waged war with the Gauls between 58 and 50 B.C., observed that the Druids among them were held "in great honor" and "engage in things sacred, conduct the public and the private sacrifices, and interpret all matters of religion." According to Caesar, Druids trained for decades, memorizing sacred verses and studying astronomy and natural philosophy. They served as judges, teachers, and political leaders, and preached that the soul was immortal, passed from one body to another.

Writing in the first century A.D., Pliny the Elder said that the Druids considered mistletoe sacred, and its branches played a role in most major rites. He described a ceremony in which a white-robed priest climbed a tree and cut the mistletoe growing on it with a golden sickle, in preparation for the sacrifice of two white bulls.

Greek and Roman observers painted a bloody picture of Druids' rituals. Pliny the Elder claimed that they ate the flesh of sacrificial victims "to secure the highest blessings of health." Both Caesar and the Greek geographer Strabo claimed that they built so called "wicker men," large wooden effigies filled with living people and set ablaze in giant acts of sacrifice.

Modern historians treat these accounts with some skepticism. As they conquered Celtic communities, the Romans had every incentive to paint the Druids—a potent cultural force, and therefore a threat to Roman rule—as strange and barbarous.

Still, there is some archaeological evidence for sacrifice among the Celts, chiefly in the form of "bog bodies" that show signs of violent, possibly ritualized deaths. In 2003, peat cutters in Ireland found two bodies, now named Old Croghan Man and Clonycavan Man, both more than 2,000 years old. They appear to have been ritually sacrificed, one with holes cut

> ∧ A Celtic sword and scabbard with a human-shaped hilt, circa 60 B.C.

The late 19th century saw renewed interest in Celtic art, exemplified by this 1890 Scottish painting of Druids bringing in ritually cut mistletoe.

through his upper arms for restraint ropes, the other disemboweled. Both had their nipples cut off. One theory holds that the two were kings who reigned during major crop failures, which would have been seen as breaches of their sacred marriages to the land. In ancient Ireland, where sucking a king's nipples was a gesture of submission, their removal could be seen as an emphatic rejection of the king's rule—and a method of preventing him from reigning in the hereafter.

Lindow Man, a nearly 2,000-year-old peat body found in 1984 in Cheshire, England, also shows signs of a brutal death. He was stabbed and strangled, his skull smashed in with a club or stick and his body dumped into a bog pool. Four grains of mistletoe pollen were found in his stomach. Had Lindow Man deliberately eaten the plant, possibly during a pre-sacrificial rite?

Once Christianity began to spread through Celtic lands in the first century A.D., Druids were either suppressed or barred from their priestly functions. But across the Celtic world, pagan imagery, symbols, and holy sites seeped into Christian practice. Druids occasionally made cameos in Christian stories: St. Patrick, the patron saint of Ireland, was said to have quelled a snowstorm summoned by a Druid wielding dark magic. Mistletoe also became linked to Christmastime, eventually yielding the seasonal practice of kissing under the mistletoe.

Celtic tradition was deeply interwoven into the cultures of Britain and Ireland and is still felt throughout those lands' history and mythology. Some scholars have speculated that deep-rooted Celtic themes helped shape the ostensibly Christian legends of King Arthur, first laid down by the Welsh cleric Geoffrey of Monmouth in the 12th century. ▪

> This early 15th-century tapestry depicts King Arthur, a semilegendary Christian king of the Britons, as one of the "Nine Worthies," who embodied medieval chivalry.

ARTIFACT SPOTLIGHT

VULGATE CYCLE MANUSCRIPT

The legends of King Arthur, Merlin, and the Knights of the Round Table flourished in England and France in the 12th and 13th centuries. Some of the most influential and comprehensive versions of these legends emerged in France between 1215 and 1240 in a series of anonymously written romances known collectively as the Vulgate Cycle. Some 200 versions have been found so far, all with minor variations that hint at the tastes and sensitivities of scribes' individual patrons. In most versions, the enchantress Viviane tattoos three names onto her groin, which prevents Merlin from sleeping with her. But a 13th-century fragment discovered in Bristol in 2019 makes Viviane's spell more family-friendly by having her engrave three names onto a ring instead.

A 14th-century French drawing of a beggar and three Knights of the Round Table carrying the Holy Grail's silver table

AMONG THE SPIRITS

Magic in West Africa

In the West African epic story of *Sujata*, dating back to the 14th century, the concept of *dalilu* is described as a secret recipe of acts, materials, and energy that creates a powerful entity. This belief among the Mande people is one of the few documented features of early magical beliefs in West Africa. Scholars today seek to understand historic practices by studying both their modern counterparts and the remnants of religions that traveled to the Americas.

Long before Christianity and Islam arrived in West Africa, many aspects of life were dictated by indigenous religions. Nearly all people worshipped a pantheon of divinities meant to protect and guide humans, particularly in matters of health, relationships, wealth, and natural disasters. In many traditional African religions, everything—from mountains to plants to inanimate objects—has a spirit.

Communication among deities, ancestral guides, and spirits is the most important aspect of the region's many religions. Yoruba people in Nigeria, Togo, and Benin use shells and nuts to facilitate communication through Ifa divination, and decisions are made in consultation with a diviner (see page 120). Across West Africa, stones, shells, animal entrails, and seeds have been used to predict the future and diagnose illnesses.

In Yoruba tradition, Orisha divinities govern every part of the human body, requiring unique offerings for different ailments. For the Kongo people, who live along Africa's Atlantic coast, medicine is a magical process that requires a *nkisi*—a charm that contains a spirit's soul, along with a type of magical power called *juju*. Juju can be good or bad, and it may be held in blessed amulets or in cursed items like food, drinks, or live animals.

Today, indigenous practices remain an undercurrent of belief in West Africa. Some secret societies still practice spirit

∧ A ram's head carved in ivory decorated the head of a Yoruba leader, known as the *olowo*, in Nigeria.

This wood-and-iron figure was stuffed with medicines by a Kongo ritual specialist and used to heal sickness, mediate disputes, and ensure peace.

possessions, use rituals to establish communication between spirits and humans, and believe in witchcraft. In the darkest chapters of Africa's history, that belief may have helped protect some communities from slavery: Because the Ashanti people were said to practice witchcraft, they largely avoided being taken captive by European enslavers.

But the same beliefs that have built rich cultures can fuel accusations that target marginalized groups or may be weaponized by politicians. Even today, witches are thought to cast spells, cause illnesses, and suck life from the young in many areas of Africa. Much of the continent has suffered from modern-day witch hunts, in which those accused as witches are killed or expelled from their communities.

In Western analysis, traditional religions and belief in witchcraft and magic have long been painted as primitive. Despite prejudiced ideas propagated by Western societies, new generations of Africans are reviving magical aspects of indigenous religions. In parts of the continent, traditional beliefs are being celebrated once again as communities attempt to resurrect cultures all but stamped out by the slave trade and colonialism.

READING THE RUNES

Shamans & Sorceresses of Scandinavia

Magic has deep roots in Scandinavia. The Sami people of modern-day Norway, Sweden, Finland, and Russia have lived in the region for millennia—possibly more than 10,000 years—and originally followed a shamanic belief system. The Sami worshipped a host of deities that corresponded with everyday survival, from childbirth to the sky. Like other Indigenous peoples around the world, the Sami held that plants, animals, and even geologic features such as rocks had souls. Natural and purposely built sacred spots across the landscape were used for sacrifices and other offerings.

For the Sami, ritual drumming could connect the human realm with the world of spirits. Powerful shamanic figures known as *noiadi* entered trances and interacted with the spirit realm, aided in their journeys by the spirits of sacred animals.

Starting in the 17th century, Christian missionaries waged a campaign of forced assimilation against the Sami, persecuting any who practiced their traditional religion and destroying their drums and holy sites. Many Sami are now Christian, with the shamanistic religion of old largely forced to extinction.

Old Nordic myths and epic poems dating to as early as the 10th century A.D. mention *seiðr*, another Scandinavian magical practice that some consider to be shamanistic in nature. According to *Eiríks saga Rauða (Saga of Erik the Red)*, which recounts the Norse exploration of North America at the turn of the 11th century, *seiðr* rituals featured a staff-wielding sorceress known as a *völva*, who entered a trance-like state as a group of singers around her chanted incantations. She then communicated with spirits and acted as an oracle for the group.

Many, if not most, practitioners of *seiðr* were female. Male practitioners risked being identified with *ergi*, an insult that denoted effeminacy and unmanliness. Some scholars explain this gender imbalance by drawing a connection between domestic chores, such as spinning and weaving, and the rituals of *seiðr*, which could be thought of as spinning or weaving spirits.

Some historical evidence suggests that

< A 17th-century Sami *runebom*, a drum struck with a reindeer antler wand

Scandinavian peoples used runes—mystical alphabetic letters or marks—for magic (see page 162). The Old Norse poem *Sigrdrífumál* references runes that ensured victory in battle when carved into a sword's hilt and others that aided in childbirth when written on an expectant mother's palms. Whether for communication or magical ends, knowledge of runes was prized. Yet over centuries, knowledge of runic magic faded, until it saw a revival in the 17th century thanks to the Swedish scholar-mystic Johannes Bureus (1568–1652).

Around the time of Bureus, an anonymous group of Icelandic authors assembled a spell book known as the *Galdrabók*, which chronicled a magic tradition unique to Iceland: *galdrastafir*, or magical staves or sigils. In combination with specific procedures, these elaborate designs could bring protection, detect thieves, or even cause someone to vomit as a prank.

∧ A recent study of Sweden's ninth-century Rök stone suggests that the runes describe fears of devastating weather.

RUNES & SIGILS

Runes are letters in the alphabets once used by ancient Germanic peoples who lived across modern-day Scandinavia, Germany, and the British Isles. These characters primarily served as a means of communication and sometimes as magical symbols. They evidently carried great power: In the Old Norse poem *Hávamál*, Odin hangs from a tree for nine days with no food, no water, and a wound from a spear stabbing, all to gain knowledge of the runes. Since the 17th century, mystics and occultists have sought to "revive" (or invent) systems of runic magic by building on details gleaned from ancient

texts, such as possible descriptions of Germanic divination by the Roman historian Tacitus.

Other magical symbols have also held sway in Scandinavia. Since at least the 17th century, Icelandic grimoires have recorded elaborate sigils known as galdrastafir (staves). In combination with specific rituals, or solely on their own, these staves are believed to have the power to grant good fortune in all areas of life—or strike fear into the hearts of others.

^ KILMAINHAM BROOCH
The roughly 1,200-year-old Kilmainham Brooch, found in a Viking burial in Ireland, combines Celtic and Viking influences.

^ VIKING SILVER
Vikings amassed vast amounts of silver, including a 10th-century hoard of 7,000 coins found in Cuerdale, England, in 1940.

< VICTORY
This manuscript page depicts Ægishjálmur (Helm of Awe), a modern Icelandic stave that ensures victory over one's enemies.

^ VEGVÍSIR
This reproduction shield features Vegvísir (Wayfinder), a 19th-century Icelandic stave that keeps its bearer from getting lost.

v THOR'S HAMMER
Vikings wore miniature Thor's hammers as religious charms, such as this ninth-century amulet found in Denmark.

RUNESTONE >
This commemorative runestone was raised in the 11th century outside Stockholm, Sweden.

^ VIKING SWORD
Various symbols, including crosses, festoon the cross guard and pommel of a ninth-century Viking sword.

MODERN RUNIC DIVINATION

In the system of runic divination created by American writer Ralph Blum (1932–2016), pebbles are carved with the oldest form of the runic alphabet, then drawn from a bag and interpreted. The interpretations below are based on Blum's 1982 book *The Book of Runes*.

f

fehu
wealth
fulfillment; nourishment

u

ūruz
aurochs
opportunity disguised as loss

⋀ RUNIC ALMANAC
This 16th-century Norwegian almanac consisting of wooden leaves is inscribed with a runic calendar.

þ

þurisaz
giant
gateway; non-action

a

ansuz
god
self-change; transformation

r

raiþō
riding
communication; reunion

k

kaunaz
ulcer or fire/torch
renewed clarity; openings

g

gebō
gift
imminent union

w

wunjō
joy
new energy; light

h

hagalaz
hail
disruption; coming to one's senses

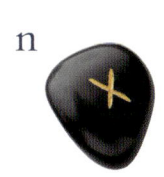

n

nauþiz
need or hardship
constraints imposed by self or others

i

isa
ice
standstill; impediments

j

jera
year or harvest
good outcomes in due time

ï

eihwaz
yew tree
defense; averting difficulties

p

perþ
fruit tree
mystery; questing

z

algiz
elk
protection; resolve

s

sōwulō
sun
wholeness; accessing life force

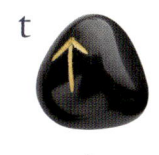

t

teiwaz
the god Tyr
the "Spiritual Warrior"; self-reflection

b

berkana
birch twig
growth; rebirth

e

ehwaz
horse
movement; progress

m

mannaz
man
the self; modesty

l

laguz
water
cleansing; going with the flow

ng

inguz
the god Ingwaz
fertility; new beginnings

d

đagaz
day
breakthrough in self-change

o

ōþila
inherited land
separation; retreat

CASTING BLAME

On Trial for Witchcraft

For thousands of years, the concept of magic and the role of its practitioners fluctuated between a powerful, accepted force in society to one held in suspicion. As the Middle Ages ended, fears and superstitions won out. The popular opinion of witchcraft began to shift into nefarious territory. Between the 14th and 18th centuries, a witch-hunting hysteria consumed Europe, with around 110,000 people put on trial for witchcraft and some 50,000 killed.

Though men were not exempt from accusations, women were most often associated with witchcraft and became an easy target of blame for the pandemics, religious unrest, and conflict shaking Europe. Historians believe women were the victims of around 80 percent of Europe's witch hunts. Older widows often became scapegoats for misfortunes that befell their neighbors, and they had little protection against such charges.

What sparked a witch hunt? The impulse might have been linked to a health crisis, a sudden tragedy, or a time of economic distress that ripped apart an otherwise tight-knit community. Scholars believe witch hunts reached a fever pitch in Europe in the late 1500s as a side effect of economic upheaval: The feudal system of farming had collapsed, and jobs and food were scarce in rural areas. Once laws allowed officials to seize the property and land of accused witches, older women became easy targets.

PROFILE

ALICE KYTELER

Later known as the Witch of Kilkenny, Alice Kyteler was an Irish aristocrat who amassed both a fortune and a series of husbands in the early 14th century. Her stepchildren, likely angry at being disinherited, accused her of witchcraft and claimed she had murdered her husbands and gained her wealth via magic. Kyteler was one of the first women accused of witchcraft in the modern record. She escaped to England, but the trial proceeded, and she was found guilty in absentia. Her "collaborators" were whipped or killed and her maid, Petronilla de Meath, was burned at the stake for the crime of heresy.

The burning of three witches in Baden, Switzerland, as painted in 1585, at the peak of witch hunt fervor in Europe

In this 19th-century Goya painting, Spanish Inquisition defendants are shown wearing the *coroza* and *sambenito*, a hat and garment meant to condemn the accused.

In the Middle Ages, some European courts had set into motion protocols of *inquisitio*, which enabled them to actively seek rule-breakers, not passively await the commission of crimes. This allowed the hunting of heretics: dissidents who argued against the Catholic Church's teachings. But the practice would soon shift to catching supposed witches.

An array of literature emerging at the time offered a guide to organizing witch hunts and trials. Inquisitors—counting in their ranks the author of the witch-hunting manual *Malleus Maleficarum* (see sidebar)—believed their work was saving the Christian population.

One of the world's earliest recorded witch hunts took place in France in the early 1300s. Both men and women—among them a number of clergypersons—were accused of making sacrifices to the devil and performing magic in Toulouse and Carcassonne. From there, witch hunts spread across France and Switzerland and into Germany, the site of large-scale condemnations.

In early trials, the accusers asserted that demonic spirits were possessing the witches. Later, accused witches were believed to be courting the devil to do his

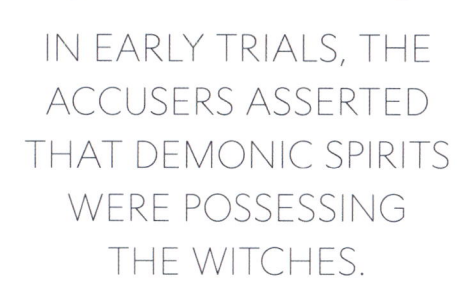

IN EARLY TRIALS, THE ACCUSERS ASSERTED THAT DEMONIC SPIRITS WERE POSSESSING THE WITCHES.

bidding. The concept of the gruesome witches' Sabbath emerged in the early 1400s: Witches were said to gather late at night to feast, smear themselves with ointments that helped them fly, have sexual relations with the devil, and plot against innocent people.

To rile up fear, inquisitors described these debauched affairs, and at trials, the accused were tortured into false confessions of wild tales—one so-called witch described attending a gathering of 10,000. By the 1500s, this witch stereotype was firmly etched in the public imagination.

For more than 350 years, the Spanish Inquisition sought to root out heretics and opposition to the monarchy. Under its auspices, witch hunts thrived—including

ARTIFACT SPOTLIGHT

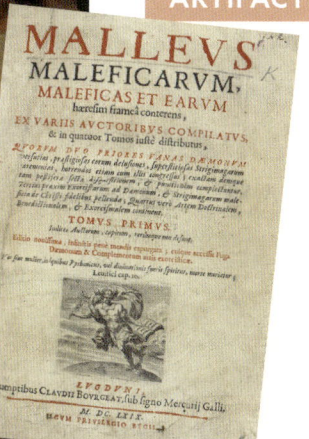

MALLEUS MALEFICARUM

In Latin, *Malleus Maleficarum* means "hammer of witches." And for more than 300 years, this book served as a guide to that end. Written in 1486 by a Dominican friar, not long after Pope Innocent VIII issued an order condemning witchcraft, it laid out folklore as fact, claiming that witches roasted their firstborn sons, invited natural disasters, and made pacts with the devil. The book also gave instructions for trying a witch in a court of law and encouraging the use of torture to get a confession. *Malleus Maleficarum* was republished 28 times before falling out of favor in the 1700s, at the tail end of Europe's witch trials.

Title page of a 1669 French edition of *Malleus Maleficarum*

An 1869 painting of a victim of the Salem witch trials of the 1690s, during which more than 200 people were accused of witchcraft

> IN EUROPE, ACCUSED WITCHES WERE NEARLY ALWAYS CHRISTIANS BEING DECLARED HERETICS.

history's largest, when for five years beginning in 1609, more than 7,000 people in Spanish Basque Country were accused of black magic. But the trial would mark a turning point. As it closed, the inquisitorial judge grew skeptical of the scope of accusations and suggested new rules to limit the reach of witch hunts.

Despite this, trials continued for more than a century. Matthew Hopkins, a British witch-hunter, was among the period's most notorious characters. Between 1644 and 1647, this so-called "Witch Finder General" may have been responsible for 230 deaths—earning him reward payment from local communities equivalent to $200,000 today. In his book *The Discovery of Witches*, Hopkins recommended submerging suspected witches in water to see whether they floated. If they did, they were guilty.

In America, the first person put to death for witchcraft, on May 26, 1647, was Alse Young, a botanist accused of starting a pandemic in the British colony of Connecticut. America's most famous witch hunt began with a man named Cotton Mather, a Puritan minister who had been documenting demonic possession of children. His work may have sparked the more than 200 accusations of witchcraft in Salem, Massachusetts, in 1692 and 1693.

In Europe, accused witches were nearly always Christians being declared heretics. But in Latin America, witch hunts targeted native peoples. In Mexico, the Spanish Inquisition put traditional healers on trial, often young women from lower social castes. And in Peru, a Catholic decree dictated the destruction of "witch doctors," leading to widespread persecution.

Witch hunts continue in the modern world. Socially marginalized individuals are often the victims of such accusations, particularly in India, where people of lower castes have been tried and killed for witchcraft. In Papua New Guinea, children are increasingly accused of sorcery. In Tanzania in the early 2000s, a human rights group estimated that 500 people a year, largely older women and people with albinism, were killed by neighbors as accused witches. Hunts have also been spurred by governments, as in the Gambia, where longtime president Yahya Jammeh imprisoned so-called witches in secret detention centers.

IN LEGEND

BROOMSTICKS & POINTY HATS

The earliest archaeological evidence of a tall, conical hat—essential to today's conception of a witch—was found in a group of 4,000-year-old Chinese mummies. These so-called Witches of Subeshi may have used the hats for falconry. The distinctive style was worn by Bronze Age priests, medieval beer brewers, and Jews living under the Roman Empire. In the early 1700s, children's books began to show wicked old women in tall hats, which became a potent symbol of black magic.

The mythology of the witch's broom may have come from a rising interest in psychedelic ointments beginning in the 14th century. These "flying ointments"—so called for the sensation they provided, and later known as "witch's brews"—were applied to armpits or genitals. In the trial of Alice Kyteler (see page 164) in 1324, investigators wrote: "In rifleing the closet of the ladie, they found a pipe of oyntment, wherewith she greased a staffe, upon which she ambled and galloped through thick and thin."

> Brooms of the time, called besoms, were handmade using twigs and straw.

WITCH TRIALS

In 15th-century Switzerland, a public denounce-ment from three neighbors was enough to brand a person a witch. Over the next three centuries, fearmongering and religious crusades turned much of Europe into killing grounds.

And witch hunts have not ended in modern times. Accusations based in fear and superstition have led to torture, detention, and dozens of deaths from Papua New Guinea to Saudi Arabia to Tanzania and beyond.

1 SALEM, MA, U.S.A.
In the Salem witch trials of 1692–1693, a series of hearings and prosecutions based on accusations of witchcraft led to the executions of 19 people and the imprisonment of many others.

2 WINDSOR, CT, U.S.A.
In 1647, Windsor resident Alse Young became the first per-son in North America's British colonies to be executed for witchcraft—with many to follow.

3 MEXICO CITY, MEXICO
In 1652, healer Isabel de Mon-toya was tried by the Holy Inquisition of Mexico City for accusations of witchcraft.

6 LANCASHIRE, ENGLAND, U.K.
The Pendle witch trials are among England's most famous. In 1612, two families, comprising a dozen individ-uals, were accused of using witchcraft to murder 10 peo-ple in the Pendle Hill area.

7 THE SPANISH NETHERLANDS
Witch hunts abounded during the 16th and 17th centuries in what was then the Spanish Netherlands (now Belgium and Lux-embourg). Between 1450 and 1685, at least 1,150 people were executed as witch-hunting committees called Hexenausschüsse went village to village seek-ing rumors of witchcraft.

8 COPENHAGEN, DENMARK
In 1590, at least four women were burned at the stake in Copenhagen for allegedly casting spells that nearly shipwrecked Princess Anne and King James VI—the same crime leveled in the North Berwick trials.

4 PERU
In 1567, a Peruvian Catholic council called for the eradica-tion of "witch doctors" due to the Taki Onqoy movement, which sought to rally huacas (deities) against Spanish rule, sparking a century-long persecution.

5 HADDINGTONSHIRE, SCOTLAND, U.K.
The North Berwick witch trials in the 1590s implicated around 70 alleged witches for conspiring to assassinate King James VI at a convention with the devil in the St. Andrew's Auld Kirk on Halloween night. (p. 175)

9 PARIS, FRANCE

Catherine Deshayes Monvoisin was an infamous alleged witch who led a network of fortune tellers in Paris, providing poison, aphrodisiacs, abortion, and magical services. She was burned to death in 1680.

10 VALAIS, SWITZERLAND

Between 1428 and 1436, hundreds of people in Valais were accused of witchcraft and at least 100 killed in what is considered the first organized witch hunt in modern history.

11 SPANISH BASQUE COUNTRY

The Basque witch trials (1609–1614), known as the trials of the witches of Zugarramurdi, were among the largest in world history, with 2,000 to 7,000 people accused of witchcraft.

12 CARCASSONNE & TOULOUSE, FRANCE

Starting in the early 1300s, in some of the earliest recorded witch trials, numerous French citizens, including members of the clergy, were accused of making sacrifices to the devil and performing magic.

13 SINTET VILLAGE, THE GAMBIA

In 2009, Amnesty International reported that recent witch hunts had led to the accusation of more than 1,000 people, some of whom were taken to secret detention centers, where they faced violent punishment and gave forced confessions.

14 GHANA

In present-day Ghana, women accused of witchcraft, often due to misfortune or mental illness, are exiled to witch camps, where they're protected from retribution but live in extreme poverty.

15 MONGBWALU, DEMOCRATIC REPUBLIC OF THE CONGO

In 2021, South Kivu province in the Democratic Republic of the Congo saw a dramatic increase in murders of women accused of witchcraft. Reports show eight women were burned or lynched in three districts within a single month.

16 TANZANIA

Between 2005 and 2011, more than 3,000 people in Tanzania were lynched for witchcraft, according to a report from the Legal and Human Rights Centre.

17 SAUDI ARABIA

In 2009, Saudi Arabia established an "Anti-Witchcraft Unit" under its religious police. Saudi woman Amina bint Abdul Halim bin Salem Nasser was arrested for practicing witchcraft and executed in 2011.

18 CHOTA NAGPUR, INDIA

In the mid-1800s, witch hunts led to mass violence against women. Approximately a thousand alleged witches were killed in central India's plains during this period.

19 CHINA

In 91 B.C., Emperor Wu of the Han dynasty initiated a witch hunt, known as the Witchcraft Incident, that led to the execution of tens of thousands of people. (p. 144)

20 PAPUA NEW GUINEA

In the mid-2010s, researchers documented 1,039 incidents in which sorcery accusations were leveled against individuals across the country, including an increasing number of allegations against children.

ROYAL REVELATION

Magicians in the Halls of Power

Around the world, rulers of the medieval period and the Renaissance took diverging approaches when it came to magic, at times persecuting suspected witches and warlocks while also relying on magicians for counsel on political, scientific, and supernatural issues. Whether they were devising prophecies, casting horoscopes, or simply entertaining noblemen, magicians often held high-status roles on royal courts, depending on how sympathetic their patrons were to esoteric arts. They even helped shape the decisions of their sovereigns.

One early, notable example comes from 13th-century Europe. Scottish physician and astrologer Michael Scot (1175–1235) made a name for himself by translating Aristotle's works into Latin from Arabic and Hebrew, helping introduce the philosopher to western Europe. By 1227, he had become the court astrologer for Holy Roman Emperor Frederick II, advising him to seek counsel during the new moon and plan acts of deception during the hours governed by Saturn, among other issues.

Centuries later, Queen Elizabeth I of England turned often to the statecraft and counsel of adviser John Dee (1527–1608/9), a polymath with a deep and abiding interest in magic. To Dee, alchemy and astrology were, like mathematics and natural philosophy, tools for understanding the universe's hidden truths. He published writings on magical glyphs in 1564, and in the 1580s worked closely with medium (and convicted counterfeiter) Edward Kelley, conducting séances and attempting to speak with angels. Their collaboration yielded a series of supposed revelations, transmitted in an "angelic" language now known as Enochian. In part, Dee gained these insights by scrying with an obsidian "magic mirror" originally made in Mexico.

Sometimes, rulers themselves became intensely caught up in magical subjects. King James VI of Scotland (later James I of England) grew obsessed with witchcraft starting in 1590, when he encountered terrible storms while sailing from Scandinavia

---

∧ This large wax disk bearing a symbol known as the Sigillum Dei (Seal of God) once held one of John Dee's "shew-stones," or scrying mirrors.

In this 19th-century painting, John Dee performs an experiment for Queen Elizabeth I. Modern x-rays reveal that the artist originally painted human skulls around Dee.

In a drawing commissioned by 17th-century Mughal emperor Jahāngīr, an astrologer is surrounded by his equipment: an astrolabe, zodiac tables, and an hourglass.

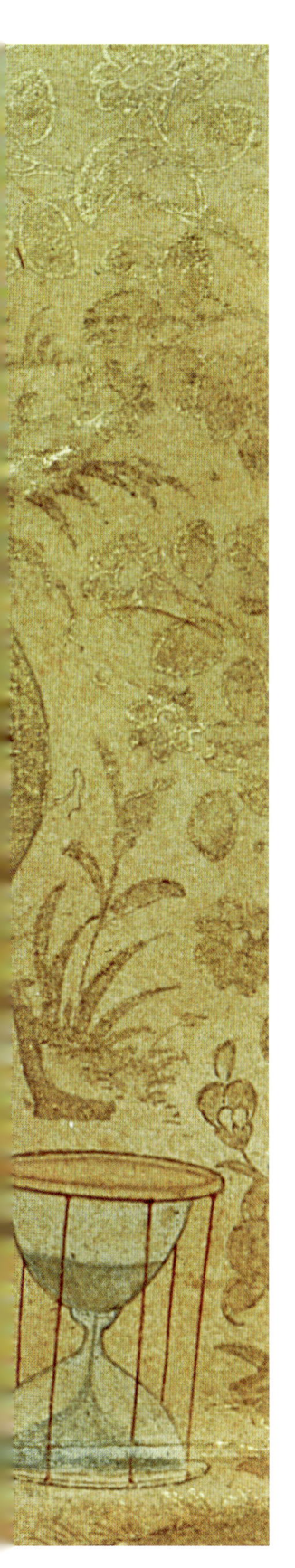

THE MUSLIM RULERS OF THE MUGHAL EMPIRE REGULARLY CONSULTED COURT ASTROLOGERS TO CAST HOROSCOPES FOR NEWBORN ROYALS AND TO ADVISE ON THE TIMING OF MAJOR EVENTS.

to Scotland with his new wife, Anne of Denmark. The storms, he grew to believe, had been summoned by Scottish witches who had meant him harm. These accusations eventually yielded the North Berwick witch trials, in which roughly 70 people from one small town, mostly women, were executed for witchcraft. James VI himself presided over some of these trials and wrote a book on the subject in 1597.

In South Asia, the Muslim rulers of the Mughal Empire regularly consulted court astrologers to cast horoscopes for newborn royals and to advise on the timing of major events. The empire's second ruler, Humāyūn (1508–1556), organized much of his life around the influence of the cosmos. He wore different-colored outfits based on the planet of highest influence on a given day, and his imperial audience hall featured a huge carpet containing concentric circles that corresponded to the planets and four elements. Some sources say he died after falling down a flight of stairs

PROFILE

RASPUTIN

The man who came to be known by only one name—Rasputin—was one of the most powerful and mysterious figures of the 20th century. Born in 1869, he began life as Grigori Novykh, an illiterate Siberian peasant. He gained his nickname, Rasputin, meaning "debauched one," before a religious epiphany made him a self-proclaimed holy man. Among the court circles of St. Petersburg, where many were fascinated by the occult, Rasputin gained a reputation as a mystic and healer. Tsar Nicholas II and his wife, Alexandra, called upon him to heal their hemophiliac son—which Rasputin allegedly did through hypnotism. Though some suspected him to be a charlatan, he maintained great influence with the royal family even as he returned to his scandalous habits. He wielded control over the appointment of religious and political officials until 1916, when a group of Russian noblemen, fearing his expanding influence, murdered him in the cellar of Moika Palace in St. Petersburg.

Rasputin enchanted the Russian royal family with his mystical powers.

from the roof of his library, where he had been consulting with his astrologers on the movement of Venus.

During his 50-year reign, Humāyūn's son Akbar (1542–1605) maintained and expanded on his father's fascination with astrology. He relied on court astrologers to help determine the timing of auspicious events, such as laying a fortress's foundation or starting a war. In the *Akbarnama*, a chronicle of his reign, Akbar's head vizier and court poet, Abu'l Fazl, emphasizes the

ARTIFACT SPOTLIGHT

DAEMONOLOGIE

Published in 1597, *Daemonologie* is a philosophical treatise and handbook on demons and witchcraft written by King James VI of Scotland (later James I of England). Written as a dialogue between two characters, the volume deals with magic, necromancy, sorcery, and witchcraft, and it contains James's classification of demons and their methods. The book includes a reprint of "Newes from Scotland," a pamphlet of the confessions given under torture in the North Berwick witch trials of 1590 and 1591. Around 1606, William Shakespeare probably consulted *Daemonologie* as he wrote *Macbeth*, which is set in Scotland and features three witches. In Act 1, Scene 3 of the play, one witch says she will sail the ocean in a sieve and summon a deadly storm; under torture during the North Berwick trials, a woman named Agnes Thompson confessed to doing the same.

Title page of a 1597 edition of *Daemonologie*, featuring the Scottish royal coat of arms

ruler's horoscope as a sign that Akbar was an ideal, once-in-a-millennium king.

Some rulers also promoted certain kinds of magical practices to safeguard cultural traditions. In China, the Qing dynasty (1644–1912) was ruled by emperors of the Manchu people, who hail from northeastern Asia, a longtime cultural home for shamanism. Among the Manchu, shamanism was the dominant religion. So when Manchu rulers established the Qing dynasty and began to rule as cultural outsiders, they adopted the prevailing beliefs of Confucianism, while also providing state support for shamanistic rituals.

Under the Qing dynasty, shamanistic rites for the imperial family were conducted in the Forbidden City's Palace of Earthly Tranquility (Kunning Gong), one of the inner court's three main halls. Every New Year's Day, the Qing emperor traveled to a *tangzi*, a small complex that had been built to the southeast of the Forbidden City, to visit an octagonal sacrificial shrine. Rituals honored ancestors, heaven, and spirits known as *enduri*; offerings included small cakes, the flesh of sacrificial pigs, wine, and blood. When making sacrifices to heaven, Manchu shamans relied on the power of a *shengan*, a ceremonial spirit pole.

Some royal advisers became experts in the occult—yet denied believing in it. In the Byzantine Empire during the 11th century, courtier Michael Psellus (1018–1078) revived study of ancient mystical texts by a group of Greek philosophers known as Neoplatonists. Psellus's interests sparked accusations of heathenism by his Orthodox Christian peers. Although he never endorsed pagan beliefs, he gained a reputation as an authority on the occult, in part because of his writings on demonology. In an annotation of *The Rime of the Ancient Mariner*, poet Samuel Taylor Coleridge (1772–1834) cited Psellus as an expert on spirits. ■

This painting from the Qing dynasty (1644–1911) shows 21 ancestors and a spirit tablet—a placard inscribed with an ancestor's name.

SCIENCE & SECRECY

Magic During the Enlightenment

It may seem logical that in the Enlightenment, scientific and philosophical advances would have left magical beliefs little room to flourish. Many of the era's leading rationalist thinkers, after all, dismissed the subject as mere superstition. In his "Essay on the Manners of Nations," 18th-century philosopher and historian Voltaire argued that magic is "the secret of doing what nature cannot do" and is therefore "an impossible thing."

In some jurisdictions, laws followed suit. The British Witchcraft Act of 1735 declared that people who claimed to perform magic, witchcraft, and fortune-telling should be prosecuted—not as witches but as frauds. The law also repealed the death penalty for those found guilty of practicing witchcraft. Just eight years earlier, Scottish woman Janet Horne had been the last person legally executed for witchcraft in the British Isles.

Still, for many Europeans at all social levels, magic persisted as an explanatory force in everyday life. In England and Wales, fortune-telling healers known as cunning folk were prosecuted with increased frequency but nevertheless remained highly valued members of society, especially in more isolated and rural communities. Many were artisans in addition to their magical trade, working as every-thing from blacksmiths to schoolmasters.

In Scandinavia, the *kloke folk* (wise folk) cured illnesses, found missing people and cattle, and told fortunes. Eilev Olsen, a 19th-century "cunning man," enjoyed decades of notoriety in the Norwegian press for his claimed clairvoyant powers. Noted wise woman Anne Johansdatter Sæther, better known as Mor (Mother) Sæther, built a national reputation in Norway for her practice despite being prosecuted for quackery three times over the course of her career (see page 285).

Despite the age's professed rationalist streak, people from perches high and low latched on to the idea of ghosts and hauntings. In Germany, tradition held that ghosts watched over treasures and that their appearance could reveal lost hoards. In the state of Württemberg, government officials in the early 18th century regularly received requests for treasure-hunting permits on the basis of ghostly apparitions. Beginning in 1783, officials in the German Hohenzollern territory conducted a lengthy investigation of the house of a man named Vinzenz Diepolt, who claimed a poltergeist was haunting him.

Even people with scientific credentials believed in—and sought to explain—the unexplainable. In two tracts published in 1705 and 1724, the physician and geologist

The intensely spiritual English poet and artist William Blake (1757–1827), who drew this scene from the Book of Revelation, fiercely criticized the Enlightenment.

This engraving, printed in 1754, depicts a Freemason made of potent Masonic symbols such as the sun, masons' tools, and stone pillars.

A Free Mason

John Beaumont (1640–1731) claimed that over the course of two decades he had been visited by spirits, which he could see by slipping into a dreamlike "extatick state of mind." During one such encounter, two female spirits wearing black-and-gold gowns stayed near him constantly for three months straight.

Some freethinking Enlightenment-era men joined secret societies that promised brotherhood and personal illumination. In 1776, law professor Adam Weishaupt created a secret society he called the Illuminati, inspired by Jesuit teachings and more esoteric works such as those of kabbalah. This short-lived society was one of several to adopt the Illuminati name over the centuries—and was far removed from its modern conspiracy-theory connotation.

Of the age's secret societies, none was of higher profile or stature than the fraternal organization known as Freemasonry. Although the group has historical roots in the medieval guilds of stonemasons, its modern incarnation traces back to England in 1717, with lodges that admitted "speculative" masons with no professional connection to the craft of masonry itself. Freemason rituals established the organization's ancient roots and spurred spiritual imagination.

Like ancient mystery cults, Freemasonry

DESPITE THE ENLIGHTENMENT'S PROFESSED RATIONALIST STREAK, PEOPLE FROM HIGH AND LOW LATCHED ON TO THE IDEA OF GHOSTS AND HAUNTINGS.

and related groups placed high priority on the secrecy of their rites. One 18th-century German society known as the Oculists developed a sophisticated cipher to encrypt its rituals, which modern Freemasons have identified as Masonic in origin. This encoded document, known as the Copiale cipher, eluded decryption until 2011. Freemasonry still exists today, with lodges active as fraternal and charitable organizations. However, membership is on the decline, amid shifting cultural mores around clubs and fraternities in general. In the United States, membership in Masonic organizations has fallen by nearly 80 percent since the late 1950s to fewer than 870,000 people in 2023.

RITES & RITUALS

CEREMONIES OF THE FREEMASONS

The secrets and ceremonies of the Freemasons have stoked the general public's curiosity for centuries, even inspiring modern novels like Dan Brown's bestseller *The Lost Symbol*. Though ceremonies vary across different groups of Freemasonry, the most consistent rites are those used to initiate a member through the fraternity's first three degrees: Entered Apprentice, Fellow Craft, and Master Mason. These initiation ceremonies are steeped in symbolism and draw heavily on the Hebrew Bible's story of the Temple of Solomon, including its two freestanding pillars, Boaz and Jachin. Initiates learn secret grips, hand signs, and code words that let them quietly identify other Freemasons.

19th-century pendant worn by a member of England's Grand Stewards' Lodge

HOODOO

African Magic in the Americas

Even as Anglo-American magical practices were pushed to the margins as folk belief, African beliefs were becoming more firmly rooted in America. Black diviners, healers, and witchcraft practitioners proliferated.

In the 1830s, the Black statesman Frederick Douglass, then enslaved on a farm in Maryland, attempted to escape. While he was hiding in the woods, an enslaved friend acting as an African conjurer gave him a root and advised him to carry it for protection from the enslavers' whips. It emboldened Douglass to fight back against a violent "slave breaker" he went on to encounter. The resistance transformed him. "You have seen how a man was made a slave; you shall see how a slave was made a man," he wrote in his autobiography.

During the transatlantic slave trade, from the 16th to 19th centuries, African traditions blended with Christian, Native American, and European folk beliefs. Out of this melting pot emerged hoodoo: a catchall term for spiritual African American traditions, including the magical interaction between spirits and religious entities known as conjure. Conjurers

---

PROFILE

ROOTWORKERS

Hoodoo rituals for protection, healing, and honoring ancestors emerged from a blend of African and Native American traditions, European folk religion, and Christianity. Illnesses were often considered manifestations of witchcraft or spirits, and those who treated them and offered other magical solutions were known as rootworkers. Their medicine bags contained organic material like roots and herbs—all that was available to them at the time. On plantations, local rootworkers might be called upon to heal, protect, divine the future, cast love spells, or offer the promise of riches. Often, their amulet was literal: High John the Conqueror, a spirit who took the physical form of a tuber root, would be carried for protection. Today, hoodoo has reemerged as a form of cultural preservation.

19th-century English illustration of jalap root (*Ipomoea purga*)

< Anthropologist Zora Neale Hurston's studies tempered fears around hoodoo and brought its beliefs into the mainstream.

deployed charms and amulets—including balls of tar, bags of dried leaves, and needles—to protect their clients from misfortune, read the future, or harm their abusers.

In the 1800s, conjure was widely practiced among enslaved people in America, serving as a connection to their ancestral land and beliefs. Both free and enslaved Black people feared violence and separation from their families, on top of an ever-present undercurrent of racism and societal marginalization.

Against this oppressive backdrop, conjure offered a means of controlling one's life and destiny. Conjure was used for healing, harming (often as rebellion or in self-defense), and protection. Conjurers were said to fly, shape-shift, control the weather, and become invisible. Beliefs adapted depending on the struggles of the individual or larger group.

Diverse spiritual and religious beliefs from central Africa contained strong themes about universal cosmologies, sacred rituals, and devotion to ancestors. As Christianity was imposed onto Black communities, practices from Africa—including divination, omen analysis, and charms—mixed with Protestant beliefs, along with healing practices adopted from Native American cultures. This birthed hoodoo and its corresponding belief systems, like the vodou religion, which came from the African kingdom of Dahomey in what is now Benin, traveled with enslaved people, and took root in the French colony of Louisiana.

In the 1920s, pioneering American anthropologist Zora Neale Hurston began researching hoodoo; her writings helped shift public perception away from then-pervasive stereotypes of nefarious witchcraft. Conjure doctors, as they were known, had an empowering livelihood, and their beliefs provided a moral code for followers.

"As we look at African American religion, certain themes appear to be inescapable: where there are preachers, there are also Conjurers; where there are conversions, there are dreams and visions," writes Yvonne Chireau in *Black Magic: Religion and the African American Conjuring Tradition.* "And where there is faith, there is, and ever continues to be, magic."

THE NEW OCCULT
Magical Movements

The last half of the 19th century saw a surge of occult interest across Europe and the United States, with the creation of new groups—and even new religions—that turned magical ideas into organized practice.

In the 1800s, Christianity was in crisis: The idea of damnation was going out of favor, and the field of geology was proving the world to be much older than once believed. Unencumbered by the constraints and punishments of orthodox religion, occult movements drew followers seeking alternate explanations.

Eastern religions found fertile ground in the West, where followers adopted mystical doctrines and began forming their own religious entities. Among those were prominent actors, authors, and artists who helped quicken the expansion of such groups.

In 1875, Russian spiritualist Helena Blavatsky and American author Henry Steel Olcott founded the Theosophical Society in an attempt to merge science, religion, and philosophy. It would usher in the first large-scale occult movement.

Influenced by Jewish kabbalah, Hinduism, and Buddhism, the society established headquarters in what's now Chennai, India, and began to prepare for the arrival of an entity known as "the world teacher" to Earth.

The founders shunned popular scientific and religious movements of the day, instead promoting mystical experience. Madame Blavatsky, as she came to be known, claimed to have psychic powers and toured the world gathering followers. Her teachings would guide the New Age of spirituality and religion that looked to the East for guidance (see page 286). But they would also have a darker impact: By creating an evolutionary theory of ancient races, including the Aryans, Blavatsky's ideas could be distorted to support ideas of racial superiority. Their inclusion in later occult movements would seep into Nazi ideology.

Soon after Blavatsky's death, in the 1890s, the Hermetic Order of the Golden

∧ A lamen (magical pendant) from a lodge of the Stella Matutina, an offshoot of the Hermetic Order of the Golden Dawn

Dawn, founded by Freemasons (see page 181), became the occult movement du jour (see page 125). Out of these groups and their teachings, religions like Wicca and a new generation of occult societies would emerge.

Born in 1875, the same year as the Theosophical Society's founding, Golden Dawn member Aleister Crowley would become the most notorious occult leader of his time. Claiming that he'd been con-tacted by a formless being, he issued a book of teachings for a new religion called Thelema, which drew from ancient Egyptian religions and encouraged followers to find their true calling. Crowley's practice of "magick" and his distaste for Christianity garnered him a lasting reputation for wickedness, sacrilege, and even evil. Even so, Crowley's influence—and his religion, Thelema—left a mark on popular culture that endures today.

∧ Starting in 1906, Swedish artist Hilma af Klint (1862–1944) channeled spirits to create 193 "Paintings for the Temple," including this 1915 work.

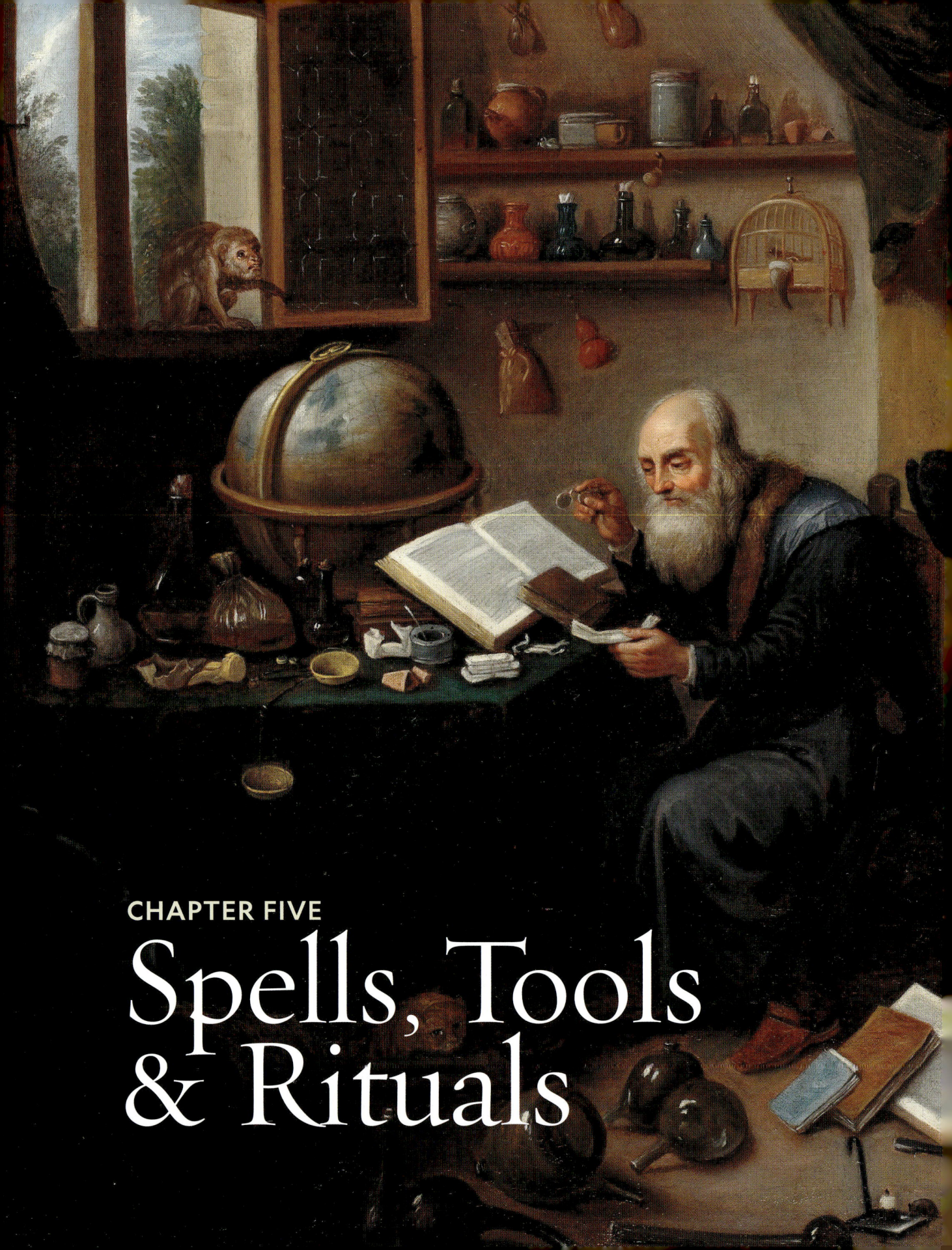

Spells, Tools & Rituals

Practical Magic

Tools of the Trade

For many, magic was more than a mystical experience—it was also a business. As a trade, the practice required scholarship, artistic skill, scientific knowledge, and possibly a bit of hand-waving salesmanship. It also required tools; much of what we know today about magic's long history comes to us through the amulets, spell books, and other objects its practitioners left behind. Working magicians used and sold objects ranging from carved gemstones to scrolls to laboratory apparatuses. With these wares and incantations, magicians and ordinary people alike attempted to access the invisible world, create elixirs, protect themselves and others from harm, and discover treasure.

Magical items are as ancient as the wands found in prehistoric graves and as modern as the healing crystals sold on the internet. Mesopotamians buried charms under their houses to keep away evil spirits. Medieval warriors bought swords inscribed with protective spells from specialty workshops. Renaissance rulers collected saintly relics that promised health and blessings. Today, we might still pick up a penny—if it's heads up—for good luck.

Spell-casting is ancient, too, but as an art it may have reached its height in the European spell books known as *grimoires*. The complicated rituals described in these tomes often demanded both a skilled practitioner and exotic ingredients. Charms and incantations have been preserved through oral tradition; in folklore, tales passed from parent to child at the hearth taught new generations how to keep their milk from going sour or the best way to bring a babe safely into the world.

Magical rituals mixed psychology, religion, mysticism, and practical know-how. In alchemy, magic even began to evolve into modern science. ▪

∧ Wedjat eye amulet, Egypt, first millennium B.C.

The witch Baba Yaga of Russian folklore used a mortar and pestle as magical tools.

OBJECTS OF POWER
Wands & Amulets

If spells are the province of skilled practitioners, amulets—objects that protect against disease and harm—might be described as the people's magic. Stones, bones, figurines, and metal objects inscribed with protective spells have been found in homes and graves around the world (see page 234). They date to prehistory and continue to be used today in jewelry or as household decoration.

Wands are some of the oldest and most recognizable magical objects: slender rods, straight or curved, that have been carved with magical inscriptions. Today, we think of them as spell-casting tools, but the first wands were more like amulets. They were apotropaic, or specifically designed to protect against evil; Egyptians used them as early as 2800 B.C. Carved from hippo ivory, ebony, or steatite, they were decorated with magically potent animals and entities such as griffins, demons, or gods, as well as text.

By Homer's day—roughly the eighth century B.C.—stories began to depict wands as instruments of magic, not just as protective objects. In *The Odyssey*, Athena disguises Odysseus as an old man by touching him with her wand. Hermes carries a caduceus, a staff surrounded by two twining serpents, as a symbol of peace. From the medieval era through the revival of the occult in the 19th century, the wand or staff became increasingly connected with sorcerous power, appearing in illustrated medieval spell books, on tarot cards, and in Wicca rituals (see page 292).

THOUGH THEY OFFICIALLY SCORNED THE BLACK ARTS, MEDIEVAL MONKS REGULARLY CRAFTED WEARABLE CHARMS TO PREVENT FEVERS, TOOTHACHES, THEFT, OR ATTACKS FROM WITCHES OR ELVES.

In addition to wands, everyday citizens of the ancient world carved figurines and charms to ward off danger. Mesopotamians fended off spirits and sickness by burying figurines of demons, gods, or animals under their houses. Dogs, associated with the healing goddess Gula, were popular. So, too, were pendants carved in the shape of the deity they intended to appease or oppose, such as the fearsome Lamashtu, a female demon, or Pazuzu, the wind demon. Ancient Egyptians wore an eye of Horus for healing or a string of cowrie shells draped around the waist for fertility. Medieval monks, though they officially scorned the black arts, regularly crafted wearable charms to prevent fevers, toothaches, theft, or attacks from witches or elves.

Plague charms were fashionable in times of epidemic. In *A Journal of the Plague Year*, published in 1772, Daniel Defoe wrote that people in 1665 wore "charms, philtres, exorcisms, amulets, and I know not what" against the Black Death. These included the word "abracadabra" written in an inverted triangle, with a letter subtracted from each line.

Because they are easily carried and decorative, people still wear amulets today. Southern Italians may sport a *cornicello*, a twisted coral charm that fends off the evil eye. Some North Africans wear a palm-shaped *hamsa*, or hand of Fatima, for good fortune. Even President Franklin Delano Roosevelt, who warned against "fear itself," carried a rabbit's foot as a lucky charm.

ᐯ Protective figures such as crocodiles, toads, and a turtle adorn a stone rod from ancient Egypt.

MAGICAL PROTECTIONS

Ancient artisans have left us a rich selection of amulets dating from Mesopotamian times onward; most were intended to be solid and long-lasting, for which historians are duly grateful. As wards, amulets were worn around the neck, carried, hung in households near doors and windows, buried under floorboards, and interred with the dead. Assyrians and Egyptians crafted protective pendants, scarabs, and the like, sometimes combined into impos-ing necklaces and breastplates; often, they entombed their mummies with scarabs tucked into bandages to shield them from the dangers of the afterlife. Medieval folk wore more perishable ink-and-paper charms against their skin. Even today, it's not uncommon to see an iron horseshoe nailed for protection above a doorway, or a person hunting for a lucky four-leaf clover.

∧ AMULET CASE
This 19th-century amulet case from India would have held rolled-up papers inscribed with holy words. Chiseled in relief on its gold and coral surface are eight rows showing human faces, birds, and floral motifs.

∨ HEI TIKI
Carved from greenstone, or pounamu, in the 19th century, this Maori *hei-tiki* pendant was worn around the neck. It represents a spiritual connection between the ancestral past and the present.

∧ TURTLE
A girl born to Plains Indian tribes around the turn of the 20th century might have worn this beaded turtle amulet for protection. Inside, a relative would have placed a piece of her umbilical cord. Turtles, to Plains tribes, represented long life and endurance.

∨ SCARABS
Ancient Egyptian scarabs were often placed within mummy wrappings or worn as ornaments. Egyptians associated the scarab beetle with the regenerative nature of the sun.

NEKHBET

The young Egyptian pharaoh Tutankhamun was mummified with layer upon layer of sacred jewelry, including this pendant of Nekhbet, the vulture goddess who was the protector of Upper Egypt.

∧ VISHNU

The Hindu god Vishnu, the preserver, rides the divine bird figure Garuda on this Nepalese amulet case made between the 17th and 19th centuries.

∨ MAYA VULTURE

This Maya vulture pendant, probably worn by a high-ranking figure, is carved from jadeite, whose bright green color symbolized life and vegetation. The Maya respected vultures and other raptors for their strength and speed.

∨ GUARDIAN DOG

Figurines such as this dog, dating back to around the eighth or ninth centuries B.C., were often placed under Mesopotamian floorboards to serve as magical household guardians.

ETRUSCAN BULLA >

Bullas, such as this gold Etruscan pendant from the fifth century B.C., held charms or perfumes in their hollow centers. This piece features Daedalus, the mythical craftsman, and his ill-fated son Icarus (on the back).

∧ BADGER

A modern Zuni fetish depicts Badger (Donashi). Aggressive and tenacious, the badger is said to have healing properties and is a reminder to stay focused on a goal.

∧ MUCH SUFFERING EYE

A copper pendant from fifth- or sixth-century Byzantium depicts an eye being attacked by a lion, snakes, a scorpion, a stork, and spears. On the reverse, King Solomon spears the destructive figure of Lilith. The pendant was intended to protect the wearer against the evil eye.

GLASS EYES

Phoenician glass eye beads, from the first centuries B.C., were probably meant to be protective as well as decorative.

< INUHARIKO

This dog-shaped papier-mâché incense case, from 19th-century Japan, would have been designed as a protective amulet. Pairs of *inuhariko* were often carried in wedding processions to bring good luck.

PRECIOUS INSCRIPTIONS

Gemstones & Scrolls

Precious stones have long been prized among amulet wearers for more than just their beauty. Carved or placed in settings and often worn as jewelry, purportedly magical stones include hematite, obsidian, carnelian, onyx, and chalcedony, as well as topaz, lapis lazuli, beryl, amethyst, jasper, and ruby. Ancient Greeks and Romans carried them for health and protection: The lion-headed Greek god Chnoubis carved on gray-green soapstone might ease stomachaches, while the image of a uterus inscribed on hematite—derived from the Greek word for "blood," after its deep red color—ensured fertility.

Even uncarved, some stones were believed to hold intrinsic magical powers. Medieval and Renaissance scholars wrote entire books, called lapidaries, on their properties (see page 196). The sapphire, they tell us, takes away envy and perfidy. The ruby's color darkens in the presence of danger. Emeralds improve memory or shatter in the presence of lust. If a wearer of turquoise falls from a horse, the stone will break instead of the rider's bones. Gemstones were not only worn—they could even be ingested. Physicians sometimes treated those who could afford expensive remedies, such as Florentine ruler Lorenzo de' Medici, with potions that incorporated ground gems.

ARTIFACT SPOTLIGHT

INCANTATION BOWLS

In what was once western Mesopotamia, archaeologists have uncovered simple clay bowls buried upside down, dating mostly to the fifth to seventh centuries A.D. Aramaic script spirals from their rims down to their centers, containing blessings, curses, or protections against demons. One reads, in part: "May you be healed, may you be protected, may you be saved … from every evil strong powerful spirit." In at least one case, the script is reversed, as if to be read in a mirror. Buried at a building's corners or entryways, the incantation bowls are thought to have been inverted to trap demons before they could rise into the household.

Aramaic inscriptions adorn the inside of an ancient Persian incantation bowl.

EVEN UNCARVED, SOME STONES WERE BELIEVED TO HOLD INTRINSIC MAGICAL POWERS.

From late antiquity onward, cautious folk in Europe and Africa employed a new means of protection: paper, parchment, or vellum scrolls, some as long as a human body. Priests and other religious figures created these as shields against sickness, injury, or the ill will of demons. Paintings on the scrolls, often taken from the Christian tradition, were seen as talismans against harm. The 15th-century English Harley Roll, for instance, depicts the wounds of Christ; it was probably designed to be draped over a pregnant woman to protect her in childbirth.

Ethiopian healers were masters of the talismanic scroll. Their traditions date to the early Aksumite Empire, which adopted Christianity in the fifth century and flourished through the eighth century. An unordained priest, a *dabtara*, wrote prayers on the scroll in black ink and paired them with such images as angels, eight-pointed stars, animals, rulers, or heroes like St. Susenyos, slayer of the demon Werzelya. A user displayed the scroll on a wall or rolled it up and carried it in a cylindrical leather or silver case for protection. To this day, such scrolls are written in Geez, the 2,000-year-old language of the empire and still the liturgical language of the Ethiopian Orthodox Church.

∧ An Ethiopian healing scroll includes prayers and images of eyes looking for divine intervention.

MAGICAL GEMS & STONES

In ancient and medieval lore, gems were said to possess magical powers that stemmed from either their carvings or simply the inherent quality of the stone. These stones ranged from minerals we recognize as gems today, such as emeralds, rubies, or topazes, to stony materials such as obsidian, coral, chalcedony, and jasper.

Stones were often used for healing. The practice, detailed in books called lapidaries, used stones to cure issues from gangrene to hair loss.

Carvings on classical-era healing stones were specific to particular ailments. A farmer bending over to cut grain appears on a carnelian gem intended to protect against sciatica in the hips. An ibis, devourer of snakes, is carved into limonite, along with the words "digest, digest, digest": suitable for throat and digestive problems. Heracles wrestling a lion, on jasper, represented the heroic fight against stomachaches.

∧ LAPIS LAZULI
Easily carved and decorative, lapis lazuli has been associated with good luck.

OBSIDIAN >
The shiny volcanic stone obsidian, seen here in an Egyptian amulet, was believed by some to bring visions.

CORAL >
Medieval sources held that coral could protect against accidents, storms, and lightning.

TOADSTONE >
Toadstones, supposedly extracted from a toad's head and useful against poison, were in truth fossilized teeth from an extinct ray-finned fish, *Lepidotes*.

∧ ONYX
Some Renaissance scholars believed the intensely dark stone onyx had a depressive effect, making it able to quench unwanted attention.

< SERPENTINE
Easily carved, as in this pendant showing Daniel in the lion's den, serpentine was connected to healing and protection.

∨ CARNELIAN
Carnelian was associated with fire, royalty, and the sun, as in this Roman carving of the sun god Sol in a chariot.

∧ RUBY
Rubies, according to some, would darken in the presence of danger and protect the wearer from poison and sorrow.

∧ GARNET
Garnets were said to protect against injury. Some legends said that the stone could emit its own red light.

SAPPHIRE >
According to medieval scholars, the sapphire (inset at right in a Germanic brooch) protected against envy and betrayal.

< EMERALD
Medieval sources claimed the emerald could improve memory, sharpen wits, and perhaps give the wearer the ability to see the future.

∧ AGATE
The agate, here carved with the Byzantine figure of St. Theodore Teron slaying a dragon, was reputed to guard against venom.

∨ DIAMOND
According to medieval lapidaries, the diamond (shown below as a raw specimen) would drive away nightmares.

SARDONYX >
Classical-age warriors wore talismans of sardonyx to war, believing it bestowed courage and protection.

∨ JASPER
Jasper (below, as a Roman carving) was connected to an array of powers, including easing childbirth and protecting the wearer from delusions.

∨ AMETHYST
Medieval lapidaries claimed the amethyst brought the wearer good hunting and fishing, as well as sobriety.

MAGIC'S SHARP EDGE

Enchanted Weapons

Weapons such as daggers, swords, and even guns were often inscribed with magical protections and formulas to bring strength. Historians have found ancient Egyptian mace heads, designed to smash skulls, decorated with elaborate symbols of power and wealth and apparently intended to convey the power of the gods to their owners. Archaeologists digging into the ruins of the ancient Chinese city of Shimao discovered 4,000-year-old jade blades buried along with human skulls—likely as a defense against evil spirits. In the 20th century, fighters in New Guinea carried daggers carved from cassowary or human bone that were believed to draw on the strength of the supernatural world.

The power of magic to protect was a common belief across time and culture. Medieval Christian, Islamic, and Viking warriors inscribed their swords and spears with religious symbols, texts, and generally straightforward declarations of prowess. The lettering could be enigmatic. The 13th-century River Witham sword, for instance, was found in an English tributary in 1825; scholars believe its double-edged blade was made in a German workshop that specialized in forging "magic" swords

IN LEGEND

EXCALIBUR

The tale of King Arthur's sword, Excalibur, has a twisty lineage. Made famous by medieval tales such as Sir Thomas Malory's *Le Morte d'Arthur* (1485), the legendary blade may have its origins in older Celtic stories describing the swords Caladbolg (able to lop the tops off mountains) or Caledfwlch (Arthur's sword in early Welsh tales). The sword was said to cut through steel; its magical scabbard protected the owner from any mortal harm. In Malory's account, Excalibur is not the sword Arthur pulls from the stone but one given to him by the Lady of the Lake that is returned to her as he is dying. Its story reflects the longstanding, real-life practice of donating a weapon to the waters after its owner passes on.

Medieval European sword

for the aristocracy. The inlaid letters +NDXOXCHWDRGHDXORVI+ along one edge still puzzle scholars. The *NDX* may refer to *Nostrum Dominus*, or Our Lord, and the *XOX* could reference the Holy Trinity, both invoked for divine protection.

Ancient swords like this are often found in rivers, bogs, or streams in the British Isles. Some are now bent into useless shapes by time and the elements, while others appear relatively unused. They seem to have been deliberately placed as votive offerings in the waters—considered liminal places between this world and the next—upon their owners' deaths.

In legends, famous swords take on personalities of their own, adding to their owners' prestige. Greek historian Priscus claimed that the fearsome fifth-century emperor Attila the Hun bore a weapon that came to be known as the Sword of

Mars, which, Attila believed, assured him victory in all wars. According to the medieval epic *Song of Roland*, Joyeuse—the sword of Charlemagne, ruler of the Carolingian empire during the eighth and ninth centuries—held a piece of the lance that pierced Christ's side in its pommel; each day the blade "reflects a score of different shades of light." A sword purported to be Joyeuse, or perhaps a composite containing Joyeuse, is on display at the Louvre.

In later eras, gun owners also sought mystical protections. Russian soldiers would guard themselves against enemy bullets with an incantation that asked a mystical maiden to shield them: "In her right hand she holds bullets of lead, in her left bullets of copper, on her feet bullets of iron. Do thou, fair maiden, ward off the guns of the Turks, the Tatars, the Circassians, the Russians, the Mordvins, or all tribes and foes."

∧ A fire-magic adept from the 19th-century Japanese novel *Hakkenden* raises his magical sword, Murasame.

SAINTLY PROTECTION
Medieval Relics

In medieval Europe, the growing power of the Catholic Church and the reorganization of medieval life around church-centered villages meant that traditional magic was shunted to society's margins. Priests condemned magical practitioners as heretics and their amulets as demonic. Yet practices once considered magical persisted, merely shifting their focus to religious relics, which flooded into European shrines, churches, and palaces in the tens of thousands throughout the Middle Ages.

Religious relics are objects, often anatomical, associated with a sacred figure; in medieval times, they were generally held to confer some of that figure's essence, power, and mystical protection upon those who venerated them. This sort of belief began long before Christianity. The ancient Greeks dug up the purported bones of the legendary hero Theseus and interred them in Athens. The Buddha's remains, we are told, were divided and preserved in eight shrines. But medieval Christianity made the veneration of relics a central part of religious life and, by extension, daily life.

ARTIFACT SPOTLIGHT

RELIQUARY OF SAINTE FOY

In the ninth century, thieves grabbed the body of the French girl known as Sainte Foy, supposedly martyred by the Romans for refusing to make pagan sacrifices, and took it to the French town of Conques. There, artisans encased her skull within a glittering, golden statue, roughly two and half feet (.75 m) tall. Through her reliquary, the saint was said to perform remarkable miracles in exchange for gifts; her intercessions reportedly cured the blind and broke the chains of the enslaved. Those who disobeyed her, on the other hand, were plagued by dark visions or even killed. For centuries, pilgrims following the Santiago de Compostela route have stopped to venerate the reliquary, now housed in a small museum.

Gold, silver, and precious stones cover the reliquary of Sainte Foy.

This 15th-century German reliquary with an Islamic perfume vessel as its centerpiece holds what was said to be a tooth of John the Baptist.

Medieval relics were typically body parts, clothing, or other objects that had supposedly belonged to or been touched by saints, the Virgin Mary, or Jesus Christ. They included teeth, hands, heads, hair, blood, chairs, swords, and entire bodies; purported pieces of the Virgin's veil, vials of her breast milk, or splinters of the True Cross were particularly valuable. To the everyday medieval worshipper, these relics retained the incorruptible health and miraculous powers of their original owners: an essence that might be transmitted by touch or simply by veneration. Some were said to give off light or perfumes.

By the eighth century, the church had ruled that every altar should contain a relic. Entire cathedrals were built around sacred items and, in turn, became the end points of pilgrimages by the faithful. Spain's Cathedral of Santiago de Compostela is said to hold the remains of St. James and draws pilgrims by the hundreds of thousands. Notre-Dame de Paris claims Jesus' crown of thorns, as well as a nail and wood from the True Cross. At least two reputed Holy Grails are displayed in cathedrals today—one in Valencia, Spain, and another in Genoa, Italy. St. Mark's Basilica, in Venice, Italy, was built around the purported remains of the saint himself, stolen from their original Egyptian resting place by two Venetian merchants in 828.

Medieval artisans across Europe crafted bejeweled reliquaries to hold such sacred objects; noblemen collected relics along with other riches and stored them in their

vaults. Frederick the Wise, the 16th-century ruler of Saxony, owned almost 19,000 relics, including, supposedly, hay from Christ's manger, a twig from Moses' burning bush, and body parts from infants murdered on King Herod's orders. In Frederick's court, as elsewhere, relics brought in money for their owners. Visitors could pay to view them, thus earning a deduction of years from their sufferings in purgatory.

Eventually, commercial practices such as these and the obvious fakery of some purported relics drew condemnation from religious reformers. Sixteenth-century theologian John Calvin, in his *Treatise on Relics*, points out that "there is not a church, from a cathedral to the most miserable abbey or parish church, that does not contain a piece [of the True Cross] … In short, if we were to collect all these pieces of the True Cross exhibited in various parts, they would form a whole ship's cargo."

By the Enlightenment, scientifically minded scholars were denouncing the worship of relics as paganism and superstition. Today, the Catholic Church continues to safeguard relics around the world but acknowledges that they are not intrinsically magical.

∧ Scenes from the life of the Virgin Mary flank a central figure of the Virgin and Child in this French reliquary shrine.

STORIES AT THE HEARTH

Folklore & Fairy Tales

For as long as people have told stories, traditional magical belief—its spells and rituals, its lures and dangers, its supernatural creatures—has been passed on in the oral tradition through folklore. Grandmothers at the hearth, elders at the campfire, and neighbors around the well dispense advice and tales to new generations, retaining key elements while adding their own twists.

Cultures around the world have folk traditions, often expressed in song or poetry. In West Africa, generational storytellers and musicians known as griots are honored for their role in passing lore and history from generation to generation. In southern India, traditional storytellers accompany tales from the culture's great epics with bowed instruments. Most familiar to Westerners are the European versions of spells and stories collected and codified by 19th-century folklorists. These recitations were often a creative blend of pre-Christian beliefs and church rites couched in repetition and rhyme, making them easier to remember.

Charms and rituals abound in folklore; like so much magical practice, they tend to

---

IN LEGEND

JINN

Jinn (or genies, as they're often known in Western stories) are powerful spirits that appear frequently in Arabic mythology and in Islamic teaching. Invisible beings of smokeless fire, they are said to live in remote places and to shift into visible human or animal form as they wish. According to Islamic lore, jinn are like humans: they can choose between right and wrong, they can fall in love, and they can be killed. They are separated into several classes, among them afreets (rebellious and malevolent), ghouls (dangerous shape-shifters), and *sila* (female and malicious). Jinn are accepted as real in many traditional Islamic societies; a 2012 poll showed that in at least 13 countries, a majority of the population believed in their existence.

Aladdin's genie of the lamp from *The Thousand and One Nights*

1238. Afrique Occidentale - SÉNÉGAL
Halamkat Sénégalais

A Senegalese griot from the early 20th century holds a *xalam*, a traditional stringed instrument.

focus on healing and protection. Old English tradition reports that to help with a dangerously delayed birth, for instance, a woman should visit a grave, step over it three times, and recite a chant that dictates a successful outcome. In Cornwall, England, those affected by arthritis or rickets might seek a cure by crawling through the hole carved out of the Mên-an-Tol standing stone—though their knees should not touch the ground. Some 20th-century African American folk healers claimed that a rattlesnake skin tied around the wrist would cure rheumatism and that backaches could be eased if you let a seventh daughter walk across your back.

Folk remedies also played into the age-old quest to find love, treasure, and lost items. European traditions promised that fern seeds, collected just before midnight on Midsummer's Eve, could draw your future spouse to your home. Bones from a dead criminal would bring luck at cards.

According to tradition, rituals might have to be repeated a certain number of times or performed in magically potent locations to be effective. Thresholds, hearths, churchyards, and crossroads held particular power, and these beliefs persist today. Scottish tradition, carried into the New World, dictates that for luck the first person across a threshold in the new year must be a dark-haired man bringing gifts. According to legend, the great 20th-century blues guitarist Robert Johnson learned his trade from a mysterious stranger at a crossroads at midnight.

European folktales often invoke elves, brownies, and other household spirits in a tradition dating back to the tutelary spirits of classical times. These tiny guardians were said to remain in the household generation after generation if they were properly respected. Brownies or pixies, a kind of household elf, were reported to come into a home at night to clean it; you could thank them with milk or bread, but other gifts offended them and drove them away. In Scandinavian lore, brownies enjoyed stealing from neighbors to benefit their own household, a belief that led to real-life acrimony and accusations of witchcraft.

More dangerous and more alluring than brownies, according to British folklore, were fairies, sometimes known as fae. The word "faerie" or "fairy" comes from an old French term meaning "enchanted." Fairies turn up in British folklore and literature as early as 1100. By the 15th century, they were standard characters in stories, poetry, and song. They might be described as diminutive, pixie-like creatures or beautiful, soulless, long-lived beings. They were said to venture out from their underground kingdoms (often in a hollow hill) through magical portals to

CINDERELLA

The Cinderella story, in its essence, has appeared in hundreds of versions around the world for at least a thousand years. Western readers know some version of Charles Perrault's 1697 story, but a very similar tale, "Ye Xian," was published in China in the ninth century. In that story, a girl mistreated by her stepmother and stepsister is befriended by a magic fish. She attends a festival where she loses a slipper. An island king tracks her down, finds that the slipper fits, and marries her. All

live happily ever after—except for the stepmother and stepsister, who are crushed by stones. Scholars don't know whether this Chinese story is the source for other Asian and European Cinderella tales; "Ye Xian" may have spread by word of mouth to the West. But Cinderella tales in many cultures might simply have arisen on their own, reflecting the universal appeal of certain archetypes: cruel stepparents, magical friends, and a poor but virtuous youngster made good.

Cinderella's stepsisters look down at her on this 20th-century cover of Perrault's "Cendrillon."

The Mên-an-Tol and surrounding stones still stand on Cornwall's Penwith Peninsula.

Fairies of the diminutive variety march with elves in a 19th-century illustration.

interfere with humans. Traditional beliefs held that the fae might carry you off to their lands; if you ate or drank there, you would never leave. Some would kidnap children and leave their own offspring—changelings—in their place.

Fairies are cited surprisingly often in accounts from European witch trials. As early as 1572, accused Scottish witch Janet Boyman claimed to have learned magical skills from the "good neighbours," which was a way of referring to fairies without offending them. In 1590, a purported Scottish witch told of serving as a midwife to a fairy queen; another, in 1597, said she learned witchcraft from her daughter, who had been abducted by fairies as a child.

Men, too, claimed to have consorted with fairies. Those judging such cases saw little difference between fairies and demons and condemned the accused accordingly.

Despite, or perhaps because of, the witchcraft connection, fairies were popular characters in literary "fairy tales" of the sort collected by the brothers Grimm (see sidebar). These tales were clearly intended and understood as fiction. Yet they passed on not only moral and cautionary lessons but also magical practices and beliefs that were a part of daily life. The perils of hearths and thresholds, the proper treatment of elves and goblins, hidden treasure, and more live on in stories that contain centuries of accumulated wisdom.

PROFILE

THE BROTHERS GRIMM

Jacob and Wilhelm Grimm, erudite scholars of language and literature, might be dismayed to learn that today their work is associated with fairy tales. Born in Germany in the late 18th century, they overcame an impoverished upbringing to become lawyers and later, following their true calling, antiquarians. Believing that folk songs and tales reflected the intrinsic nature of a people, they collected and published 156 such stories in multiple editions of their book *Kinder- und Hausmärchen (Children's and Household Tales)*. Jacob Grimm also wrote a groundbreaking work on language, *Deutsche Grammatik (German Grammar)*, which outlined the connection among Indo-European languages that is now known as Grimm's law.

A young huntsman plays the flute for gnomes who will grant him his wish, from the folktale "The Gnome."

GRIMOIRES

Magic in Writing

Spell books, or grimoires, are written records of spells, charms, and conjurations: instruction manuals for the student of magic. They have existed since the first scribes put quill to papyrus, and they flourished in the Renaissance and Reformation, when the printing press democratized magical knowledge.

The 19th-century word *grimoire* probably derives from an older French word for a book written in Latin, *grammaire*. While many of the most famous spell books were originally written in Latin, written spells themselves predate the Romans. The Egyptian Book of the Dead, a collection of protective spells that were painted on coffins and mummy wrappings as well as papyrus scrolls, is considered a spell book (see page 236). Traditions from ancient Judaism, early Christianity, and Islam, as well as classical Greece and Rome, all fed into spell-book texts as the years went by. The angel Raziel, according to some medieval writings, taught Noah the art of astrology via a book of magical lore. And an early medieval papyrus claiming to be the "Eighth Book of Moses" contains mystical instructions and charms, such as a ritual to protect the user from fear and anger.

The medieval Testament of Solomon, attributed to the biblical king, explained how to control demons; copies have been found with handwritten notes about performing exorcisms. *The Key of Solomon* (also known as *The Clavicule of Solomon*), a grimoire containing illustrated spells and dating to the 15th century, purported to be a text found in the biblical king's tomb. This remained popular in its many versions into the 19th century. To conjure angelic spirits, the text advises to "let them see the pentacles, and say: Obey ye, obey ye, behold the symbols and names of the creator; be ye gentle and peaceable, and obey in all things that we shall command ye. They will then immediately talk with thee, as a friend speaketh

< *The Book of Saint Cyprian*, a grimoire

Angels line up in *The Sworn Book of Honorius,* a 15th-century version of a grimoire.

A 20th-century Wiccan grimoire bears lines from a poem by occultist Aleister Crowley.

unto a friend. Ask of them all that thou desirest, with constancy, firmness, and assurance, and they will obey thee."

With the invention of mechanized printing in the late 15th century, grimoires proliferated. They offered their users charms to find love (carnal and otherwise), as well as spells for locating treasure, growing fruitful crops, avoiding injuries and illnesses, reeling in fish, and successfully pilfering from neighbors. One of the most popular spell books, the 18th-century French *Petit Albert*, explains how to use a disembodied hand taken from a felon (a Hand of Glory) to become invisible. *The Dragon Rouge,* or *Grand Grimoire*, a notorious French spell book of the same era, became famous for its dark recipes, which include how to summon demons and put them to work.

Unsurprisingly, the Catholic Church took a dim view of these handbooks of the occult arts; it added many to the church's Index of Prohibited Books and destroyed them when possible. Grimoires nonetheless spread widely in Protestant lands and in cheaply produced underground versions through the centuries.

Twentieth-century occultism, syncretic religions in Latin America, and the Wicca movement have all kept spell books in circulation. The spells and charms of the *Book of Saint Cyprian* were popular in Brazil in the 1950s and '60s. An American version of the *Grand Grimoire*, printed in Pennsylvania in 1910, includes instructions about bathing as well as a prediction that "We are approaching the termination of the present civilization … and are entering upon a new epoch of human history and might, destined to develop powers in man, now latent mainly, but which are destined to revolutionize the globe." Gerald Gardner's *Book of Shadows* (see page 292), written in the mid-20th century, is still influential—and, like many other grimoires, widely available. ▪

An 18th-century painting imagines a wizard, his spell book, and the fantastical creatures it allows him to conjure.

THE MADRID CODEX

Now housed in the Museo de América in Madrid, the medieval Madrid Codex is a record of astrology and divination: one of the few documents to survive from Maya culture before the 16th century, when Spanish conquistadores and their diseases devastated the Maya population of Mexico and Central America. Intricately detailed painted figures cover both sides of a long, folded paper made from bark. Not strictly a grimoire, it is nevertheless part of the worldwide tradition of illustrated rituals, containing detailed artwork of ceremonies and predictions as well as practical depictions of such crafts as beekeeping and weaving.

˅ THE GODS OF CREATION

Itzamnaaj (top left) was the lord of the heavens and inventor of books and writing. His wife Ix Chel (top right) governed childbirth, healing, and weaving.

< SKYWATCHER

A skywatcher, in blue at the top of the panel, watches the stars through a viewing tube.

DIVING GOD >

The upside-down Diving or Descending God, in the upper left corner of the blue section, was probably connected to bees, beekeeping, and the spirit world.

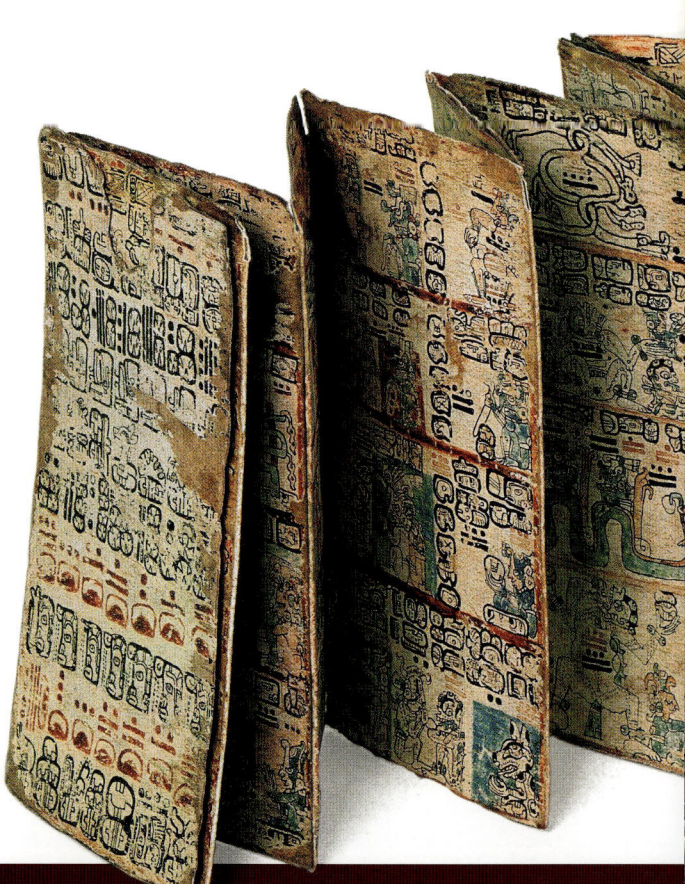

STINGLESS BEES

Ten pages of the codex show the cultivation of sacred stingless bees, whose honey was used for trade and in ceremonies.

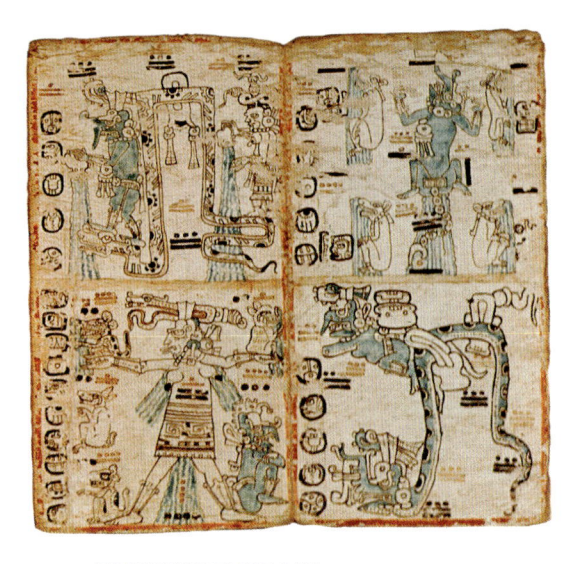

BRINGING THE RAIN

Chaak, god of rain, lightning, and thunder, and creator goddess Ix Chel bring water to the Earth. Chaak was frequently invoked in the water-dependent Maya culture.

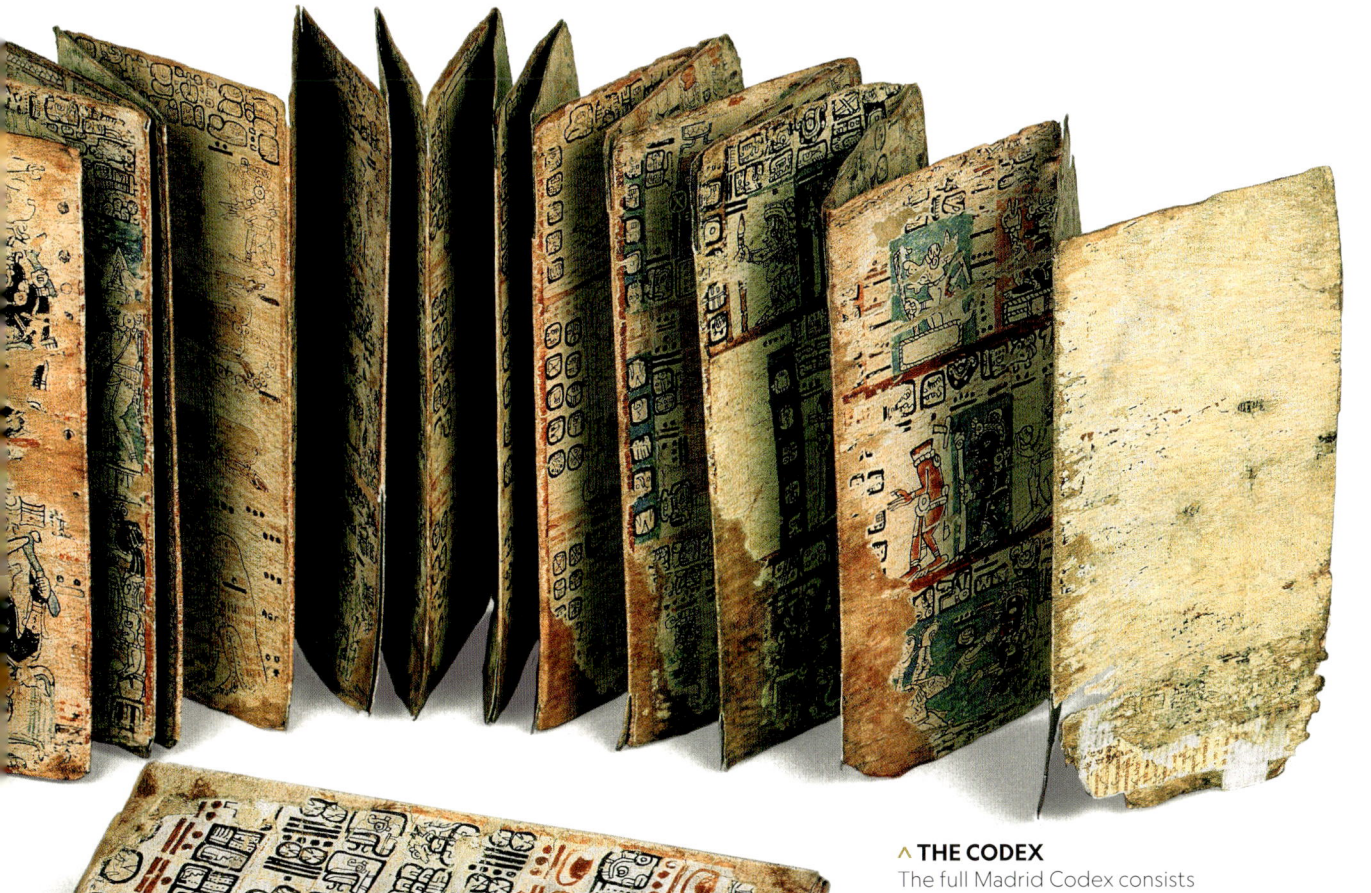

THE CODEX

The full Madrid Codex consists of 56 illustrated panels.

CURSES

The Art of Ill-Wishing

It may say something positive about the human spirit that most magical inscriptions and amulets are designed not for harm but for protection, prosperity, and healing. In medieval times, purported witches were sometimes accused of cursing people or households, but evidence for deliberate ill-wishing is scarce. Nevertheless, the curse is a recognizable subset of magical incantation—and the ancient Greeks and Romans were masters of the art.

We know this because they inscribed their curses on lead tablets or other durable materials that remain legible to this day. The aggrieved party hired a professional to carve the curse onto a thin sheet of lead with a stylus. They would then heat the lead until it was soft, fold it, and sometimes coat it in herbs or with hair from the intended target. Finally, they'd bury it in a pit, pool, or grave, where it would be close to the spirits of the underworld; only the spirits or gods could effect the curse.

It is not always clear what offense the cursed person had committed. No fewer than four tablets found in the Sicilian city of Morgantina ask the gods to take an enslaved girl to hell without specifying what she has done. Some curses target opponents in the courtroom or rivals in sports. Charioteers, beware, for one tablet proclaims, "I adjure you, daemon, whoever you are, and I command you to torment and kill the horses of the green and white [teams] from this hour on, from this day on, and to kill Clarus, Felix, Primulus, and Romanus, the charioteers."

Christian Europe forbade pagan magic, but Christian maledictions were another matter. Medieval scribes cursed book thieves in writing: "Whoever to steal this volume durst / May he be killed as one accursed / Whoever to steal this volume tries / Out with his eyes, out with his eyes." Gavin Dunbar, the archbishop of Glasgow, ordered a lengthy curse on raiders to be read from pulpits along the Anglo-Scottish border in 1525. "I curse them going, and I

^ A Doric Greek inscription on a curse tablet wishes ill on an opponent in court.

curse them riding," it thunders. "I curse them standing, and I curse them sitting."

Aggrieved parties today can visit a curse-maker in Hong Kong. For a fee, customers pay someone known as a "villain hitter"—typically an elderly woman—to produce a jinx by whacking an enemy's picture or written name vigorously with a shoe. Even if the proceedings don't actually yield a curse, observers say, they may at least provide some psychological satisfaction for the customer.

∧ The legendarily cursed sailing ship *The Flying Dutchman* looms through the fog in a 19th-century painting.

ALCHEMY
The Science of Transformation

Alchemy stands with astrology as one of the most enduring forms of learned magic. This practice, dating to early Mesopotamia, encompasses both the mysticism and the science of transmutation: the transformation of an element, such as a metal, into a higher form. Although alchemists often couched their instructions in deliberately confusing and esoteric terms in order to impress the uninitiated, the art was in essence a proto-chemistry that combined such metals as mercury and lead with corrosive salts and other materials that would dissolve, coat, or alter the color of the metals. Practitioners typically aimed to produce either elixirs, such as potions of immortality, or precious metals such as gold.

The very word "alchemy" is itself something of a mystery and a transformation. The *al* clearly comes from Arabic for "the"; the *chem* is unclear, but it may derive from the Greek word for "fluid." While the word reflects Western alchemy's roots in the ancient Near East and Greece, the practice was more widespread than its origin would indicate: It includes a long tradition in China and India as well.

In ancient China, alchemy was mainly devoted to producing elixirs for health or immortality. Many early emperors sought such concoctions. In the third century B.C., Qin Shi Huangdi, first emperor of the Qin dynasty, issued demands that his subjects find him immortality potions. (He died at age 49.) Over the centuries, Chinese alchemists wrote treatises on making elixirs from cinnabar, gold, or sulfur; scholars estimate that at least six emperors died after ingesting the toxic mixtures. Ninth-century poet and alchemist Po Chü-i lamented of his friends: "All fell ill or died suddenly / None of them lived through middle age. / Only I have not taken the elixir; / Yet contrarily live on, an old man."

Meanwhile, in the Mediterranean world, alchemists were more concerned with changing metals into purer, precious substances, such as gold. Medieval and Renaissance alchemists were heavily influenced by Greek texts

∧ A three-headed beast represents the elements of the philosopher's stone.

黄道漸漸開明

臨爐施條

陽氣漸進

身中陽火漸漸條暢

A Qing dynasty alchemist contemplates an elixir of longevity in a 17th-century silk painting.

IN THE MEDITERRANEAN WORLD, ALCHEMISTS WERE CONCERNED WITH CHANGING METALS INTO PURER, PRECIOUS SUBSTANCES, SUCH AS GOLD.

from the first centuries A.D. attributed to an Egyptian sage known as Hermes Trismegistus. Most likely there was no such person, but the name is attached to a wide range of writings, known as hermetic texts, on astrology, magic, and alchemy.

Islamic scholars also delved into alchemical studies. The Muslim alchemist Jābir ibn Hayyān, who might have been an eighth-century apothecary, wrote influential papers on purifying and distilling reactive substances such as sulfur or ammonium chloride while also linking them to numerology. By the late Middle Ages, European alchemists attributed hundreds of alchemical texts, translated into Latin, to Geber, as he became known.

Renaissance experimenters picked up the medieval alchemical ball and ran with

ARTIFACT SPOTLIGHT

THE EMERALD TABLET

The Emerald Tablet, an alchemical text attributed to the (possibly mythic) ancient Egyptian savant Hermes Trismegistus, inspired many medieval alchemists. Its true source was probably an Arab manuscript from the seventh to ninth centuries. The author claimed to have received it from "an old man sitting on a golden throne, who was holding an emerald tablet in one hand." Translated into Latin in the Middle Ages, it famously contains the phrase "That which is above is like to that which is below," usually shortened to "as above, so below." Occultists later appropriated the adage to indicate the invisible connections between the heavens and the earth.

Tabula Smaragdina (Emerald Tablet of Hermes Trismegistus), 1609

it. In 1267, English philosopher Roger Bacon named alchemy one of the branches of experimental science. Like many of his contemporaries, Bacon believed in the existence of the philosopher's stone, a mythical substance that could turn base metals into gold or produce an elixir of immortality. The famed 16th-century German-Swiss physician Paracelsus (see page 280) linked the seven key metals of alchemy—lead, tin, iron, gold, copper, mercury, and silver—to astronomical counterparts, and wrote of their chemistry as a kind of drama. Of Mars (lead), he wrote, "The six occult metals have expelled the seventh from them, and made it corporeal … imposing on it great hardness and weight."

European rulers of this era both feared and desired alchemy, since those who could create or counterfeit gold clearly posed a threat to the economy. In 1404, Henry IV of England passed the Act Against Multipliers, which prohibited the transmutation of base metals into gold or silver. Some 80 years later, his successor Henry VI began licensing alchemists, hoping they could create gold to pay for his wars. (They could not.) Rudolf II, a 16th-century Holy Roman Emperor, had

∧ The Muslim alchemist Jābir ibn Hayyān (circa 721–815) teaching chemistry at the School of Edessa, Greece; illustration from 1867

LIKE OTHER MAGICAL PRACTICES, ALCHEMY FADED AS THE SCIENTIFIC REVOLUTION TOOK OVER— ONLY TO MAKE A COMEBACK WITH THE OCCULT WRITERS OF THE 19TH AND 20TH CENTURIES.

his own alchemical laboratory in Prague. He patronized such scientists as Tycho Brahe (see page 224) and Johannes Kepler (see page 117), as well as leading alchemists of the day, including Elizabethan court magician John Dee (see page 172). Dee and his shady assistant, Edward Kelley, demonstrated alchemical transformations at Rudolf's court as well as other royal venues across Europe.

Perhaps the most surprising alchemist of the scientific age was Isaac Newton, who devoted many years to the subject in the late 17th century. To the English physicist, alchemy was one among many natural sciences, worthy of exploration in his search for scientific connections. Like other alchemists before him, Newton sought the secret of the philosopher's stone, studied alchemical manuscripts, and experimented using his own furnaces. His assistant Humphrey Newton wrote, "He rarely went to bed … the fire scarcely going out … till he had finished his Chymical Experiments."

Like other magical practices, alchemy faded as the scientific revolution took over, only to make a comeback with the rise of occult interests in the 19th and 20th centuries. Alchemy, said 19th-century writer Ethan Allen Hitchcock, was not about chemicals at all, but rather was a coded metaphor for the transformation of humanity. ▪

NICOLAS FLAMEL

Chief among legendary alchemists is 14th-century French scribe Nicolas Flamel. According to 17th-century accounts, Flamel discovered a mystical tome that allowed him to create the philosopher's stone in his own laboratory not once but three times. Realizing that such knowledge could be corrupting, he hid the book. The story of Flamel's discovery is explored in the book *Exposition of the Hieroglyphical Figures*, published in 1612. *Exposition* was attributed to Flamel, but modern scholars say there is no evidence that Flamel, who became a prosperous property owner, wrote the book or ever experimented with alchemy in real life. Today's readers may recognize Flamel and his stone from their fictionalized counterparts in J. K. Rowling's Harry Potter series (see page 327).

Nicolas Flamel, not an alchemist in real life, depicted with alchemical tools

Alchemists tend to furnaces and stills in an illustration from a 15th-century British manuscript.

THE MEDIEVAL ALCHEMIST'S TOOLS

Alchemists and their helpers spent long, hot hours in their laboratories. Depending on a practitioner's wealth and status, these workshops might consist of anything from a single room to the entire floor of a building. At the heart of the lab were furnaces, where the alchemist and his assistants heated and mixed base substances in the pursuit of precious metals and medicines. Sixteenth-century Danish astronomer Tycho Brahe, a well-funded scientist, dedicated the basement of his famed observatory at Uraniborg to an alchemical lab with 16 furnaces. Another workshop from the same era, found beneath a collapsed house in Prague in 2002, consisted of a room for drying herbs, a distillation and furnace room, and a glass-blowing room, where the alchemists could craft their own instruments.

Specialized devices and references cluttered alchemical chambers. In Isaac Newton's case, according to his assistant, "the laboratory ... was well furnished with chymical Materials, as Bodyes, Receivers, fends, Crucibles &c [sic], which was made very little use of, the Crucibles excepted, in which he [fused] his Metals: He would sometimes, though very seldom, look into an old mouldy Book."

^ HOURGLASS
An hourglass, such as this 18th-century version, helped the alchemist time chemical transformations.

< RUBY GLASS BEAKER
Alchemists spurred innovations in glassmaking, including the production of valuable ruby-colored glass.

< CUCURBIT
Cucurbits, such as this Islamic example from the 10th to 12th centuries, were gourd-shaped containers that held material to be distilled.

MINIATURE COPPER ALEMBIC >
The alchemist's alembic was a distillation device consisting of a cucurbit, a head, and a receiving vessel connected by a pipe.

^ CRUCIBLE
This German clay crucible would have held melted metals.

< MORTAR
This 16th-century German mortar was both decorative and useful for holding alchemical ingredients.

^ PESTLE
A 14th-century bronze pestle from Iran was used to grind materials in a mortar.

v RETORT
This hand-blown Italian glass retort was used to collect and condense gases from heated liquids. The distilled liquid drained down the long neck.

< ALEMBIC
A simple English alembic, reconstructed from glass fragments, has a sharp downward spout for draining distilled liquids into a receiving vessel.

v BRONZE SCALES
Careful alchemists would weigh and record their materials.

< FURNACE
A Sphinx-like figure decorates a German alchemical furnace.

BELLOWS >
Bellows, reproduced here from a 16th-century model, were essential in keeping alchemical fires burning.

KNOCK ON WOOD

Modern Rituals & Charms

Rituals and charms are not just things of the past. Citizens of today's high-tech world may not think of themselves as superstitious, but anyone who has ever said "knock on wood" or made a wish while blowing out a birthday candle has participated in a magical ceremony. In the United States, for instance, about a quarter of the adult population believes that crossing your fingers or carrying a four-leaf clover can bring good luck. A smaller but still significant fifth thinks that walking under a ladder or breaking a mirror invites bad luck.

In China, spoken words can hold magical double meanings. The number four is held to be bad luck, because the word for "four" sounds like the word for "death." Similarly, the number eight brings good fortune, because the word for "eight" sounds like "lucky."

Why do people carry good luck tokens or believe in lucky words in a supposedly rational age? Scientists say it's because human psychology hasn't changed, even if education has advanced. We are still anxious in an uncertain world, still aware that random events can bring tragedy, and still seeking the quick comfort of apotropaic items and actions just like our many-times-great-grandparents. In one set of experiments, psychologists found that subjects who said out loud that they would not get into a car accident were likely to think that they had "jinxed" themselves (unlike other experimental subjects who talked about neutral outcomes). Just thinking about the crash brought the fear to the front of their minds. But when the subjects were invited to knock on a wooden table afterward, the fear disappeared. The avoidant action seemed to push away the bad luck.

Charms have a similar soothing effect on the troubled mind. In many countries, circular blue glass charms still decorate household objects to ward off the evil eye. Lucky rabbit-feet were popular in the United States through the late 20th century—despite jokes that they hardly brought luck to the rabbit.

These types of lucky amulets boast a lineage dating to ancient Mesopotamia. Today's bad-luck beliefs and avoidant actions may be similarly archaic, but tracing their

∧ The Chinese New Year knot is said to represent long life.

Passersby have made a ritual of petting the bas-relief of a dog at the feet of St. John of Nepomunk, on the Charles Bridge in Prague.

IN THE UNITED STATES,
ABOUT A QUARTER OF THE ADULT
POPULATION BELIEVES THAT CROSSING
YOUR FINGERS OR CARRYING A FOUR-LEAF
CLOVER CAN BRING GOOD LUCK.

origins can be tough. For instance, responding to a sneeze by saying "bless you" or with some other acknowledgment is an old, yet unexplained, practice. In his first-century A.D. *Natural History*, Pliny the Elder asks, "Why is it that we salute a person when he sneezes—an observance which Tiberius Caesar, they say, the most unsociable of men … used to exact when riding in his chariot even?" Perhaps superstitious folks believed the sneezer was expelling evil spirits, or perhaps plague-era people were reacting to threatening symptoms—but there is no solid evidence for either. A more matter-of-fact explanation may be that responding to an utterance, even an involuntary one, is simply good manners.

Similar mysteries become attached to other common actions and items. Since at least the 15th century, people have linked the wishbone (furcula) found in most birds to luck and divination—but exactly why is unknown. The phrase "knock on wood" or "touch wood" is often connected to pagan beliefs in the sacred spirits of trees—but again, evidence is lacking. The phrase "touch wood" dates only to the 19th century. Crossing your fingers to ensure good luck, or to take away the onus of a white lie, is attributed to early Christians emulating the cross—but written records of the practice in Europe go back only about 100 years.

Many people still believe that spilling salt brings bad luck, possibly for the simple reason that it used to be valuable. Tossing a pinch of the spilled salt over your left shoulder to deflect the curse may reflect the notion that it would deter the devil who lurked there. But again, hard evidence is scarce for these historical explanations. Psychologists say that the tossing action, like knocking on wood, satisfies a physical need to throw away bad luck. The resulting relief is its own reward.

< Blue eye amulets are believed to ward off the evil eye.

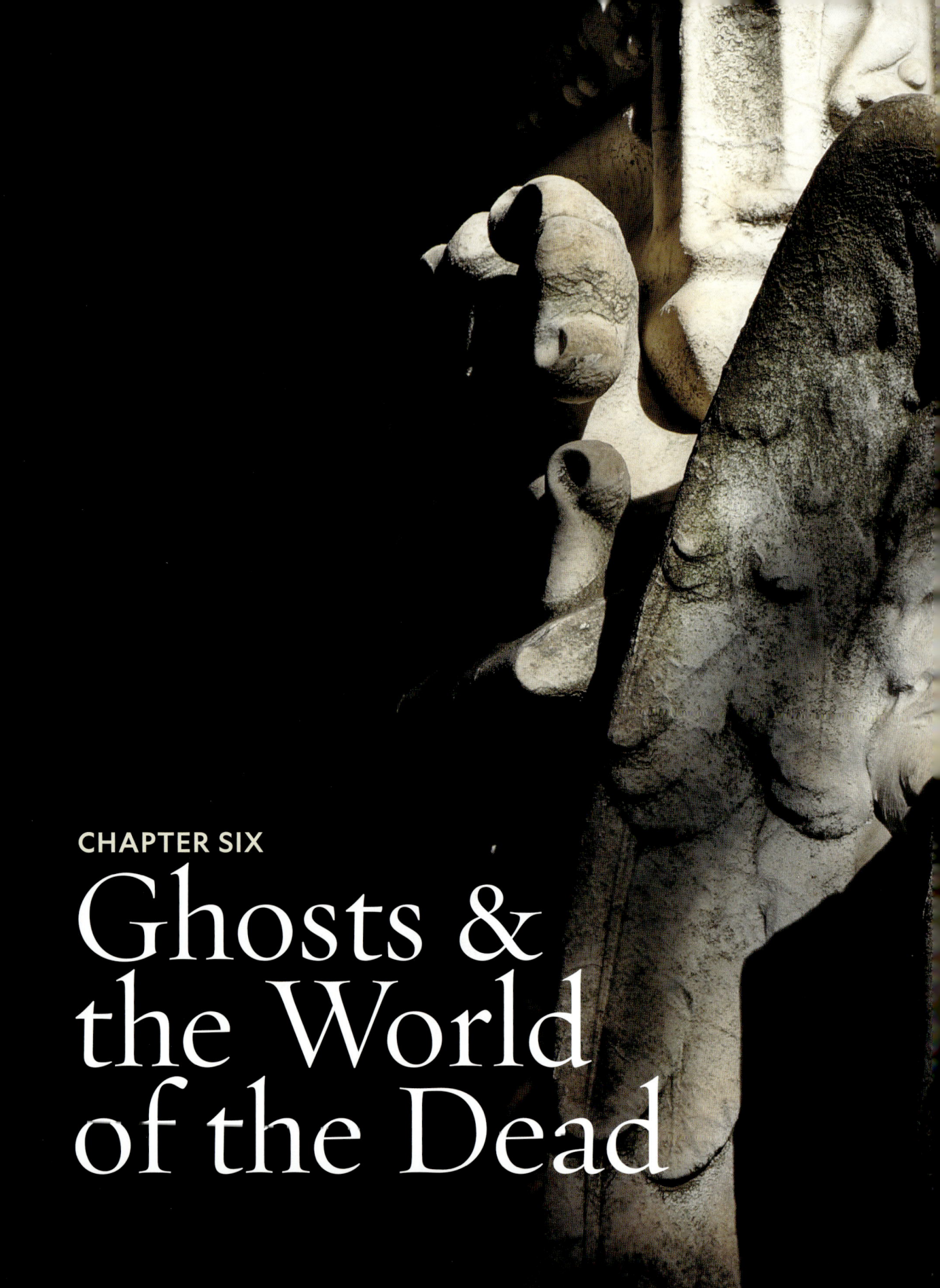

CHAPTER SIX

Ghosts & the World of the Dead

An angel gazes out over Montjuïc Cemetery in Barcelona, Spain—one of innumerable forms of art meant to honor the dead.

Crossing Over

Death & the Afterlife

Many of the oldest magical practices attempt to understand—and reach beyond—the veil of death. Over tens of millennia, ancient cultures from Egypt to the Aztec Empire came to a profound recognition: In death, the body and soul transformed. Awareness of our own mortality triggered cultural practices that distinguished between the dead and the living. Specific locations—often caves, in regions like modern-day Kenya, England, and Israel—became known as places of the dead, a concept that eventually extended to notions of the afterlife and otherworlds. Bodies came to be disposed of in increasingly deliberate and complex ways, whether to commemorate ancestors, prepare the dead for the world beyond, or settle grim cosmic debts.

Over time, traditions on every inhabited continent connected death to great and powerful natural forces, assuming a transition between worlds that could be mediated by ritual. Protection could be obtained for the afterlife. The spirits of the dead could be asked to intercede on behalf of the living. With the right necromantic rituals, some practitioners warned—or promised—the dead could even be brought back to life.

And as humans grappled with the boundary between life and death, they envisioned beings that could cross that boundary. Such restless spirits—from ghosts to poltergeists—could haunt one's home or taunt the wayward traveler with the threat of an untimely death. Undead creatures such as ghouls and vampires could rise from their graves to terrorize and feed on the living. Around campfires, over séance tables, and in ever more elaborate holidays and other spectacles, stories of these astounding and unnerving creatures frightened, cautioned, and entertained. ▪

∧ Soapstone scarab inscribed with a blessing related to the Egyptian deity Amun-Re

In the popular medieval allegory known as the Dance of Death, a skeleton dances with people from all walks of life, showing the inescapability of death.

BURYING THE BONES

Ancient Mortuary Practices

Mortuary practices, many intended to ease the deceased's passage to the afterlife, seem to have arisen deep in prehistory. The oldest widely accepted human burials date to more than 90,000 years ago, and some sites created by Neanderthals—our extinct sister species—contain simple burials that are more than 45,000 years old (see sidebar). While some of these sites contain the reddish pigment ocher and evidence of fire—both hints of symbolic ritual practices—many early burials were simple and unadorned. It is only by roughly 30,000 years ago that we begin to see elaborate mortuary practices.

Around that time in what is now Wales, for example, the body of a young man was buried in the back of a cave, covered in ocher. When geologist William Buckland unearthed these remains in 1823—calling them the Red Lady of Paviland—he found 40 to 50 fragments of mammoth ivory alongside the body. Some scholars interpret these fragments as pieces of proto-magic wands, wielded either by the man in life or by those who interred him. And more than 30,000 years ago in what is now the town

THE EARLIEST BURIALS

In the Shanidar Cave in Iraqi Kurdistan, archaeologists unearthed Neanderthal skeletons more than 45,000 years old, covered in dirt within either natural or artificial depressions. In Israel, the Qafzeh Cave contained *Homo sapiens* skeletons buried between 90,000 and 120,000 years ago. One of these burials held the bones of a young adolescent as well as the remains of a hunted large deer—some of the clearest known evidence from this time period for grave offerings. In what is now Kenya approximately 78,000 years ago, people buried a child—now nicknamed Mtoto, after "child" in Swahili—within the mouth of a cave known as Panga ya Saidi. The position of Mtoto's skull indicates that something supportive, such as a pillow, was placed underneath the head when the body was laid to rest.

Cast of a child's skull found in the Qafzeh Cave, Israel

of Vladimir, Russia, two children were buried at what's known as the Sunghir site alongside an extravagant set of grave goods: thousands of ivory beads, mammoth-tusk spears, and hundreds of arctic fox teeth. How these children died, or why they were given such an elaborate burial, remains a mystery.

But even as burials became more intricate, they remained rare. Perhaps people who received elaborate interments played especially important roles in their societies—or perhaps their deaths were so ominous that the ritual of burial was required to cleanse the cosmic slate. According to the archaeological record, burials became more commonplace only around 11,000 years ago or so, with the emergence of proto-cemeteries: dedicated spaces where large numbers of people were formally buried over time.

Burial wasn't the only ancient mortuary practice; many cultures also defleshed the

dead. In 1953, British archaeologist Kathleen Kenyon uncovered seven human skulls in ancient Jericho. Between 9,250 and 10,100 years ago, these skulls were filled with soil and then covered in plaster to model the living person's face. Shells were embedded in place of the eyes. Archaeologists surmise that the people who prepared these skulls venerated their ancestors, possibly attributing some kind of power to the dead within the realm of the living.

At least occasionally, this defleshing of the dead seems to have veered into ritual cannibalism. At Gough's Cave in Somerset, England, archaeologists have found butchered large mammals mixed in with cracked human bones, some of which may have been chewed on by other humans. The remains, more than 14,000 years old, include cups made from human skulls. Were these cups war trophies, tools used to absorb the essences of departed ancestors, or something else entirely?

∧ Grave goods at the Sunghir burial site include a belt made of arctic fox teeth and a pin, a horse figurine, and a disk carved from ivory.

EGYPTIAN TOMBS

Preparing for the Afterlife

Every night, according to ancient Egyptian belief, the sun god Re shuttled the dead across the underworld in his ferry. He began this route after vanishing below the earth's surface in the west at sunset and ended it by rising the next day in the east.

The journey through the underworld was filled with danger. Each night, Apep, the serpent god of darkness, would threaten the boat and its newly deceased passengers. Upon his defeat, the boat arrived at a harrowing series of tests: gates that opened only to the correct incantation, a labyrinth, the Hall of Two Truths, and, finally, the weighing of the heart. If the deceased's heart—holding a lifetime of deeds—balanced a scale with a feather, he or she was cleared to move into the afterlife.

Belief in this journey and the ensuing spirit world shaped every aspect of Egyptian mortuary rituals. The practice of mummification (see page 239), used largely by

BOOK OF THE DEAD

In the 1800s, German archaeologist and linguist Karl Richard Lepsius discovered writings scattered across Egyptian burial sites that he assumed were scripture. In the original Egyptian, these texts were titled "The Chapters of Going Forth by Day," but when published in 1842, they would become known as Book of the Dead. The hieroglyphs were magical spells meant to usher the dead into the afterlife. These spells had been written on papyrus, inscribed on mummies' bandages, and etched into sarcophagi. Some were intended to animate the figurines sent into the afterlife with the dead, others were read by priests during funerary rituals, while still others were used to preserve body parts. The earliest date back to 2300 B.C., about a thousand years before the complete work was compiled.

This pectoral, once sewn into the chest wrappings of an Egyptian mummy, includes a spell addressing the heart.

This wooden stela, made in roughly 900 B.C. for the tomb of a scribe named Aafenmut,
depicts Aafenmut (right) making an offering to the sun god Re-Harakhty.

nobility, was predicated on the conviction that the body would be needed again in the afterlife. To ensure the dead could successfully reach the next world and thrive there, tombs were filled with things they would need to achieve these ends.

Key among these were a collection of amulets and charms, which promised protection and guidance. Amulets, often related to the gods, were worn both in life and death for protection, healing, and good luck; in death, they would be carefully placed on different parts of the body and blessed by priests. The most popular, a scarab, was placed over the heart of the dead to ensure it wouldn't speak out against

them at the tribunal to determine entry into the afterlife.

In Egyptian society, magic was used to tackle the most dangerous and uncertain aspects of life from birth to death. Thus, tombs were furnished with copies of spells taken from the celebrated funerary text Book of the Dead (see page 236). Methods of harnessing magic were outlined in this guidebook to the afterlife that contained incantations crucial for surviving the fraught journey between worlds. (Particularly useful were spells 144 and 146, which provided the means for passing through the first gates of the underworld.)

Egyptians expected to be reunited with

∨ The family tomb of an Egyptian craftsman features the jackal god Anubis—the divine embalmer—overseeing a mummification.

the dead in the afterlife. But since the only way to maintain communication until then was via magic, some spells were intended for use by the living. To bequeath the deceased with provisions, for example, living visitors recited the incantations written on the tomb aloud, believing the enchanted words would instantly resupply bread, beer, fowl, and other foodstuffs necessary in the underworld.

Sometimes, the living could commune with their deceased loved ones a bit more closely. Spirits known as *ka* were thought to visit the mortuary chapel, which was often built next to a tomb. A spirit could enter via a false door and inhabit a statue

of the dead; mourners left them offerings of food and drink.

Each tomb, meanwhile, was stocked with a variety of goods to outfit the dead for a luxurious stay in paradise: food, clothing, animals, and *ushabtis*, or small statues that could be animated in the afterlife as servants with the correct spells. The afterlife was thought to be a bucolic version of Earth, with clean rivers, mountains, sunshine, and fields of barley stretching many feet high. But these fields needed harvesting, and the reanimated ushabtis would perform the required manual labor. Over time, more and more laborers would be included in a tomb, and by around 1000 B.C., a single person could be buried with one ushabti for every day of the year.

Between the powerful inscriptions on a tomb and the objects permanently enshrined in it, deceased Egyptian nobility were certain to be well supplied in the afterlife. ◾

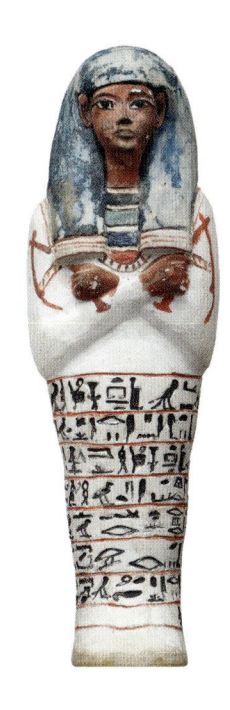

∧ An ushabti, or servant for the afterlife, dedicated to a 13th-century B.C. artisan

MUMMIFICATION

Mummification was not for the timid, since the process involved emptying the body of blood and organs. Only the heart would be left inside, while the other organs were placed in jars and buried next to the body. The hollowed-out body was cleaned and packed with natron, a type of salt, for a 40-day period of dehydration. Next, the dried body was coated with resin, wrapped in many yards of linen, and decorated with protective amulets. A final layer of resin sealed the mummified body before it was placed in a sarcophagus.

To ensure that the dead would make it safely to the underworld, priests presided over the mummification process. The practice was not limited to ancient Egypt: Evidence of similar rituals in modern-day Chile dates back 2,000 years earlier than that found in Egyptian tombs.

A mummy bandage from Tutankhamun's embalming cache, 1336–1327 B.C.

EGYPTIAN GODS

Diverse and fantastical deities provided the foundation of religion in ancient Egypt; each was associated with a different natural force and worshipped through elaborate ceremonies. Few held more power than Re-Atum, a blend of the sun god, Re, and the creator god, Atum. His strength came from a source called Heka, a type of magic used by gods, pharaohs, priests, and ordinary people. Heka helped Re move across the heavens, protected and sustained the universe, and could be summoned during religious rituals. As both a form of power and a deity, Heka was associated with a scepter. To show their magical powers, gods and pharaohs were often depicted holding Heka's scepter.

Other gods, like Thoth, who contained all knowledge, were also thought to possess magical powers. Thoth reigned over magical texts, secrets, and spells, while Isis, the goddess of magic, was one of the most prominent and powerful figures in ancient Egypt. By the time the Romans ruled Egypt, the belief that Isis controlled fate entirely had become widespread; her name was worshipped as far away as England and Afghanistan.

∧ SAKHMET
Two of this lion-headed goddess and two cobras adorn this necklace piece from around the 12th century B.C.

∧ HORUS
Egyptian leaders worshipped Horus, who was both pharaoh and sky god, and often used his image for protection.

∧ BES
Often found carved into amulets, cups, and beds, the god Bes guarded homes from evil spirits, protected pregnant women, and promoted childbirth.

HATHOR >
The goddess Hathor, usually depicted as a cow, represented love, music, and fertility. In cobra form, she could protect against enemies.

< OSIRIS
The god of the underworld was represented by this ceremonial flail, which was buried with a mummy to usher the soul into the afterlife.

^ HEKA

Both a god and a power, Heka (far left in this first-century B.C. stela) was the embodiment of magic. Ancient Egyptians believed Heka could be harnessed for both ritual and informal needs.

ᵛ AMUN

This sculpture of Amun, the god of the air, was likely commissioned by King Tutankhamun to stand in Karnak Temple, built in Amun's honor.

^ PTAH

Patron god of artisans, Ptah was the most important god of the city of Memphis, the first capital of ancient Egypt.

< ISIS

This aegis, a sacred collar-shaped carving, depicts Isis, a powerful, omnipresent goddess who was healer, mother, and mourner.

< BASTET

The cat-headed goddess Bastet ruled over pregnancy and childbirth, while the earlier lion-headed Bastet was regaled as a protective warrior.

NEPHTHYS >

Known as the goddess of death and decay, Nephthys aided the dead in their journey to the underworld and healed the sick.

THOTH >

Worshiped by scribes, Thoth, the god of knowledge, often appeared as an ape or a man with an ibis head.

HALLOWEEN
Pagan & Religious Origins

From trick-or-treating to ghost stories, no date on the U.S. cultural calendar is as closely associated with magic and the occult as October 31: Halloween. Nominally the eve of All Hallows' Day, a Christian feast date honoring the saints, the pop-culture Halloween is a celebration of all things spooky, scary, and supernatural.

Some scholars trace Halloween back to Samhain (pronounced SAH-win), an ancient Celtic new year's celebration that fell on November 1 and was marked with feasting and games. Samhain marked the first day of winter and the end of the farmer's year: Vegetation withered, the harvest was gathered, and the darkness of night grew longer, necessitating the gathering of fuel for winter fires.

Because of its connection with the ending of the growing cycle, the occasion came to also serve as a festival of the dead. Samhain features prominently in Irish myth as a date of magical significance, when spirits journeyed to the afterlife, the barrier between mortal and supernatural realms weakened, and ghosts walked among the living.

The date was also associated with other-worlds, supernatural realms in Celtic tradition that were inhabited by deities and other magical beings. In one story known as the "Echtra Nerai" ("The Adventure of Nera"), set on Samhain, the hero, Nera, speaks with a hanged corpse and helps him get a drink of water. Nera then inadvertently enters the otherworld through a cave in Ireland's Hill of Cruachan, emerging with a warning that fairy folk will attack Nera's king one year hence.

According to some scholars, Samhain became Halloween because of the intervention of the Catholic Church. In a letter sent in 601, Pope Gregory I encouraged Catholic missionaries in Britain to reconsecrate pagan temples and reframe pagan holidays as Christian celebrations. Samhain became All Hallows' Day (All Saints' Day), a feast that commemorates the saints of the church who have reached heaven. October 31, then, became known as All Hallows' Eve.

But this rebranding didn't stamp out the day's associations with the wandering dead. Before the Christianization of earlier Celtic beliefs in the sixth century, people lit bonfires to guide wayward spirits and made them offerings of food and drink, just as Nera had helped to slake a corpse's thirst. These practices continued during All Hallows' Eve, morphing by the 16th century into a forerunner to trick-or-treating: households giving food and drinks to mummers, masked and costumed people

Celtic beliefs in "otherworlds" inspired fairy tales such as this 1920 Irish story of a prince forced to journey through a realm of giant toads.

In 19th-century Ireland, Halloween was a night of revelry and games such as bobbing for apples, as recorded in this 1833 painting by Daniel Maclise.

who imitated the spirits by performing various antics. Along the way, All Hallows' Eve morphed into Hallow E'en, then later, Halloween.

By the late 19th century, Halloween traditions were observed throughout the British Isles and had started to gain traction in the United States, following the growth of the country's Irish American population. But not all early expressions of the holiday resemble what we see today. Against the backdrop of Victorian-era modesty, Halloween's associations with the spirit world led to playful fortune-telling rituals that young people used to glean insights into their future romantic partners. In ceremonies known as "dumb suppers," young women summoned spirits they hoped might reveal the identities of their future husbands. To call on these specters and tempt them to reveal the future, the women staged unusual rituals: meals held in complete silence that were set up at odds with traditional customs, with chairs turned backward and dessert served first. In another Halloween love ritual, a woman could learn of her future beau by walking backward under moonlight while gazing into a hand mirror.

In the early 20th century, one popular Halloween game—an ancestral cousin to bobbing for apples—called for hanging a stick from the ceiling with string and then impaling an apple on one end and a lit candle on the other. With their hands behind their backs, partygoers attempted to take a bite from the apple as the stick spun around. The first person to succeed would marry; a run-in with the candle foretold bad luck.

Though the modern Halloween places less emphasis on love, one constant has remained: a belief that the day is suffused with magic.

SPELLBINDING SYMBOL

JACK-O'-LANTERN

The beloved carved pumpkin known as a jack-o'-lantern has come to symbolize Halloween. It is thought to have Celtic roots, tracing back to Samhain traditions of carving frightening faces into root vegetables such as turnips, potatoes, and beets to ward off spirits. Pumpkins did not become the vegetal canvas of choice for jack-o'-lanterns until the tradition jumped to the United States. The name comes from 19th-century Irish folk stories about Jack, the spirit of a boy who wasn't good enough for heaven or bad enough for hell, said to wander the countryside with nothing but a lantern. Jack-o'-the-lantern, as he was sometimes known, appeared as a ghostly light in the dark, leading fishermen and wayward travelers to boggy or watery graves. Some think these lights may have been caused by the spontaneous burning of methane-rich swamp gas in marshes, produced as vegetation decayed.

VAMPIRES
From Folklore to Hysteria

Few monsters loom as large in modern popular culture as the bloodthirsty vampire. Amalgams of 19th-century literary characters such as Dracula and centuries-old folklore traditions, these creatures feast in the dead of night, their fangs slipping into innocents' throats and draining their life force. They were once human but now exist beyond both life and death, with many sleeping in coffins or graves before their nocturnal hunts. Some are beautiful, others grotesque.

Despite their strength and power, they have vulnerabilities—including, most famously, a wooden stake through the heart.

Stories of blood-drinking monsters and the living dead can be found around the world. In Greek mythology dating as far back as the sixth century B.C., a female monster with male genitalia known as Lamia feasted on children's blood and flesh. In the medieval Anglo-Saxon poem *Beowulf*, the monstrous Grendel "quickly seized a sleeping man …

[and] drank the blood from his veins." In the Philippines, folklore tells of a creature that disguises itself as a beautiful maiden, marries an unsuspecting man, and then sips his blood with a proboscis-like tongue.

The vampire as we know it today is based in Slavic folklore dating to at least the 11th century A.D., from regions including modern-day Poland, Romania, Serbia, and Bosnia. In Slavic traditions, if a dead person had been denied Christian burial or had lived as a sorcerer, murderer, or any other kind of grievous sinner, their unclean soul could latch on to a corpse and stalk the living. At night, this *upiór*, as it was known in Poland, would rise to suck people's blood and attack household animals. Slavic myths also describe the *strzyga*, a ruddy-faced, female demon that fed on blood and harassed the living. A person's odds of becoming a strzyga (or a male *strzygoń*) after death increased if they had two rows of teeth or no pubic or armpit hair.

Destroying a corpse suspected of being an upiór required exhuming the body, driving a wooden stake through its heart, and burning it. In other cases, a suspected

< The Greek monster Lamia, as shown in a 17th-century "game book"

In myths and legends, many creatures eat human flesh and drink blood, including the monster Grendel (illustrated here) in the heroic poem *Beowulf*.

AS VAMPIRE HYSTERIA PEAKED IN THE MID-18TH CENTURY, GOTHIC AUTHORS FOUND INSPIRATION IN THE FABLED BLOODSUCKERS.

upiór or strzyga would have a sickle placed over their neck, their legs mutilated, or iron nails pounded into their skull—all to keep the corpse from rising.

The modern vampire myth crystallized in the mid-1700s, amid what's now known as the vampire epidemic, when apparent disease outbreaks in modern-day Serbia and Bosnia combined with longstanding folk beliefs, misinterpretations of the decomposition process, and a government turnover to fuel a mass hysteria.

During an eight-day span in 1725, nine people in the Bosnian town of Kisolova died suddenly. Townspeople suspected that a recently deceased peasant named Petar Blagojević had risen from the dead and sucked their blood. Local clergy and a visiting official from the Habsburg Empire, which had recently taken control of the area, opened Blagojević's grave to find his body unusually fresh—and his mouth seemingly full of liquid blood. The townspeople hastily staked the body and burned it. Reports of Blagojević's exhumation quickly made their way to the Habsburg capital of Vienna, where pamphlets ran with the lurid tale of the "vampyri."

The vampire epidemic didn't become a true sensation, however, until seven years later. In 1731, 13 people died suddenly in the town of Morawa, in modern-day Serbia; villagers insisted the tragedy was the work of vampires. In early 1732, Habsburg

SCIENCE OF THE VAMPIRE

While vampires are the stuff of myth, researchers have suggested some scientific explanations to help explain the origins of vampire stories. During decomposition, a human's gums and nail beds recede, which can create the illusion that teeth and fingernails are growing after death. Diseases can also create vampiric symptoms; rabies, for example, can bring about sensitivities to sunlight and pungent foods such as garlic, as well as an urge to bite. It's also possible that some of the deaths that triggered the vampire epidemic were caused by pellagra, a disease that leads to sunlight sensitivity, anemia, and foul breath. It's caused by diets overly high in corn—a crop introduced to eastern Europe during the 18th century.

A 13th-century skeleton staked with an iron rod through the chest in Bulgaria

officials dispatched military surgeon Johann Flückinger to the scene. The autopsies he conducted found some of the corpses to be unusually plump, fueling suspicions that they had risen to feed on blood. Villagers then treated the corpses as vampires: cutting off their heads, staking them through the heart, and burning them. Flückinger also uncovered the story of a local infantryman who, according to villagers, had died years earlier but rose soon after his death to kill four people and suck the blood of local livestock.

Flückinger's reports, and others that followed, captivated intellectuals and the general public alike. As vampire hysteria peaked in the mid-18th century, gothic authors found inspiration in the fabled bloodsuckers. After first appearing in the 1748 poem "The Vampire" by Heinrich August Ossenfelder, the creature jumped into the English canon with works such as John Polidori's 1819 story "The Vampyre" and Joseph Sheridan Le Fanu's 1872 novella *Carmilla*. The modern vampire's urtext is arguably *Dracula*, the 1897 novel by Bram Stoker (see page 251), which has inspired endless variations on the vampire myth across all forms of media.

Vampires' modern allure is tied to the subversive thrill of their inherent sexuality: the seduction required to feed on another's

∧ In this 1890s engraving, Romanians shoot a corpse in an effort to keep it from rising again as a vampire.

Count Dracula reached pop-culture icon status thanks in part to movies such as the 1931 film *Dracula*, starring Helen Chandler and Bela Lugosi.

very life, as well as the intimacy of penetrating another and exchanging bodily fluids. Even in Ossenfelder's 1748 poem, a male vampire narrator tells a "dear young maiden" that when he gives her a "vampire kiss," she will "start to tremble and … sink down into [his] arms." Many scholars have found *Dracula* to be sexually, even homoerotically, charged. Early in the novel, a man nearly submits to three female vampires at once, having "closed [his] eyes in a languorous ecstasy and waited—waited with beating heart." The sexualized vampire is a mainstay of modern pop culture, from *Interview with the Vampire* to *True Blood* to *Twilight*. These works are just some of the many that have kept the creature undead and well in our imaginations.

∧ Bram Stoker's 1897 novel *Dracula* popularized the link between eastern European vampires and bats.

IN LEGEND

DRACULA

No work of fiction has defined the modern vampire myth more than *Dracula*, the 1897 gothic horror novel by Irish author Bram Stoker (1847–1912). Told through letters, newspaper articles, and diary entries, the novel tells the story of a team that hunts down and kills Count Dracula, a wealthy, powerful vampire from Transylvania (modern-day central Romania) who attempts to move to England. One of the most influential English-language novels ever written, *Dracula* cemented the modern archetype of the vampire—including the creature's strengths, weaknesses, and association with bats—and contributed to the modern link between vampires and sexuality. Though Stoker's inspiration for Dracula remains debated, some scholars have drawn parallels with a real historical figure: Vlad III Dracula (1431–1476; aka Vlad the Impaler), a military governor in Romania who gained a reputation for ruthlessness in wars with the Ottoman Empire.

Sixteenth-century portrait of Vlad III Dracula

ZOMBIES

Trapped Souls

In the 17th and 18th centuries, there was only one escape for enslaved Africans toiling on any of the 8,000 sugar, coffee, and cotton plantations in French-colonial Saint-Domingue: death. In the richest colony on Earth, today called Haiti, it was estimated that half the enslaved population would die within a few years of arriving. Death was not to be feared, however; in death, many believed, they would be transported back to freedom in Africa.

But with death came the risk of being turned into a *zonbi*, or zombie. In the kingdom of Kongo, where many Haitians trace their roots, it was believed that a spirit could be bottled up and used by priests in ceremonial magic. The term *nzambi*, or spirit god, in the Kongo language became *zonbi* in Haitian creole. To enslaved Haitians, becoming a zonbi in Saint-Domingue meant their soul would be trapped on the plantation for eternity, permanently enslaved.

In Haiti today, zombies persist both in folklore and religion. Some vodou followers believe corpses can be reanimated by

MARIE LAVEAU

In 19th-century New Orleans, a vodou priestess named Marie Laveau (1801–1881) peddled magical charms, spells, and advice to her diverse clientele, from enslaved people to upper-class white society. Laveau claimed to have been gifted her talents from a rattlesnake, and she often provided her patrons with a silver dime to be worn as a necklace or to put in a shoe for protection. On Sundays, Laveau's followers would dance and worship in downtown Congo Square, where she'd conjure deities and oversee spirit possession. Nearly 150 years after her death, the Vodou Queen remains an omnipresent deity, revered by modern vodou practitioners.

1973 portrait of Marie Laveau, New Orleans Historic Voodoo Museum

sorcerer priests known as *bokor*. In the vodou religion, the soul has multiple parts: One holds personality, and the other is the immortal soul. Upon death, the latter joins the spirit world, while the personality lingers near the grave, risking zombification. Because these spirits could retain the skills and knowledge of their owner, the bokor could provide customers with the zonbi best suited to their needs—whether for benevolent or nefarious aims.

The concept of a zonbi migrated from Haiti into global popular culture. Zombies arrived in America in 1929 in the pages of *The Magic Island*, a bestseller by travel writer William Seabrook, who learned about vodou on a visit to Haiti. In Bela Lugosi's 1932 film *White Zombie*, a woman is turned into a zombie by a Haitian plantation owner.

Today, zonbi are enlisted to help with religious celebrations like the annual Rara festival. Bands parade to cemeteries, where a ritual asks guardian spirits for the loan of recently deceased spirits. Those zonbi spirits are captured in a bottle and provide energy and strength to the humans who carry out the festivities. After the festival, the zonbi are offered food and drink before being returned to their graves.

In the centuries since Haiti's 1791 revolution, the idea of zonbis as perpetually enslaved walking-dead creatures has persisted in politics and popular culture. Rural migrant laborers coming into the cities might be derisively called zonbis because of the grueling nature of their menial work. The zonbi appears both in Haitian literature and as a joke on the street, where the image of a mindless cog in a labor machine remains a strong reminder of the country's history.

∧ Zombies remain fixtures of 20th- and 21st-century Haitian art, as in this 1946 painting by Haitian artist Hector Hyppolite.

MUMMIES

Consumption & Curses

Beginning in the 1400s, a public fascination with mummies fueled a dark trade in Europe. Because mummified remains (see page 239) were believed by Europeans to have powerful medicinal properties, the practice of consuming them was popular for centuries in countries including Italy, France, and England. Catherine de Médicis sent explorers to Egypt to collect mummies for such use, and traders sold both real mummies and powdered substances they'd pass off as mummy dust.

Ground mummies were turned into a pigment called "mummy brown," used in paintings from the Renaissance to the Romantic period of the 1800s.

But it wasn't until Napoleon Bonaparte returned to Europe after invading Egypt at the end of the 18th century that Egyptomania was officially sparked. The treasures of his conquest—statues, obelisks, and the Rosetta Stone, which would prove the key to translating hieroglyphics—began a flow of Egyptian goods into private collections

IN LEGEND

THE CURSE OF THE MUMMY

The curse of the mummy loomed large over Egypt's explorers. Once the hieroglyphic code was cracked, grave robbers and smugglers could translate the ancient pleas and curses on pillaged tombs. Disturbed spirits were said to cause untimely deaths, so some mummy recipients sent back their purchases out of fear. In 1922, the tomb of King Tutankhamun was opened by British explorer Howard Carter, who likely started the rumor of a curse to dissuade would-be tomb raiders. When George Herbert, the funder of Carter's expedition, died from an infected mosquito bite within the year, King Tut's curse became enshrined in the public imagination.

Howard Carter (left) and George Herbert at the doorway of Tutankhamun's burial chamber, 1923

across Europe. Travelers, scientists, and soldiers could acquire a mummy in Egypt and bring it home. There was even a market for "mummy seeds"—actual plant seeds, like wheat—that allegedly came from inside the mummy's bandages (but were more likely placed there later).

Queen Victoria's reign in 19th-century England was marked by a public fascination with death, and the elaborate burial rituals of ancient Egypt appealed to these sensibilities. Victorians began incorporating obelisks, pyramids, scarabs, and sarcophagi motifs into their lives and architecture. Secret societies like the Freemasons and the Hermetic Order of the Golden Dawn (see page 125) embraced the Book of the Dead (see page 236), adopted pseudo-Egyptian rituals, and dressed in pharaonic robes to align with the ancient civilization's mysticism.

In the 1830s, public fascination with mummies reached a fever pitch when a British surgeon named Thomas Pettigrew began hosting public mummy unwrappings. The audiences, according to a review in an 1834 journal, felt "delight in witnessing the unrolling of endless bandages, smiling at the hieroglyphics, and then staring at the dried remains of a being who moved on the earth three or four thousand years ago." In 1852, Pettigrew reversed his process by mummifying the Duke of Hamilton, per his wishes, in accordance with Egyptian techniques and interring him in an ancient sarcophagus.

The influence and persistence of Egyptomania was in no small part due to its presence in the arts. In 1827, Jane Webb wrote *The Mummy!*, taking cues from Mary Shelley's *Frankenstein* (see page 259). Writers including Percy Shelley, Oscar Wilde, Edgar Allan Poe, and Arthur Conan Doyle joined the trend. Thousands of years after ancient Egyptians walked the earth, their mystique continues to inspire artists, leaving a trail of mummy dust through literature, Hollywood, and culture at large.

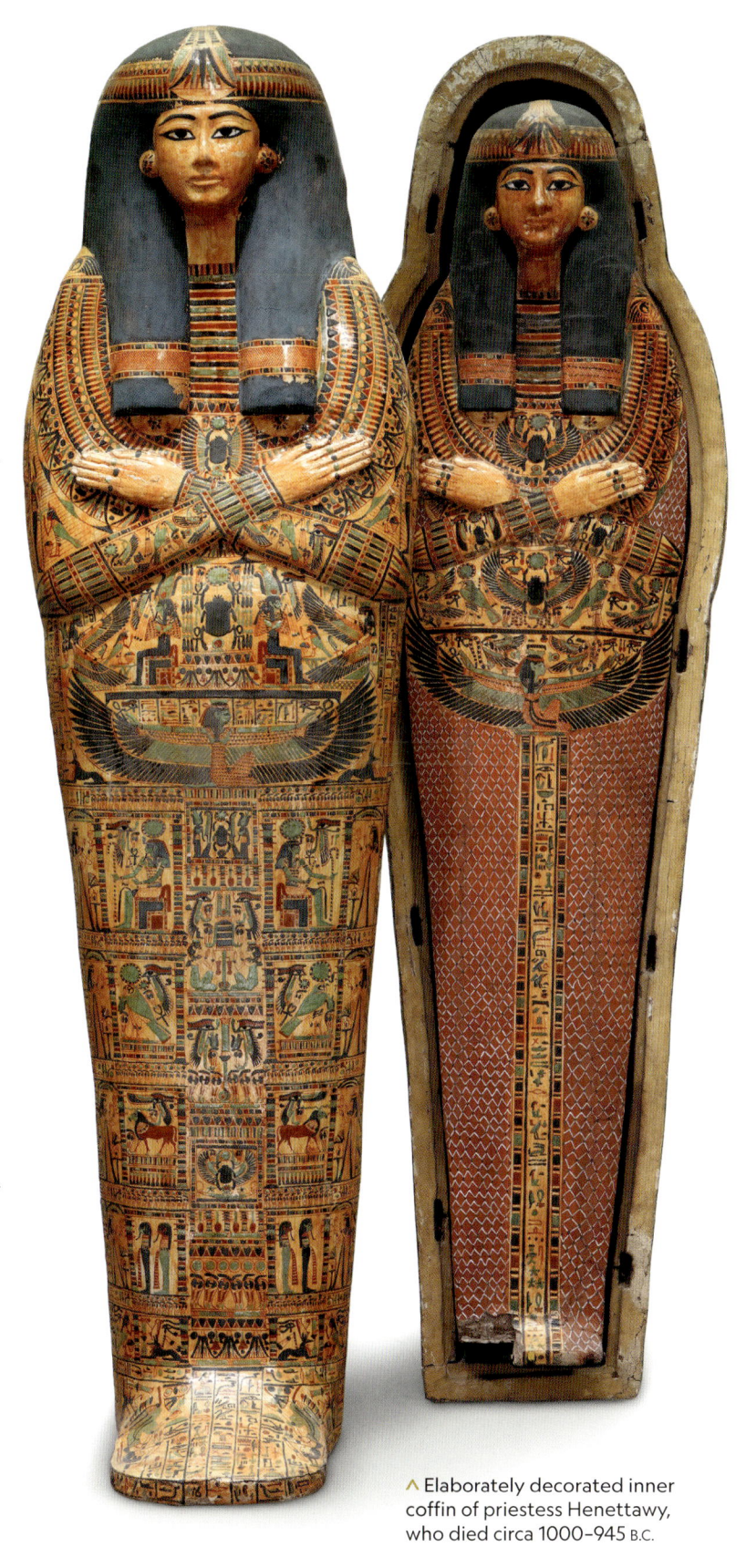

⋀ Elaborately decorated inner coffin of priestess Henettawy, who died circa 1000–945 B.C.

GHOST STORIES

Tales of the Undead

Stories of restless spirits and hauntings have captured human imagination since antiquity. In a letter to a Roman senator, the first-century A.D. lawyer Pliny the Younger recounted the story of an Athenian house plagued by an old man's chain-rattling ghost—a haunting resolved by finding and interring the man's chained-up, unburied remains. In the storied collection of folktales from the Middle East and surrounding areas, *The Thousand and One Nights*, first published in English in 1706, an Egyptian merchant named Ali travels to Baghdad, where a haunted house kills any-

one who sleeps there. (When Ali stays there, however, the jinni (genie) haunting the residence showers him with gold.) And in *The Tale of Genji*, the pioneering Japanese work by 11th-century poet Murasaki Shikibu, a lover of the story's hero dies after being violently possessed by a jealous spirit.

In the West, ghost stories as we know them today are literary creatures dating back to 18th-century Europe and the rise of gothic fiction. Stories in this genre typically pit humans against forces of supernatural evil or embodiments of human folly, within bleak settings that provoke unease. The first such story in the English language—and one of the earliest literary horror stories—was the 1764 novel *The Castle of Otranto* by Horace Walpole. Its spooky plot elements include a person killed by a huge falling helmet, a breathing portrait, and a gigantic spirit who brings a castle's walls down as he declares a prophecy fulfilled.

By the early 19th century, bound compilations of ghost stories from folklore were published and circulated widely. Among the most influential of these works was *Das Gespensterbuch (The Book of*

< Ali receives gold from a jinni in this engraving from a 19th-century English edition of *The Thousand and One Nights.*

This 1892 illustration depicts the vine-encircled spirit of Yūgao, a maiden in *The Tale of Genji* who dies after being possessed.

A ghostly vision stands in an otherworldly courtyard in this 1903 work by Russian painter Viktor Borisov-Musatov.

Ghosts), a five-volume collection assembled by Johann August Apel and Friedrich August Schulze between 1810 and 1815. The legacy of *Das Gespensterbuch* endures through another book: *Fantasmagoriana*. Published in 1812 by French geographer Jean-Baptiste Benoît Eyriès, this French-language anthology of ghost stories featured tales that were translated from Apel and Schulze's collection.

Fantasmagoriana's claim to fame is that it inspired the single most important ghost-story reading in literary history. During the cold and dreary summer of 1816, several English writers decamped to Lake Geneva, Switzerland, where they spent most of their time indoors. These authors included poet Lord Byron, who brought his personal physician John Polidori, and poet Percy Bysshe Shelley, along with his partner, Mary Wollstonecraft Godwin (see sidebar), who would become his wife. One evening, after reading stories from *Fantasmagoriana*, Lord Byron challenged each member of the group to come up with their own ghost story.

Polidori's submission grew into the short story "The Vampyre" (1819), which helped inspire the 1897 novel *Dracula* (see page 251). Mary's contribution came to her in a nightmare: the vivid image of a scientist resurrecting a dead body with electricity and then, in terror, rejecting his creation. In 1818, she went on to publish her groundbreaking novel *Frankenstein*, a landmark of science fiction and gothic horror.

Ghosts, ghouls, and other sources of horror abounded in 19th-century urban legends, which merged older folkloric traditions with mass media and the anxieties of modern city life. Perhaps the best known ghoul of Victorian urban legend was Spring-Heeled Jack, a mysterious being that robbed and terrorized people and then escaped by jumping enormous distances. Stories of the shadowy figure first appeared in the late 1830s, in newspaper reports on a string of unusual assaults in northwest London, in which a cloaked figure grabbed, kissed, or clawed at women before jumping away. Among the lower classes especially, Spring-Heeled Jack—also known as Jumping Jack—became considered a ghost or demonic figure. By the late 19th century, the legend spread beyond London into the towns and countryside, where the character became a kind of boogeyman.

MARY SHELLEY

A Romantic novelist and pioneer of the science fiction genre, Mary Wollstonecraft Godwin Shelley (1797–1851) gave the world the groundbreaking horror story *Frankenstein; or, The Modern Prometheus,* first published in 1818. The daughter of political philosopher William Godwin and women's rights advocate Mary Wollstonecraft, she grew up surrounded by literary excellence. In 1814, Mary ran away with English Romantic poet Percy Bysshe Shelley, and the couple married in 1816. After Percy's untimely death, Mary edited and published many of her husband's poems. She also wrote other novels, including the early dystopian work *The Last Man* (1826), a prescient story of a 21st-century plague.

Portrait of Mary Shelley by Richard Rothwell, circa 1840

SPIRITUALISM
Communicating With the Dead

For millennia, religious and occult figures have claimed to have a direct line to the spirit world. In the 19th century, such claims would echo around the globe as the movement of Spiritualism gained traction. Spiritualists believed that the dead could be channeled through a living medium who would relay their messages by voice, writing, or physical phenomena like moving objects.

In upstate New York in the mid-1800s, sisters Kate, Leah, and Margaret Fox first performed their mysterious spirit rappings (see page 264). Soon, mediums were making contact with the spirit world in living rooms and on stages across America. These lively events often included messages transmitted via chalkboards, taps, and disembodied voices. Some mediums would emit shapes or a substance they called ectoplasm from their bodies, often through their mouths and noses (this ghostly manifestation was often gauze or even animal organs).

The core beliefs of Spiritualism were espoused by Andrew Jackson Davis, an American clairvoyant regarded as the father of the 19th-century movement.

Davis took cues from the teachings of Austrian healer Franz Anton Mesmer (see page 285), who claimed that an invisible magnetic force among all living things could be controlled if the subject was in a hypnotic state (which came to be known as mesmerization), and Swedish philosopher Emanuel Swedenborg, who described contacting a spirit world parallel to Earth. At a time of rigid religiosity, Spiritualism provided a path of self-determination, allowing followers to directly communicate with the world beyond.

Eras of grief and suffering would enliven belief in Spiritualism. The American Civil War was a boon for the movement, as believers clung to the hope they could communicate with their dead loved ones; spiritualists would claim two million new followers in the war's wake. Queen Victoria attended séances, and it was rumored that Mary Todd Lincoln held them in the White House. By the 1880s, an estimated eight million spiritualists lived in the United States and Europe.

In 1886, two men attended a séance

∧ Talking board for communicating with spirits

Spiritualists such as author Sir Arthur Conan Doyle believed that spirits made their presences known as ghostly "extras" within photographs.

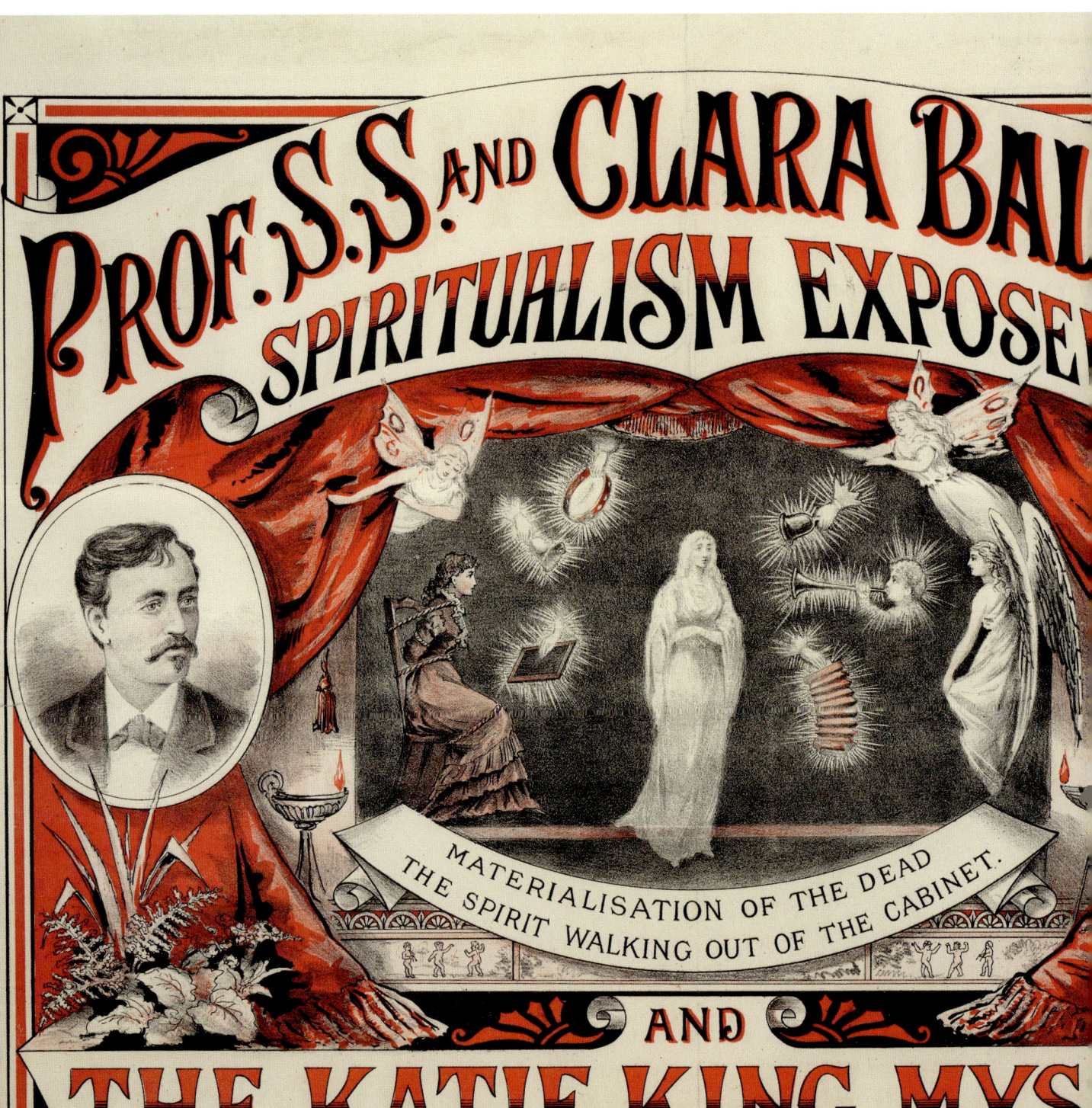

W. AUBERT. LITH, LONDON.

In the late 1800s, spiritualists and skeptics were fascinated by tales of a spirit named Katie King that had supposedly materialized in front of mediums.

IN 1922, ENRAGED BY A MEDIUM WHO HAD CLAIMED TO CHANNEL HOUDINI'S DEAD MOTHER IN A SÉANCE, HOUDINI MADE IT HIS MISSION TO UNMASK THE MOST UNSCRUPULOUS SPIRITUALISTS.

with medium Helen Peters and emerged with a new idea to help the general public contact the spirit realm. The Ouija board allowed two people to guide a small, raised table over the board's letters and numbers, spelling out answers to questions posed to the beyond. The invention, wrote a local Ohio paper that year, was "setting whole communities of eminently sober and respectable Ohio people on their heads." As with the Civil War, World War I (1914–18) heavily boosted the ranks of spiritualists across the world—and made the Ouija board a bestseller.

But by that time, the movement had made enemies of scientists and magicians, who disapproved of fraud being perpetrated on grieving people. Many associations formed at this time to tackle the challenge of proving or disproving mediums and their alleged spirit communications.

The debate would pit two of the most famous figures of the era against each other. From his own training, magician Harry Houdini (see page 318) recognized many of the techniques mediums employed. In 1922, enraged by Jean Elizabeth Leckie, a medium who had claimed to channel Houdini's dead mother in a séance, Houdini made it his mission to unmask the most unscrupulous spiritualists. He dispatched a team of undercover investigators to towns across America and revealed the mediums' secrets at his sold-out shows. Opposing Houdini was his one-time friend, the writer—and husband of Leckie—Sir Arthur Conan Doyle, who was convinced he could communicate with his son who had died in World War I. Despite Houdini's doubts about the veracity of mediums, he did hope that spirit communication would someday be possible. Both men swore to convey secret messages to their loved ones after their deaths, but no contact from either man's spirit was ever reported.

Today, spiritualist churches can be found in more than 30 countries. The National Spiritualist Association of Churches, founded in 1893, boasts congregations in some 20 U.S. states. And an estimated one-third of Americans claim they have communicated with the dead.

SPIRITUALIST SIBLINGS

Starting in the mid-19th century, belief in spiritualism was propelled by three sets of siblings who claimed to be able to communicate with the deceased. Their influence turned the budding religious movement into a global phenomenon.

< The Fox sisters, from left to right: Margaret ("Maggie"; 1837–1893), Kate (1828–1892), and Leah (1814–1890)

THE FOX SISTERS

In 1848, in a small farmhouse in upstate New York, sisters Margaret and Kate Fox told their neighbor an incredible story: Every night, they said, ghostly raps on the walls and furniture of their room could answer questions they posed. Before long, they were performing with their sister, Leah, in front of hundreds who came to watch them communicate with the spirit world. Their story fueled a religious movement as influential followers, including *New York Tribune* editor Horace Greeley, proclaimed their belief. Before her death, Margaret Fox confessed they had made the rapping sounds by cracking their toe knuckles (a confession she later recanted).

THE DAVENPORT BROTHERS

In the 1860s, brothers Ira and William Davenport toured the United States and Europe with their new device: the spirit cabinet. The brothers were bound by ropes and locked inside the cabinet, which was seven feet (2.1 m) tall and six feet (1.8 m) wide. Once the doors closed, incredible sounds emanated from within: a tambourine's jingle, a bellowing trumpet, loud bells. Phantom hands emerged from a hole in the center of the cabinet. When the doors were reopened, the brothers sat bound in their ropes, seemingly immobilized. Arthur Conan Doyle called them "probably the greatest mediums of their kind," but Harry Houdini believed that the Davenports were particularly agile and could manage to slip from nearly any bond, likely with the help of oil and a secret hinge in the stick they were tied to.

> The Davenport brothers: Ira Erastus (1839–1911), left, and William Henry (1841–1877)

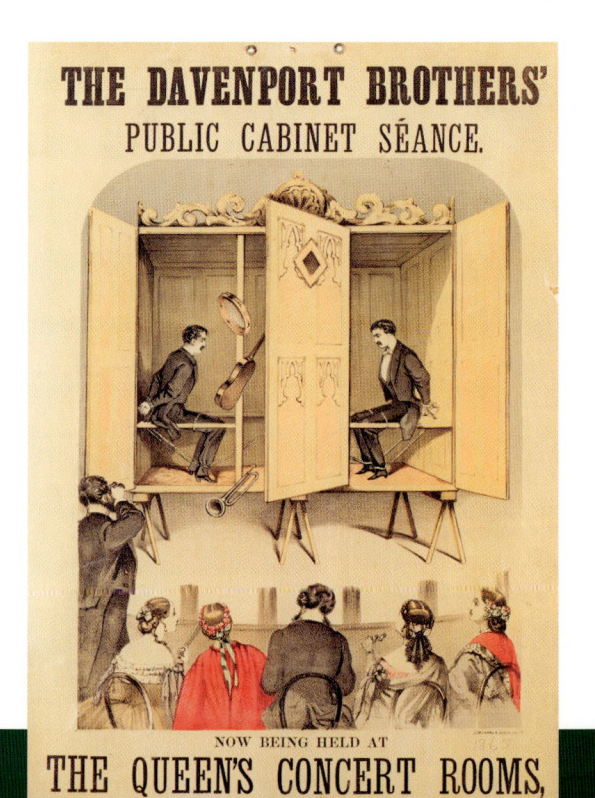

MINA CRANDON & WALTER STINSON

As the wife of a respected Boston surgeon, Mina "Margery" Crandon wasn't a typical medium. But in 1924, she became the top contender for a psychic research prize offered by *Scientific American*. The magazine promised $2,500 to anyone whose communications with the spirit world could withstand the scrutiny of their judging panel, including faculty from Harvard and MIT and medium skeptic Harry Houdini. Crandon claimed she could communicate with her deceased brother, Walter Stinson, and held numerous séances that fooled the judges. "'Margery' Passes All Psychic Tests," screamed a headline in the *New York Times*. Charming and well-spoken, Crandon convinced most of the highly esteemed panel that she was the real deal. But Houdini wasn't fooled, and when she demurred from further tests, Margery was denied the prize money and was not allowed to claim the title of a true medium. She was later unmasked when a thumbprint she had claimed as Walter's turned out to match that of a local dentist.

∧ Mina Crandon (1889–1941) and Walter Stinson (1884–1911).

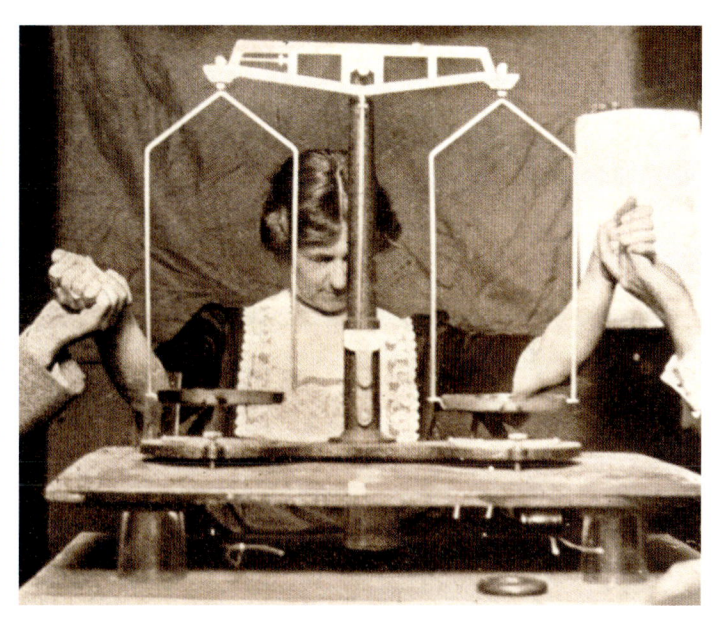

> At a test held in 1925, Crandon attempted to psychically balance weighted scales.

> In 1925, Harvard researcher Mark Wyman Richardson (right) tested whether the ghostly voice of "Walter" was really Crandon (left) whispering.

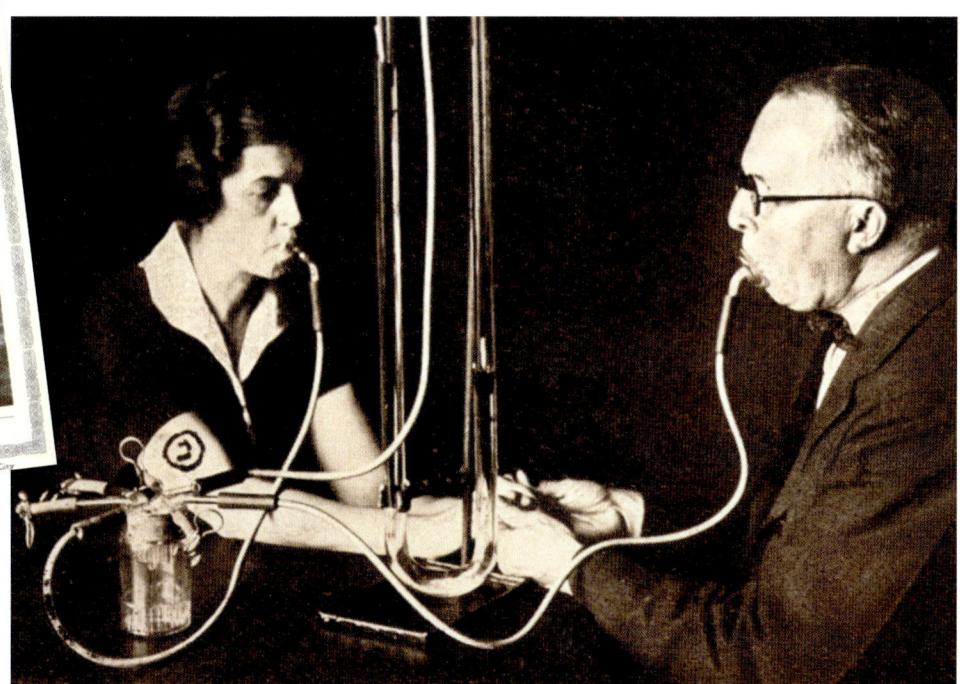

HONORING THE DEAD

Modern Funerary Rites

Around the world, funerary rites continue to bridge the divide between the living and dead, honoring the departed while letting the living grieve and support one another.

The Philippines is home to a rich tapestry of funerary customs, as diverse as the more than 7,100 islands that comprise the Pacific nation. Today, Indigenous Igorot peoples practice a wide range of customs honoring the dead, including *sangadil*, or propping up the deceased in wooden chairs. This symbolizes the departed person's final connection to the living world.

Among millions of Filipino Catholics, All Saints' Day (November 1) and All Souls' Day (November 2) are spent at loved ones' graves. During this two-day period known as Undas, families gather for joyous reunions, eat the favorite foods of their departed loved ones, and leave offerings.

This same period is celebrated in Mexico, among other countries, as the Día de los Muertos: the Day of the Dead. Though it focuses on death, the Day of the Dead is a merry holiday that treats passing away as an everyday part of life, with colorful decorations that feature skulls and other death

---

PROFILE

LA CATRINA

In the early 1900s, Mexican illustrator José Guadalupe Posada sketched an image of La Calavera Garbancera, a skull-like depiction of an Indigenous woman attempting to pass as European under a French hat. The drawing appeared in newspapers in Mexico as a satire of classism and corruption in the wake of the Mexican Revolution. Legendary Mexican muralist Diego Rivera was drawn to Posada's work; he renamed the figure La Calavera Catrina, which means "the elegant skull," and used her as the star of his famed 1947 mural, "Dream of a Sunday Afternoon in the Alameda Central." La Catrina soon became the face of the Day of the Dead holiday, and her gaping smile can be seen across the Spanish-speaking world.

Detail from "Dream of a Sunday Afternoon in the Alameda Central" by Diego Rivera, 1947

icons. Families also build temporary altars called *ofrendas* to honor their ancestors and decorate graves with candles, the departed's favorite foods, and marigolds, whose bright color and fragrance guide souls back to their families' homes. Aspects of this tradition may be rooted in Aztec legend, which held that souls must pass through nine grueling levels to reach Mictlán, the underworld ruled by the powerful goddess Mictēcacihuātl. The living could aid their loved ones' journeys by making offerings of flowers and food.

Other cultural traditions place death firmly within the cycle of nature. In modern-day Madagascar, the Merina and Betsileo peoples honor their dead every five to seven years through a ceremony called *famadihana* (turning of the bones). After receiving a message in a dream from the deceased, living family members remove bodies from ancestral crypts and carefully rewrap them in fresh silk shrouds.

Without the practice of famadihana, the spirits of the deceased cannot complete their transition from the living realm to the ancestral one.

Similarly, modern-day Tibetan Buddhists have long practiced "sky burial": offering up a person's dismembered body on a rocky ledge. If vultures leave the body untouched, the person is believed to have committed great sins during life. The practice is thought to have been shaped by the harsh environmental conditions of the Tibetan Plateau, where both land for burial and fuel for cremation are scarce.

Along with traditional practices, new rituals are continually emerging. In recent decades, thousands of families in South Korea have opted to convert the ashes of their cremated loved ones into commemorative beads kept in containers. Similarly, companies in the United States and elsewhere make artificial diamonds from cremains.

FUNERARY TRADITIONS

Death is universal—and so is the human impulse to honor the dead. Over thousands of years, cultures around the world have developed diverse rituals and ceremonies to commemorate the departed and let the living grieve. In managing the transition from life to death, honoring the spirits of ancestors, and providing peace and support to families and loved ones, these rituals are among our most sacred and meaningful cultural practices. These funerary traditions, modern and ancient, show astounding diversity in the ways humans honor their loved ones and process their grief.

SESANDO >
In Timor, a bamboo zither called a *sesando* is thought to hold supernatural powers. The instrument is played at weddings and funerals.

GRAVESITE SCULPTURE >
Important hunters and warriors of the Bongo tribe were honored by effigies erected at their graves in what's now South Sudan.

^ FUNERARY MASK
This funerary mask from the pre-Inca Sicán culture of Peru, circa A.D. 1000, was buried with the body of a ruler in a huge mud-brick platform mound.

< POST FROM BURIAL SHIP
Two upper-class Viking women found on a 10th-century ship in Norway were buried with items likely considered magical, including a staff and a wagon.

AMULET OF ANUBIS >
The jackal-headed god Anubis watched over the afterlife, death, and gravesites, and his image was considered a powerful amulet.

< CINERARY URN
Embellished with battling terra-cotta warriors, this Etruscan urn was meant to hold the ashes of a man named Aulus Latinius.

MUMMY MASK >
In the first century B.C., the Paracas people of Peru entombed their dead in layers of woven cloth and a painted mask.

< FUNERARY CROWN
Philip II, the duke of Burgundy, was laid to rest in 1404 with this gold crown inlaid with pearls and precious stones.

LOCKET >
To commemorate a loved one's death in 1706, this locket's owner commissioned a piece of jewelry containing a woven piece of hair. Jewelry was often used as a remembrance.

^ SHARK RELIQUARY
This wooden shark head has a hollow center to hold the skull of a deceased chief in the Solomon Islands. The shark is revered as a guardian and link to the spirit world.

^ MOURNING CORSAGE
This tintype portrait of Abraham Lincoln was worn by a mourner as a memento mori of the assassinated president during the funeral tour that carried his body across America in 1865.

TOMB GUARDIANS >
These fierce spirits known as *qitou* guarded the tomb of a Chinese grave during the Tang dynasty, keeping out intruders and preventing the soul of the dead from wandering.

^ BURIAL URN
Carefully decorated urns depicted individual faces, between the seventh and third centuries B.C. in what's now Poland.

CHAPTER SEVEN

Healing, Dreams & the Mind

For centuries, people have ascribed magical meaning to patterns, such as this labyrinth at the Chartres Cathedral in France.

Mysterious Currents

Engaging With the Magical

At its core, magic is about engaging and harnessing the wild, unseen forces of the interconnected cosmos. Throughout history, some of the most common reasons people have attempted to wield this power relate to health: to enhance reproduction, to stave off death and disease, to ensure a long life, and to focus—or even alter—the mind.

These impulses run deep, and many practices have been employed to realize them. For at least 10,000 years, ancient peoples of Europe may have conducted rituals to ensure fertility. Through the centuries, herbalists and healers around the world built up remarkable toolkits for the treatment of disease (of the 25 plants included in a 16th-century Aztec medicinal text, at least 16 probably worked as advertised, according to one 1975 study). And from dreams to yoga and psychoactive drugs, ancient cultures found ways to alter their consciousnesses. Some of the earliest evidence of people using mind-altering drugs—discarded betel nut fragments found in a Thailand cave—goes back 9,000 years.

But simply evaluating ancient medical practices by modern, Western scientific standards misses the forest for the trees. For many cultures past and present, how we heal is inextricably linked to how we envision the greater order of things: the flow of energy, the relations between the elements, the power of gods and demons juxtaposed across plants, rocks, minerals, and animals, all with the capacity to help and hurt. In their collective efforts to cast out disease and secure good health, humans have long engaged the mysterious currents that flow through us and around us. In other words, we have engaged with the magical. ▪

ʌ Tibetan singing bowl, meant to align the energy of its users

Meditation, like that practiced within Buddhism, is meant to sharpen the mind and bring practitioners to a spiritual zenith.

NEW LIFE

The Magic of Reproduction

Long before modern medicine, our ancestors likely turned to the spiritual realm, performing sacred rites to ensure successful childbirth. There is no more spectacular emblem of this practice than the legendary Venus of Willendorf. Discovered in Austria in 1908, the 4.4-inch (11 cm) figurine's generous curves were likely carved from Italian stone during the last ice age some 30,000 years ago.

Few ancient finds have enchanted archaeologists like the assortment of exaggerated female forms collectively known as Venuses. With no written record to illuminate their significance—or to indicate how ancient societies viewed concepts like gender and sexuality—scientists can only speculate about the figures' uses. Prominent reproductive organs suggest that they were made as talismans in fertility and reproduction rituals.

Around 200 Venuses have been found in ancient human settlements across the globe, spanning a range of 20,000 years.

RITES & RITUALS

THE SCENT OF MAGIC

In ancient Greece and Rome, magic and the divine were inextricably linked by smell, an invisible yet forceful presence. The Greek Magical Papyri, written in Greco-Roman Egypt from the first century B.C. to the fourth century A.D., describe many rituals involving aromatic plants. Garlic was a must for one chariot-wrecking ritual; to see visions, a rose or lily perfume was required. In the epic poem *Argonautica*, the enchantress Medea helps the hero, Jason, nab the golden fleece by crafting a "sweet air" that enchants the monster guarding it. By the fourth century B.C., Greek medical texts also referenced scent, noting that certain smells could unbalance the body's humors and bring about disease. Particularly noxious and "hostile" odors, known as *miasmata*, were thought to trigger pestilences. On the other hand, some strong-smelling perfumes, including a cinnamon-myrrh blend known as *megaleion*, were thought to bring about healing.

Greek alabastron (perfume bottle) made of glass and gold, first century B.C.

Venus figurines (left to right): mammoth-ivory Venus of Lespugue, found in France; limestone Venus of Willendorf, found in Austria; one of the mammoth-ivory Venuses of Avdeevo, found in Russia

Willendorf's is particularly voluptuous—and possibly for good reason. A recent study found that Venus figures became more rotund the closer they were found to glacial climates. To survive the extreme cold, pregnant women would need more body fat. Perhaps one prehistoric woman braved the Ice Age with this figurine held close, hoping for a healthy birth.

In Poland, an artifact carved from an antler some 10,900 years ago shows what appears to be a woman with her legs spread wide. The carving was likely used in rituals, perhaps involving fertility. It appears to have been crafted by a group of people, indicating that ancient Europeans may have viewed perpetuating the species as a collective effort.

Fertility rituals are omnipresent throughout the historical record. In most ancient civilizations, goddesses were bestowed with the power of reproduction and creation of the universe. Natural elements, from water to the moon, were also thought to influence fertility.

A seventh-century B.C. clay tablet found in Assyria, which stretched from the Mediterranean to Iran, held a list of 3,000 omens that foretold the future via unusual births. "If a woman gives birth and the baby has no right ear: the prince's days will end," one said. No left ear, on the other hand, would portend the prince's long reign. Reports show the king was often notified about these omens.

In Hellenistic Italy, life-size "votives" of infants carved in terra-cotta were offered to deities to ensure reproductive success. During the Middle Ages, women in countries including England and France wore charms, amulets, and rolls inscribed with prayers to that same end.

Compendium Medicinae, a 13th-century text considered the first survey of medical knowledge that included Greek and Arabic medical texts to arrive in the monastic libraries of medieval Europe, contains a remedy for sterility that "never fails": The man must recite the Lord's Prayer at a certain hour, then extract the juices of comfrey and daisy and use them to inscribe a particular biblical passage on an amulet worn during conception. This would ensure a son if worn by a man, a daughter if worn by a woman.

Even today, cultures around the world turn to particular ceremonies, foods, and rituals to ensure reproductive success. In Naples, Italy, women still line up to sit in the "miracle chair" of St. Maria Francesca to be blessed; they later return to cover the walls with photos of their babies. In China, women have eaten bird's nest soup, made of the saliva of cave-dwelling swiftlets, for thousands of years to guarantee reproductive success. In West Africa's Ashanti culture, a doll-like good luck charm known as an *akua'ba* is carried by expectant mothers and those struggling to conceive. And in Tamil society in Sri Lanka, women offer the deities silver charms of children in cradles, along with a sweet rice pudding, in the hopes of good reproductive fortune. ■

THE EBERS PAPYRUS

Dating to around 1550 B.C., the Ebers Papyrus is one of the oldest surviving medical texts of the ancient world. An extraordinary record of medical practice in ancient Egypt that stretches some 66 feet (20 m) long, the papyrus contains 108 columns of text, including nearly 900 prescriptions and educational references. The document describes about 80 medical conditions, including heart disease and diabetes, along with a remarkably detailed description of the heart and the "vessels from it to every limb." Among its many recommended remedies are magical cures that draw on Egyptian mythology; one headache cure, for example, calls for rubbing the head with the ashes from burnt catfish skulls. Unusual though it may appear, this prescription symbolically defeats a demon that, according to one story, gave the Egyptian god Horus splitting headaches.

A column of the Ebers Papyrus details 18 different burn remedies.

This Indian book cover, circa 1700, depicts a common fertility motif: the "Tree of Life" teeming with birds and insects.

HINDU MAGIC

From Mantra to Tantra

Hinduism has a long and rich tradition of employing magic and sorcery, particularly for healing the body and expanding its abilities. Dating to roughly 1200 B.C., the ancient Atharva Veda—one of the sacred Hindu texts known as the Vedas—provides a litany of hymns and spells that seek to cure disease or ensure long life. One treatment for jaundice involves the ritual use of the hair and skin of a red cow; yellow-feathered birds are called upon to absorb the person's sickened hue. An incantation to cure leprosy reads: "O colorer, do thou color this leprous spot and what is pale." The "colorer" in question is thought to be the spice turmeric. The Atharva Veda recommends amulets for everything from protection from demons (with a lead amulet) to ensuring long life (with a gold one). Sacred utterances known as mantras hold enormous power in the vast structure of Hindu magical practice. Even a simple sound like *om* can be considered a deeply powerful distillation of spiritual wisdom. Spiritual practitioners, known in some contexts as *mantra-sastris*, devote themselves to studying and perfecting the mantras. According to one 19th-century English source, these practitioners claimed to have extraordinary powers—including the ability to bring the dead to life, make impenetrable armor, and transform milk into wine or plants into meat.

During the medieval period, India saw the rise of the religious philosophy known as Tantra, which grew out of Hindu, Jain, and Buddhist traditions between the sixth and eighth centuries A.D. According to its tenets, the feminine energy Shakti provided the creative power of the god Shiva and animated all of material reality. Tantric yogis sought to let Shakti in—and tap into her power—through awakening Kundalini, a primal feminine energy, and letting it move from the base of the spine up through the body's energy centers, known as chakras. Over time, Tantra swelled to include many rituals, including mantras, yantras (linear magic diagrams), and mandalas (radial magic diagrams). Those who master forces known as *siddhis* can gain magic powers, such as immortality or the ability to fly.

< Shakti is personified by goddesses including Parvati, the goddess of love, fertility, and devotion (seen here in a 15th-century bronze statue).

Tantric teachings pointedly hold that all aspects of existence can be sacred if imbued with sacralizing intent. At their most transgressive, Tantrists ritualize acts that violate all the taboos of traditional Hinduism, including meditating while sitting atop fresh corpses. In a sexual ceremony known as maithuna, a man and woman have sex after ritually transforming into Shiva and Shakti. These seemingly hedonistic rituals require suppressing the natural avoidance of taboos—and focusing instead on transmuting the experience into a unity with the divine.

Healing magic continues to remain a force in parts of India today. In rural villages, exorcists and folk healers known as *ojhas* claim the ability to cure ailments such as joint pain, headaches, and malaria by invoking or casting out spirits, chanting, and administering herbal medicines and charms.

∧ In Hindu tradition, the god Vishnu once took the form of a fish to recover the Vedas after a demon had stolen them.

HUMORS & HEALERS

Medieval Medicine

Medieval medicine in the Christian and Islamic worlds built upon Greek and Roman practices—notably the fifth-century B.C. teachings of Greek physician Hippocrates and the second-century A.D. teachings of Roman and Greek physician Galen. Galen believed that diseases stemmed from imbalances of the four humors: phlegm, blood, yellow bile, and black bile. To rebalance them, fluid was removed through such practices as bloodletting.

Medieval medicine also relied on the revered 10th-century Islamic philosopher-physician Ibn Sina, known in the West as Avicenna, who laid the foundation of early modern medicine with his *Al-Qānūn fi al-tibb (Canon of Medicine)*. This gigantic encyclopedia of medical knowledge placed Galen's teachings within Aristotle's philosophical framework, also providing groundbreaking descriptions of illnesses like heart disease.

Throughout medieval Europe, folk practitioners and trained physicians alike recommended charms, astrological talismans, and amulets for everything from bleeding to toothaches—much to the

---

PROFILE

PARACELSUS

Theophrastus Bombastus von Hohenheim, better known as Paracelsus (circa 1493–1541), was a German-Swiss physician and alchemist who is known today as the father of medicinal chemistry. Rejecting the time period's prevailing medical wisdom, Paracelsus called for letting wounds drain in the open and denounced the use of the period's common, but often ineffective, salves and pills. Drawing on his alchemical expertise (see page 218), Paracelsus advocated for the therapeutic use of inorganic salts and metals, such as mercury as a treatment for syphilis. Though these substances were known to be toxic, Paracelsus specified that "solely the dose determines that a thing is not a poison"—foreshadowing the modern science of toxicology.

Portrait of Paracelsus by unknown artist, Germany, 16th century

chagrin of Catholic clergy, who worried about demonic influence. Under the wings of supportive monarchs, from England to the Holy Roman Empire, alchemists toiled to create elixirs that cured illnesses and prolonged life (see page 218). Dark magic was seen as a source of misfortune and disease, particularly impotence; a 12th-century book of Catholic canon law, written in what is now Italy, weighed the case of a man who claimed he couldn't impregnate his wife because he had been hexed.

Natural materials were a regular part of medieval medicine around the world. Books called lapidaries extolled the healing properties of precious stones (see page 186); manuscripts called herbals served as references on medicinal plants. In Europe, herbals drew heavily from earlier Greek and Roman works, while compendia of Chinese herbal medicines stretch back to the third century B.C., featuring more than 10,000 formulas and 1,892 distinct herbs. By the 15th century, Aztec physicians in what is now Mexico had developed an enormous working knowledge of botanical remedies, with one 16th-century catalog listing more than 4,000 medicines.

Around the world, plant-based medicines were often created within a magical and religious framework; European teachings held that herbs resembling parts of the body could be used to treat ailments in those same parts. Lungwort, for instance, was seen as a remedy for tuberculosis, since its spotted leaves resembled a diseased patient's lungs. In Anglo-Saxon England, herbal remedies were paired with poems called metrical charms. The so-called nine herbs charm, dating to the ninth or 10th century A.D., called for treating wounds with a paste of plants such as mugwort, crabapple, and fennel. The charm was sung three times: once over the ingredients, once into the wounded person's ear, and once into the wound itself.

In many communities around the world, women took on the role of village healer: curing common ailments, aiding in labor and delivery, and preparing botanical treatments. But starting in the late 14th century, midwives and healers in Europe were increasingly prosecuted on charges of witchcraft (see page 164).

∧ The 12th-century materia medica *The Four Tantras,* the foundation of Tibetan medicine, includes recipes for medicinal pills, powders, and other drugs.

MAGICAL & MEDICINAL PLANTS

Every culture on Earth regards plants with reverence, for their magical and medicinal values alike. Many have long been used to treat disease in the form of recipes passed down through the generations to create medicinal reference texts known as herbals. In some cases, modern scientific studies have borne out these plants' potency, either to counteract illness or alter the mind. But the allure of these plants is derived from not only their biological mechanisms but also the powerful symbolism that comes with their outsize role in many long-standing spiritual practices.

> LAVENDER

Lavender's attractive aroma, long used in perfumes, also has strong associations with love spells. When the scent is inhaled, it can help bring on a sense of calm and reduce pain and nausea.

< HENBANE

A highly toxic nightshade, henbane was used as an ancient anesthetic. Its leaves, rich with psychoactive compounds, were used in hallucinogenic flying ointments. In modern witchcraft, it is believed to create feelings of love and is used to consecrate ceremonial vessels.

< VERVAIN

Also known as verbena, this "holy herb" has long been a staple of magic and medicine. In ancient Rome, altars to Jupiter were swept clean with vervain, and it was used to treat ailments including epilepsy and fever. Common in amulets in medieval Europe, its powers were thought most intense if the plant was harvested on the summer solstice.

^ WORMWOOD

A key ingredient in the liquor absinthe, wormwood has been used medicinally for more than 3,000 years. In the Egyptian Ebers Papyrus (see page 276), wormwood appears in several treatments for digestive ailments. It also features in several recipes in the *Trotula*, medieval Europe's most comprehensive text on women's health.

> BELLADONNA

This highly toxic and psychoactive plant has long been used for medicine and magic. Women in Renaissance-era Venice dropped belladonna tinctures into their eyes to dilate them. In witches' flying ointments, it may have given the applicant vivid visions of flight—and subsequent exhaustion.

∨ PEYOTE

For millennia, this small, spineless cactus, which contains the hallucinogen mescaline, has been used by Native Americans as a religious sacrament. Dozens of tribes across North America now use peyote as a sacrament for healing.

< ALOE

Associated with good luck throughout much of South America, this popular household succulent is often hung above doorways in stores and homes. Medicinally, it is widely used to treat skin problems and acts as a laxative when swallowed.

∧ GARLIC

Garlic was once worn to protect against the plague. Magically, the herb is used in a wide variety of protective rituals. Allicin, the compound that's responsible for the smell of freshly ground-up garlic, is a potent antimicrobial agent.

< YARROW

Common yarrow and its sister species grow throughout the Northern Hemisphere. It is popular in European folk medicine for healing wounds, reducing inflammation, and inducing sedation. Its genus name, *Achillea*, comes from *The Iliad*; Achilles uses yarrow to treat soldiers' wounds.

∧ SAGE

Sage and other plants in the genus *Salvia* have long been used in traditional herbal remedies as a diuretic, wound cleaner, and pain reliever. In modern Western witchcraft, sage is burned as incense to promote purification and general spiritual health.

∨ HAWTHORN

In Celtic countries, hawthorn is a pagan fertility symbol used to decorate maypoles and May Day garlands. Magically, it has been used to promote both fertility and chastity. The plant has been used to treat heart disease since the first century A.D.

> LADY'S MANTLE

Medieval alchemists considered the droplets that form on this plant's leaves the purest form of water: a key ingredient for the philosopher's stone (see page 221). Today's witches consider it an all-purpose magical amplifier, especially for love spells.

< MISTLETOE

Druids (see page 154) considered mistletoe sacred. Though toxic if ingested, it is associated with protection against such misfortunes as lightning and fires. It may have anticancer properties; extracts are used in some European countries as a part of cancer treatments.

< MANDRAKE

This plant's long taproot sometimes resembles a human body, leading ancient and medieval cultures to believe it contained reproductive power. It contains hyoscine, a potentially lethal hallucinogenic substance used in anesthetics since the first century A.D.

∧ ROSEMARY

Rosemary was no less than a medieval wonder drug, with one 14th-century Venetian book listing it as everything from a snake repellent to a diarrhea cure. Modern witches burn the plant as a cleansing incense or carry it in sachets to help with memory.

> APPLE

Apples have long featured in spells associated with love: whether to strengthen an existing relationship, enamor a crush, or divine a future love's identity. Apples also have strong historical ties to Samhain, the Celtic New Year festival (see page 242).

THEORIES & REASON

Cures & Curses in an Enlightened World

Despite the Enlightenment's foundation in reason and logic, magical healing practices abounded in Europe throughout the 18th century and well into the 19th century. In England and Wales, entrepreneurial magic practitioners known as cunning folk, or *dyn hysbys*, served a variety of roles in village life. Many were primarily tradespeople, artisans, clerks, or schoolmasters. But for a small fee, cunning folk offered a wide variety of magical services on the side: fortune-telling, finding lost property, divining a future love's identity, protection from black magic, and the diagnosis and treatment of illnesses. Some also dabbled in sleight of hand and ventriloquism.

Cunning folk often could read and write—all the better for making and selling written amulets—and were well known for their libraries of magical books. Some were born into the craft—especially those who were the seventh child of a seventh child, a branch of extreme magical potency on the family tree. And though they theoretically risked persecution, many cunning folk

---

PROFILE

ELIZABETH BLACKWELL

A long-underappreciated pioneer in the history of medicine, the Scottish herbalist Elizabeth Blackwell was the first woman to produce a commercially sold herbal, a reference on medicinal plants. Her two-volume *A Curious Herbal*, published between 1737 and 1739, contained 500 etched illustrations of plants and 125 explanatory texts. The books represent a stunning synthesis, reflecting what was then cutting-edge knowledge of the plants' properties, as well as the largest English-language compilation of medicinal plant images available at that time. Despite her masterwork, the historical Blackwell remains an enigma. Her family background and birth date are debated, and some sources say that she wrote the work to raise funds to free her husband from debtor's prison.

Elizabeth Blackwell's illustration of a red poppy

practiced openly. English cunning man Richard Morris (1710–1793), for example, was paid to recover lost cattle from the time he was 12 but was never held to account. Eventually, he amassed enough wealth to buy considerable amounts of property.

Many *kloke folk* (wise folk) of Scandinavia also practiced openly, including in roles as healers. The Norwegian herbalist Anne Johansdatter Sæther (1793–1851), better known as Mor (Mother) Sæther, was prosecuted for quackery three times from 1834 to 1844, in part over her use of tinctures made of aloe (a powerful laxative), valerian and hops (mild sedatives), and turpentine. At her third trial, she received a reduced sentence, possibly thanks to public outcry. In 1845, Sæther received royal permission to practice her craft over the objections of health officials, who decried her lack of formal medical training. Two of Sæther's concoctions—a "glandular oil" and an ointment for gout—were sold in Norwegian pharmacies well into the 20th century.

As scientific knowledge of health and disease rapidly advanced, astounding theories of medicine could spread like wildfire—and be denounced in real time as magical thinking. In the late 1700s, the German-born physician Franz Anton Mesmer became notorious for his ideas of "animal magnetism," a precursor of hypnosis (see page 260). In 1778, Mesmer set up shop in Paris, where his practice exploded in popularity as a place of healing. In 1784, King Louis XVI created a royal commission to evaluate animal magnetism, led by American scientist-statesman Benjamin Franklin. After testing Mesmer's ideas, the commission found that the effects attributed to animal magnetism stemmed from people's *belief* that the treatment worked: a dramatic early demonstration of the placebo effect (see page 298).

⌃ In this 18th-century engraving, German doctor Franz Anton Mesmer demonstrates his new theory of animal magnetism with a *baquet*, a water-filled vat holding iron rods.

THE NEW AGE
Mysticism Meets Modernity

In the 1970s, a new religious movement swept through Europe and the United States, drawing inspiration from history and cultures around the globe. Leaders of this so-called New Age movement promised that the world was entering a new dawn of harmony and peace. The movement was inspired by a variety of esoteric and occult groups that traced their roots to Helena Blavatsky, co-founder of the Theosophical Society (see page 184). In the late 1800s, Blavatsky announced that at the turn of the 20th century, a new age would begin, heralding the arrival of a messiah later in the century.

In 1970, an American philosopher named David Spangler would develop the crux of New Age philosophy. Astrological changes, he declared, had put Earth's movement into an Age of Aquarius, which released a spiritual energy to end the world's worst woes, from poverty to war. Previously, he explained, the world had been in an Age of Pisces, characterized by

RITES & RITUALS

CRYSTAL HEALING

Ancient Sumerians, who sealed messages in cylindrical crystal tubes, may have been the first to employ gemstones for ritual purposes. Ancient Egyptian, Chinese, and Hindu cultures turned to crystals for religious and medicinal uses, harnessing energy the stones were believed to hold and their abilities to bring good fortune. Pliny the Elder wrote about crystal divination in the first century A.D. (see page 103); centuries later, medieval lapidaries prescribed stones and crystals for various ailments (diamonds for nightmares) or as good luck charms (emeralds for increasing wealth). Today, someone might wear a tourmaline bracelet to decrease anxiety or place tumbled pieces of aventurine on the body to alleviate muscle cramps. Though no scientific studies support their healing properties, scientists have explored the idea that crystals might convince patients that a treatment is more effective out of sheer belief—making the placebo effect the real gem.

Head of a bull carved from chalcedony, Sumeria, circa 3000–2000 B.C.

Christianity and violence. Another leading figure of the movement, Peruvian-American anthropologist Carlos Castaneda, incorporated mystical secrets into the mix—including the power of hallucinogenic plants to communicate with alternate realities—which he claimed to have learned from a Native American shaman.

Tenets of the New Age, such as peace and gender equality, hit a nerve in an era defined by the Vietnam War, the civil rights struggle, and the feminist movement. Followers quickly amassed in the United States, Canada, Europe, and Australia. They preached that individual actions affect the living entities around them, including plants and animals.

The movement would promote tarot reading, astrology, and other spiritual tools; meditation and yoga were considered quasi-religious practices. New Age devotees eschewed Western medicine and looked to the East for guidance, practicing Chinese acupuncture and adopting eating plans like India's Ayurvedic diet. New Age treatments included an energy-healing technique called Reiki, positive affirmations, and aura readings. In the 1980s, crystals became popular for encouraging medical and spiritual transformation (see sidebar).

Not everyone was happy about the New Age tendency to adopt global practices: Critics in the Native American community accused the movement of appropriating their beliefs by selling dream catchers and marketing sweat lodges.

Nevertheless, the movement continued to grow, bringing experiments with psychedelic drugs, which were sometimes used to reach new levels of spiritual awareness. New Age mediums also practiced "channeling" as a way to speak to spirits and ancient gods.

In the wake of Blavatsky's prediction, various messiahs and prophets were anticipated to appear and officially launch the New Age. These unfulfilled visits quelled the religious movement's stride, and its popularity ebbed in the late 1980s. Still, New Age beliefs continue to permeate society, from medicine to diet to spiritual practices.

∧ A song from *Hair,* a musical exploring 1960s hippie counter-culture, declared "the dawning of the Age of Aquarius."

BEFORE CHRISTIANITY

Neo-pagans' Pull Toward a Magical Past

I n Latin, the word *paganus* referred to someone who lived in a rural area. But in the fourth century A.D., European Christians began using *pagani* to refer to those who didn't ascribe to their world-view. Pagans, according to early Christians, were those who didn't believe in the god of Abraham, also considered the father of Jews and Muslims. Many so-called pagans adhered to long-standing magical beliefs that were considered heretical by ever more dominant Christians. In polytheistic societies ranging from India to North Africa, Indigenous peoples were called pagans by foreign conquerors. Starting around the 15th century, in much of the world besides sub-Saharan Africa and South Asia, Abrahamic religions largely succeeded in eradicating the traditional beliefs of their communities' pagan inhabitants.

In later centuries, however, these extinguished religions attracted the interest of the world. During the Renaissance of the 14th century, European society became fascinated by the classical gods of ancient Greece and Rome. In the 18th century, the ideas, art, and mythologies of pre-Christian religions inspired the creative classes. A century later, occult groups adopted

PROFILE

ÁSATRÚ

W hen Viking settlers landed in Iceland in the late ninth century, they brought with them a pagan religion called Ásatrú. But by A.D. 1000, King Olaf Tryggvason had declared Christianity the state religion. Nearly a millennium later, however, Ásatrú was revived in 1973 by priest and singer Sveinbjörn Beinteinsson and was recognized once again as an official religion of Iceland. Its followers worship Norse gods and goddesses and celebrate them with the seasons. Though at first the organization had only a dozen or so members, in recent years Ásatrú has become one of the fastest growing religions in Iceland, now claiming more than 5,000 followers. In 2014, the religious body announced it would build Iceland's first pagan temple in a thousand years.

A bronze statue thought to be the Norse god Thor, Iceland, circa 10th to 12th centuries

A historical reenactor dressed as an Iron Age Briton watches a wicker man burn during a festival in England reviving an ancient Celtic ritual.

imagery and symbolism from those times. Aleister Crowley's religion, Thelema (see page 185), revived ancient Egyptian gods, and German groups looked to early Germanic religions for guidance.

When in the early 20th century small groups of people began worshipping the deities of these previously extinguished religions from Europe, North Africa, and West Asia, neo-paganism was born. Among its most popular branches were Wicca (see page 292) and Druidry. In the United States and England, Wicca adopted what was believed to be a pre-Christian witch religion; Druidry looked to the Iron Age for rituals. The Ancient Order of Dru-

ids had been founded in London in 1781 to worship priestlike Iron Age figures, but the movement experienced a rebirth after archaeological discoveries related to ancient Celtic society came to light in the mid-1900s.

In 1939, Gleb Botkin, an immigrant to the United States during the Russian Revolution, founded the Church of Aphrodite, which worshipped the Greek goddess of love and followed "the laws of the cosmos." It was the first pagan group recognized as a religion by a modern state. With the rise of New Age beliefs (see page 286) in the 1970s, paganism grew increasingly popular.

In 1971, the Pagan Federation organized

Some 40,000 witchcraft practitioners are thought to live in the Brazilian state of Rio de Janeiro, including Wiccan high priestess Jussara Gabriel.

these groups, defining adherents as "followers of a polytheistic or pantheistic nature-worshipping religion." Today, a majority of pagans fixate their beliefs on a connection with the earth and their ancestors, sometimes calling themselves followers of "Native Faith"—though a less welcoming component includes neo-Nazis and white supremacists, who portray Celtic and Viking societies as a glorified white warrior race.

Almost all pagans celebrate natural events like solstices to connect with the planet, recount important mythologies, and worship goddesses. But not all pagan religions are the same: Some believe in one god, some in multiple, and others in no god at all. Many pagan religions have no place of worship, and followers conduct their practice at home.

Magic found a fertile foundation in neo-paganism. Without a church or book to follow, these religions center on rituals and sacred spaces, sources of energy and connection. The goal is transformation, which may be intended to improve the earth or an individual. Often, rites are performed in a circle, usually centered around a firepit or an altar, where magical energy is channeled through talismans and in dance, chants, and prayers. A ritual may follow a series of eight steps, beginning with purification and grounding to prepare participants to depart from their typical reality. Once the energy is harnessed, the ritual's final steps help them return to everyday life.

RITES & RITUALS

ROMUVA

In Lithuania, "ethnic religions"—beliefs and belief systems historically associated with an ethnic group—have become so well established that in 1993, when then President Algirdas Brazauskas was being sworn in, folklore and customs of the pagan movement known as Romuva were incorporated in the ceremony.

Followers of Romuva worship the natural world and its deities. They celebrate the summer solstice, perform rituals around the sun, and observe the day of the dead. Scholars believe some Romuva traditions come from worship of an earth goddess during the Neolithic period, and of the sky god, a tradition that arrived with Indo-Europeans around the Bronze Age. The modern Romuva movement began in 1967 and gained footing in 1990, after the Soviet collapse. Soon, members appeared in dozens of communities, and the movement continues to grow today.

Wildflower garland worn during a traditional Lithuanian summer solstice celebration

THE WITCH'S CAULDRON

Brewing Modern Wicca

In the late 1930s, a man named Gerald Gardner claimed to have been part of an underground witch cult that had survived centuries of persecution in England. The group, he said, performed rituals in the New Forest, and he ascribed their beliefs to *The Book of Shadows,* an esoteric text compiled from 17th-century manuscripts and the rituals of famed occultist Aleister Crowley (see page 185).

Gardner had worked as a British civil servant across Asia, where he'd become interested in Indigenous religions and begun reading the teachings of figures like

Crowley. Gardner's beliefs would form the basis of a neo-pagan tradition called Wicca. In the late 1940s, Gardner formed his first group of followers, which he called a coven. Their tenets and rituals were modeled on those they believed to have been practiced by witches in pre-Christian history.

In 1951, archaic laws banning witchcraft were repealed in the United Kingdom, and Gardner was free to openly form his new religion. As his following grew, they became the first to perform modern pagan witchcraft publicly. Three years later, Gardner published a book called *Witchcraft Today*, outlining his theology of a mother goddess and a horned god. The book would inspire covens across the world, each led by a high priestess and a high priest.

Three decades earlier, Egyptologist Margaret Murray had argued that the witches persecuted in Europe for centuries had been practicing pagan rituals from pre-Christian times. Gardner, influenced by Murray, claimed his beliefs traced back to those European witches, and thus to pre-Christian religions from Europe, North Africa, and western Asia. Scholars

< Prominent Wiccan Gerald Gardner (1884–1964) is widely considered the father of modern witchcraft.

The Horned God, Wicca's primary male deity, draws inspiration from Cernunnos, the Celtic "lord of wild things" (seen here on an ancient silver bowl).

TODAY, WICCA IS THE LARGEST NEO-PAGAN RELIGION, PRACTICED LARGELY IN THE WEST.

have since debunked Murray's claims, showing that the practices of ceremonial magic adopted by Wiccans have evolved not from pre-Christian religions in Europe but from earlier and more far-flung belief systems such as those in Hellenistic Egypt.

Though it was later disproved, the connection between Wiccans and witch hunts remains a strong part of modern Wiccan identity, fueling a mission to transform the concept of a witch into a more positive ideal. Their guiding principle is summarized into one sentence: "An ye harm none, do what ye will"—they're permitted to do as they wish, so long as no others are harmed.

As Wicca spread, its tenets evolved. One of Gardner's disciples, Doreen Valiente, shaped the core of Wicca's theology around her own feminist beliefs and her interest in the spirituality of goddess worship. Valiente would come to be known as the mother of modern witchcraft (see sidebar).

The American zeitgeist of the 1960s fed into Wicca, inspiring a variety of spin-offs: Dianic Wicca followed the teachings of the era's women's movement, while the Minoan Brotherhood espoused the gay rights crusade. Environmentalism and Wicca merged seamlessly, as both valued living in harmony with nature.

Despite pushback by evangelical Christians, who publicly compared Wiccans to satanists, the religion continued to grow. In the 1970s, books encouraged independent Wicca practice without the need for a coven, which attracted solo practitioners and helped its principles gain an even wider following.

Wicca came to Hollywood in the 1990s, featured in movies such as *The Craft* and television shows including *Buffy the Vampire Slayer*. Soon, Wicca was a trend among teenagers.

PROFILE

DOREEN VALIENTE

In the 1930s, two decades before she would come to be known as the mother of witches, teenager Doreen Valiente quit her British convent education; it was the beginning of her boundary-breaking life. Valiente had long harbored an interest in occultism and psychic phenomena when she first contacted Wicca's founder, Gerald Gardner, in the 1950s. Before long, she was the high priestess of his coven and was helping him edit and publish the group's official doctrine, *Book of Shadows*. Valiente coined what's known as the Wiccan Rede, the guiding tenet of the religion that instructs followers on the religion's moral code, and published multiple books on the subject until her death in 1999. Her influence brought feminism, environmentalism, and solitary practice into Wicca.

Doreen Valiente holding a knife and bell while displaying her altar setup, 1962

Some Wiccans, such as this one in Salem, Massachusetts, worship the ancient Egyptian deity Isis as a form of the Goddess, especially during healing rituals.

EIGHT SEASONAL
FESTIVALS CALLED SABBATS
FIT INTO THE WHEEL OF THE
YEAR, OR THE CALENDAR,
CELEBRATING FIRE, LIGHT,
FERTILITY, REBIRTH,
AND HARVEST.

Today, Wicca is the largest neo-pagan religion, practiced largely in the West. An estimated 800,000 Americans call themselves Wiccans, but their religious beliefs change from one follower to another: Some Wiccans worship just one goddess, while others are polytheistic and pray to deities across the world's religions and mythologies. Most practice "the Craft," as it's known, solitarily. Yet their numbers continue to rise thanks to social media, which has made it easier for far-flung

SPELLBINDING SYMBOL

THE PENTACLE

The history of the five-pointed pentagram traces back thousands of years to tombs and coins found in Egypt, Mesopotamia, and Greece. The symbol may have been used for health, for protection from evil, or to represent a variety of religious and occult beliefs. But a pentagram star bound in a circle—known as a pentacle—is the iconic symbol of Wicca. Each point represents an element: air, fire, water, earth, and spirit. The pentacle may be used to represent the goddesses and gods, and to protect its wearer. In 2007, the U.S. government officially approved the pentacle for use on Wiccan soldiers' headstones.

Modern pewter pentacle pendant

For centuries, images of witches and fairies conducting mysterious ceremonies have appeared in popular culture, as in this 19th-century painting by Carleton Grant.

witches to learn about Wicca and commune with their fellow practitioners.

An average Wiccan meeting might revolve around an altar holding incense, a chalice, a pentacle star, a wand, and a knife. The rituals' intent is to harness magic to the will of the practitioners. Deities hailing from pre-Christian religions in Europe are worshipped, and rituals can include the practitioner becoming possessed by these divinities. At the end of a ritual, attendees share a communal meal.

Eight seasonal festivals called sabbats fit into the Wheel of the Year, or the calendar, celebrating fire, light, fertility, rebirth, and harvest. On each sabbat, a transformation takes place, both of the earth—during the solstice and the equinox—and of the participants, as a time of reflection and renewal. A "cone of power" is used to conduct energy and imbue the ritual with magic.

In Wicca, magic is seen as a way to tap into the spirit world, or the energies of the earth. The sabbat known as Lammas celebrates a pagan holiday that marked the start of grain harvest in Ireland. In honor of the Celtic god Lugh, people bake breads, decorate altars with scythes and crops, and perform ritual prayers to thank the earth for the harvest.

HARNESSING ENERGY

Healing & Meditation

Cultures around the world continue to use rituals to encourage healing and positive energy—arguably a modern expression of magic. In Western medicine, we regularly see the power of ritual in the form of the placebo effect. With the right context—perhaps the sage counsel of a doctor—inert substances such as sugar pills can trigger real therapeutic benefits. Likewise, the perceived quality of doctors' bedside visits can help or hurt patient outcomes. Shaping a patient's expectations seems to cause that person's brain to activate regions that anticipate a treatment's intended effect. Among other things, these responses can quell anxiety or cause the brain to release its own pain-dulling opioids. This effect almost certainly shapes the power of healing rituals of all stripes.

FENG SHUI

Practitioners of the ancient Chinese art of feng shui (which means "the way of wind and water") carefully arrange buildings, objects, and the spaces between them to enable the flow of chi, the vital life force in Taoism, an ancient Chinese religion and philosophy. The five elements—wood, earth, fire, water, and metal—help shape this flow.

Water stops and retains chi; wind scatters it. Creating the optimal flow of chi within a given space ensures health and good fortune.

Following the guidance of feng shui masters, the Forbidden City in Beijing was built along a north-south axis, with its entrance facing south. Modern buildings make use of the practice, too: The entrance to Paris's Louvre Museum, a sleek glass pyramid, took design cues from feng shui, with the pyramid representing the fire element.

MEDITATION

Many cultures practice meditation, a broad family of mental exercises that encourage contemplation, inner focus, and a detachment from the self that yields mental silence. Some forms call for the meditator to focus on regularly repeated mantras, while others rely on specific breathing exercises or focusing on the body's many physical sensations.

All major religions feature some form of the practice, and records of meditative exercises stretch back more than 3,000 years. The Zhuangzi, a collection of Taoist teachings assembled by the third century B.C.,

< 17th-century bronze of Patañjali, the Hindu sage credited with the Yoga Sūtras (page 301)

A bronze guardian lion stands near the Gate of Supreme Harmony in China's Forbidden City, which was built along a north-south axis according to feng shui principles.

Incense (depicted here by Italian painter Vittorio Zecchin) and aromatherapy in religious and spiritual rituals are thought to enhance a state of healing.

describes meditative exercises that promise a mystical "unity with the Tao," or a oneness with the workings of the universe. More than 1,600 years ago, the Yoga Sūtras—attributed to the Hindu sage Patañjali—described the goal of yoga as *citta vṛtti nirodha*: a complete mental stillness that eliminates the veils between one's inner divinity and the greater divine.

In the last 60 years, meditation inspired by Hindu and Buddhist practices has grown increasingly popular in the West. The Beatles' celebrated 1968 trip to India sparked a surge of interest in a form of Hindu meditation known as transcendental meditation. Since the 1990s, psychiatrists have embraced a Buddhism-inspired technique called mindfulness meditation as a healing supplement to psychotherapy. Scientists have found health benefits to meditation, including reduced stress and improved memory (see page 305).

AROMATHERAPY & ENERGY HEALING

Newer traditions straddle the line between medicine and mysticism to create a modern kind of magic. Aromatherapy, the use of plants' essential oils for healing, draws on centuries of worldwide study of the magical and medicinal power in strong-smelling plants (see page 274).

As both a word and a modern practice, aromatherapy stems from French chemist René-Maurice Gattefossé (1881–1950), who praised essential oils' healing properties in his 1937 book *Aromathérapie*. Today, adherents use a variety of plant oils to address a wide range of ailments. Though aromatherapy's medical benefits remain scientifically debated, there is some clinical evidence that it can help reduce stress, anxiety, pain, and nausea.

Aromatherapy is often integrated into a practice known as energy healing or vibrational medicine. This tradition posits that a vital flow of unseen and unmeasurable "subtle energy"—similar to chi in Chinese tradition or the life breath prana in Hindu tradition—courses through the body; rebalancing it is thought to encourage healing. Energy healing practices include acupuncture, the Japanese "laying on hands" tradition Reiki, the movement-based Chinese tradition qigong, and therapeutic touch.

CURANDEROS

For centuries, *curanderos*, or shamans, located mainly in Latin America, have pulled from magical beliefs rooted in pre-Hispanic Indigenous cultures and used household remedies, plants, and prayers to heal the mind, body, and spirit. On the U.S.-Mexico border, curanderos have sometimes served another role: fighting for their communities during periods of racial discrimination and political strife. Curandera Teresa Urrea was said to be able to miraculously cure cancer, blindness, stroke, and paralysis. As word of her magical abilities spread, she became an outspoken advocate for Indigenous people and is credited with inspiring fighters during the Mexican Revolution in the late 1800s.

Traditional healing is still widely practiced among Mexicans in the United States, who often face barriers accessing health care. Some providers are taking note, and new programs have started incorporating traditional healing into the medical system, making health care more accessible and less intimidating for otherwise excluded communities.

A Mexican *curandero* blows an *atecocolli* (conch shell trumpet) to gather energies for a healing ritual.

WAVELENGTHS

Your Brain on Magic

With increasing frequency, scientists are studying a wide range of spiritual practices and phenomena that either are or were once considered magical. What happens in the brain when people experience something as entrancing as a magic trick or as profound as deep meditation? Emerging areas of research highlight the incredible complexity—and enduring mysteries—of our biology and psychology.

SLEEP, DREAMS & SLEEP PARALYSIS

Some of our most magical everyday experiences come to us during sleep. Sleep is essential for maintaining memory and concentration, as well as for cycling waste products out of the brain. During sleep, we experience magical escapes from the everyday world in the form of dreams: conscious experiences that our brains synthesize as part of their general maintenance. Humans can't resist ascribing prophetic and spiritual meaning to the images embedded in them. More than 4,000 years ago, the Sumerian ruler Gudea claimed that his dreams commanded him to build a temple to the god Ningirsu. According to one 20th-century account, the shamans of Siberia's Chukchi people use sleep as a time to communicate with spirits.

Our most intense dreams happen during a phase known as rapid eye movement (REM) sleep. To keep the body from responding to the dreams of REM sleep as if they were real, the brain triggers a temporary, reversible muscle paralysis. This paralysis can get out of sync with the dream itself, to the point that a dreamer may start waking up before the paralysis wears off. People who experience this often report terrifying hallucinations: feelings of pressure on the chest, choking, suffocation, the presence of "shadow people," even out-of-body experiences.

AFTER-DEATH COMMUNICATIONS

Psychologists have examined the connections people feel to their recently departed loved ones' spirits, bonds beyond death that verge on the magical. In a classic 1971 study, psychologist William Dewi Rees found that among 293 Welsh people who had lost spouses, nearly half reported that they had seen, heard, or felt the presence of their departed loved one. These feelings were especially potent if the surviving spouse was over 40 and had enjoyed a long marriage.

These signs, called after-death communications (ADCs) or sensory experiences of the dead (SEDs), are considered normal, healthy parts of the grieving process. People

Irish artist, poet, and mystic George William Russell (1867–1935) believed that dreaming let people see "windows which open into eternity."

In Mahāyāna Buddhism, the bodhisattva Mañjuśrī personifies supreme wisdom and is said to manifest in dreams.

who experience these connections tend to have less risk for loneliness, appetite loss, and sleep problems during their bereavement. These benefits are highest among people who can contextualize the signs within their existing religious or spiritual beliefs.

Because these experiences are filtered through cultural practices, they vary widely around the world. In 1969, a Japanese team found that some 90 percent of recent widows between 20 and 60 years old reported feeling the presence of their spouse. Japan's high rate of such experiences might have stemmed partially from the ubiquity of ancestor worship in Japanese culture.

BRAIN WAVES & THE MAGIC OF MEDITATION

In meditation's emphasis on attaining unity with a powerfully interconnected cosmos, the practice promises transformative experiences that scientists have begun to chart in the brain. Meditation can affect the tempo and strength of brain waves— patterns of activity that oscillate during different activities and states (such as sleep). During high-level tasks like recalling a memory, portions of the brain's cortex sync up and oscillate between 3.5 and 7 times per second, with the rhythm stronger among expert meditators than it is in beginners.

Mindfulness meditation is thought to affect three sets of brain circuits: attention control, self-awareness, and emotion regu-lation. In addition, studies consistently report that a brain region known as the anterior cingulate cortex (ACC) lights up during mindfulness meditation. The ACC detects perceptual conflicts that emerge from incompatible streams of information. It should be no surprise, then, that this region also lights up in a literally magical context: the moment of wondrous befuddlement that comes after the climax of a well-executed magic trick.

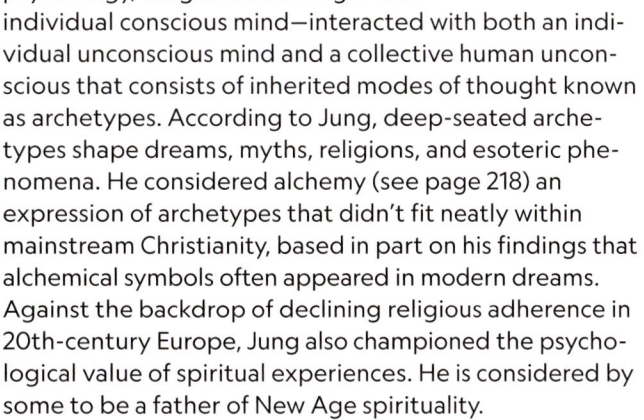

PROFILE

CARL JUNG

Carl Jung (1875–1961) was a pioneering Swiss psychologist and psychiatrist, considered one of the most influential of the 20th century. Jung's method of psychoanalysis, known as analytic psychology, taught that the ego—the individual conscious mind—interacted with both an individual unconscious mind and a collective human unconscious that consists of inherited modes of thought known as archetypes. According to Jung, deep-seated archetypes shape dreams, myths, religions, and esoteric phenomena. He considered alchemy (see page 218) an expression of archetypes that didn't fit neatly within mainstream Christianity, based in part on his findings that alchemical symbols often appeared in modern dreams. Against the backdrop of declining religious adherence in 20th-century Europe, Jung also championed the psychological value of spiritual experiences. He is considered by some to be a father of New Age spirituality.

Carl Jung at his home in Küsnacht, Switzerland, circa 1960

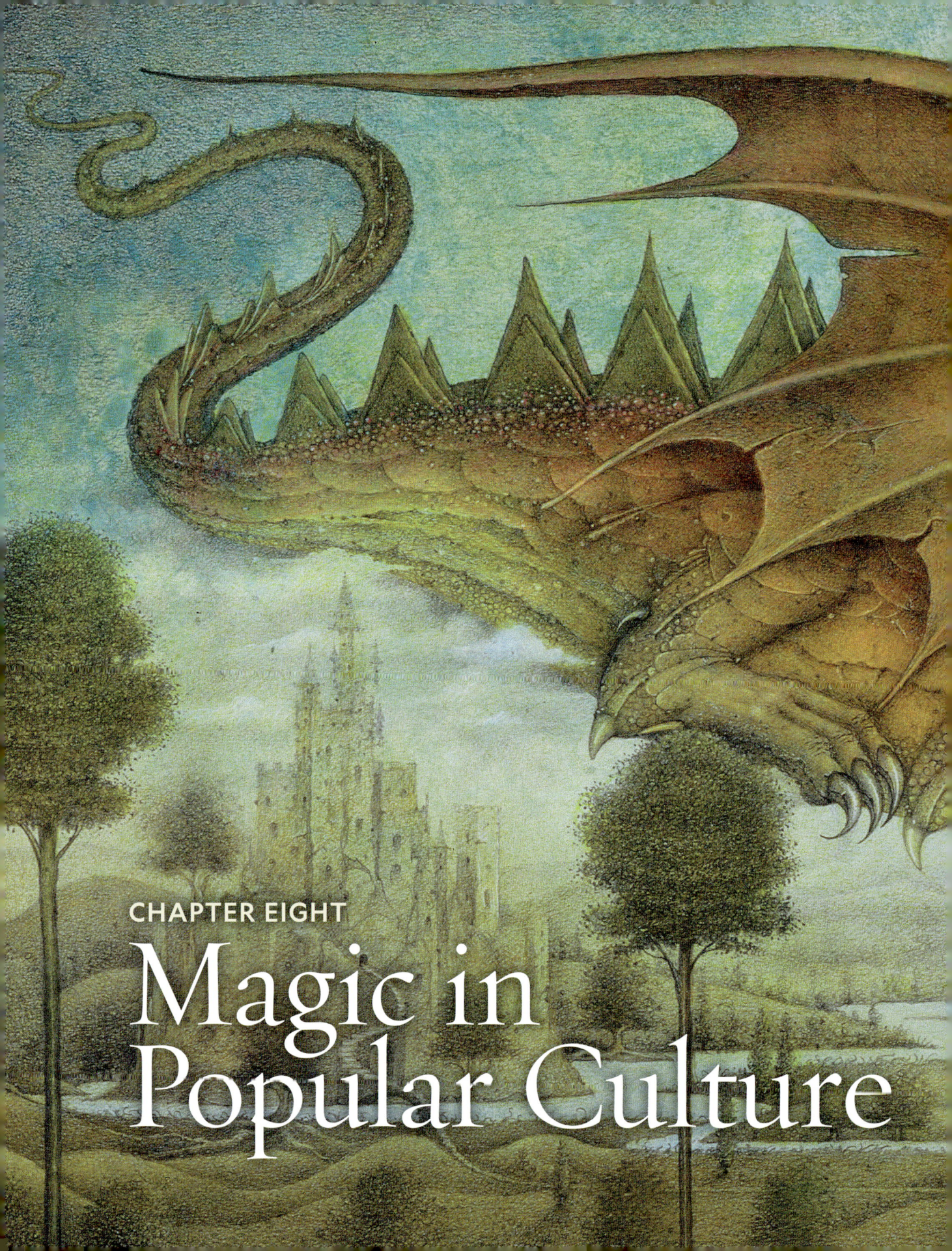

CHAPTER EIGHT

Magic in Popular Culture

Dragons and many other magical creatures and concepts abound in modern entertainment: a testament to magic's continued allure.

Tricks & Illusions

Magic as Performance

In the 1800s, magic hitched a ride on the wave of early pop culture and never looked back. Moving away from the variations on religion, superstition, and folk culture that had defined magical practice for millennia, it merged into the mainstream. Over the past two centuries, magic has transformed itself time and again alongside modern media: from street corners to the stage to the silver screen to the internet.

As mass entertainment boomed during the industrial revolution, magic took center stage. Few magicians would reach such heights as Harry Houdini, a Hungarian immigrant to the United States who pioneered both stage magic and the attention-grabbing publicity stunt. As a performance art, magic made the public question its own eyes: The events unfolding in front of them appeared to defy the laws of nature, transforming the world into a more wondrous place.

Moving pictures brought a new kind of magic to an even wider audience. Magicians have long pioneered and utilized the latest technologies, and behind the scenes of movies, they created the visual tricks and tools that would become industry standard. Through film, music, and literature, magic has given us iconic tropes like the good witch and the haunted house. Fairy tales morphed into films and illusions became theme park rides, while occult beliefs seeped into music and counterculture.

Today, we need look no further than our phones to see how our tech-obsessed world continues to celebrate magic, from Witch-Tok—one of many magic-related TikTok rabbit holes—to video games and cult television shows. Its next act may still be a mystery, but we can be certain that magic will continue to surprise and delight us all. ▪

∧ In an 1880s trick, a canister of eggs is opened anew to instead reveal cages with live birds.

KELLAR

IN HIS LATEST MYSTERY

SELF DECAPITATION

COPYRIGHT 1897 BY
THE
STROBRIDGE
LITH. CO.
CIN'TI. & NEW YORK.

Magician Harry Kellar (1849–1922) wowed American audiences with a "self-decapitation" illusion, in which his head appeared to float separately from his body.

FROM STREET TO STAGE

The Dawn of Modern Magic

The art form of modern magic is built on creating moments of wonder through illusion and sleight of hand. The craft's roots go back millennia, through a long line of tricksters and jugglers. Some 2,000 years ago, Roman conjurers performed a routine known as *acetabula et calculi*, in which small balls disappeared and reappeared beneath cups, a forerunner to the modern cups and balls routine (see page 312).

For centuries, magicians plied their trades on street corners and at fairgrounds—sometimes facing risk of persecution. Published in 1584, *The Discoverie*

of Witchcraft was one of the first Western texts that methodically compiled the methods behind magic tricks. The book's author, Englishman Reginald Scot, wrote it to stop what he considered to be baseless witchcraft prosecutions.

In the early 1700s, showmen began touring Europe with oil-lamp image pro-

PEPPER'S GHOST

In December 1862, the Charles Dickens play *The Haunted Man and the Ghost's Bargain* debuted a groundbreaking illusion invented by Henry Dircks and John Henry Pepper: a semitransparent ghost appeared on stage next to live actors. The effect was created by placing an angled, half-silvered mirror between the audience and the stage. When backlit, the mirror looked transparent and was thus unseen. However, the mirror could reflect light coming up from underneath it: In this case, the reflection was of a brightly lit actor concealed within a hidden compartment in the stage. This setup created the illusion of a semitransparent ghost on the stage. This illusion, now known as Pepper's ghost, is still widely used today, In everything from Disneyland's Haunted Mansion ride to teleprompters.

Advertisement for Pepper's ghosts at the Royal Polytechnic Institution, circa 1885

jectors known as magic lanterns, paving the way for modern stage illusions and special effects. The pace of innovation quickened by century's end, when the imagery went from quaint scenes—a spinning windmill, for instance—to more mystical sights. Just as gothic literature was delving into the supernatural (see page 256), exhibitors began using magic lanterns to stage "ghost shows" that featured projections of spirits and skeletons.

The French showman Étienne-Gaspard Robertson elevated the ghost show in 1799 with his *Fantasmagorie*, or *Phantasmagoria*. For six years, Robertson ran a show that used magic lanterns to create a terrifying, 90-minute experience, most often in an abandoned Paris chapel. After plunging his guests into darkness and locking the doors behind them, Robertson and his crew summoned lightning, spectral skeletons, and witches to descend upon the shocked audience. The spectacle was convincing: At one point, *Phantasmagoria* was shut down by local police amid fears that Robertson could resurrect King Louis XVI.

By the 19th century, magicians established themselves as mass entertainers. Ventriloquist and magician Richard Potter (1783–1835) was one of the United States' first Black celebrities and its first successful native-born stage magician. Born in Massachusetts to a white father and a formerly enslaved Black mother, Potter trained in Europe as an acrobat before returning to the U.S. and performing on his own by 1811. In performances in the States and Canada, he swallowed molten lead and danced on eggs without breaking them.

Despite their success, Potter and his contemporaries were often seen as lower-class entertainment. That changed with the work of French clockmaker and magician Jean-Eugène Robert-Houdin (1805–1871), considered the father of modern magic. Robert-Houdin's formal mannerisms and dress (often tails and a top hat) helped legitimize magic as upper-crust entertainment. In his purpose-built Paris magic theater, which opened in 1845, Robert-Houdin worked miracles for the French elite. In one trick, a small orange tree—an ingenious clockwork contraption—grew blossoms and real oranges before the audience's eyes.

^ By the late 19th century, magic lanterns were regularly used to project illustrations of popular stories (in this case, the fairy tale "Puss in Boots").

JUGGLERS & CONJURERS

Magical Influence From India & China

Modern magic is the child of cross-cultural exchange, and no history of the art form would be complete without highlighting the enormous influence of performers from India and China. In 1812, an enterprising captain of the East India Company brought a troupe of Indian magicians and jugglers to England. That troupe, led by a juggler who became known in English sources as Ramo Samee (perhaps more accurately spelled Ramaswamy), went on to wildly successful tours in England and the United States. Samee and other Indian magicians sparked an intense European fascination with Indian magic, juggling, and fortune-telling.

For many centuries, Indian street performers have been performing a version of cups and balls, a trick known today as *cheppum panthum*. In it, a seated magician uses a wand to make balls disappear and reappear beneath three or four distinctively shaped cups.

INDIAN ROPE TRICK

Dating back to at least the 10th century A.D., this celebrated trick is a feat claimed to have been performed by the magicians of India, in which a boy climbs up a rope whose end is magically floating in midair, and then vanishes. (Some descriptions say the boy was magically dismembered upon reaching the top of the rope, with the trick concluding with his resurrection.) The trick's notoriety grew beyond India in the 19th century after Western magicians learned of it; through the 1930s, the British magicians' association known as the Magic Circle sought to debunk it. Though it has long been known as "the most famous trick never performed," the rope trick's legend endures. In the 20th and 21st centuries, performers inside and outside India have dreamed up workable, scaled-down versions of the illusion.

A 1927 poster of magician Howard Thurston performing an Indian rope trick

CHINESE MAGIC MADE ITS WAY TO THE WEST IN THE LATE 19TH CENTURY, THANKS TO CHINESE MAGICIAN CHING LING FOO.

Similar traditions can be found in China, where stage tricks such as sword-swallowing and juggling had cemented themselves as court entertainment by the second century B.C.

Chinese magic made its way to the West in the late 19th century, thanks to Chinese magician Ching Ling Foo (1854–1922). Born in the port city of Tianjin as Zhu Liankui, he toured cities across Asia in the 1880s. A breakout performance at the 1898 World's Fair in Omaha, Nebraska, made him a darling of the American vaudeville circuit. For all his feats—which included eating fire and making birds seemingly die and come back to life at his command—he was perhaps most famous for making a huge, water-filled bowl appear out of nowhere.

Among Western audiences, fascination with Asian cultures led to a great appetite for the exotic and racialized, a cultural phenomenon that 20th-century academics termed Orientalism. White Western magicians frequently used face paint and caricatured costumes to appropriate the identities of Indian fakirs, Chinese conjurers, and Arabian sorcerers. In one of his earliest performances, Harry Houdini (see page 318) appeared in dark makeup as an "authentic Hindu fakir" at the 1893 World's Columbian Exposition in Chicago.

One of the highest-paid magicians of this era was the conjurer known as Chung Ling Soo: the stage name for white American magician William Ellsworth Robinson, who donned makeup and a long, braided wig to make audiences think he was Chinese. Previously, Robinson had performed as an Arab magician named Achmed Ben Ali, but he changed his masquerade for the Folies Bergère in Paris—and copied the act of Ching Ling Foo. In 1904, Ching Ling Foo accused Robinson of being an impostor and challenged him to a duel, but the confrontation never materialized. Robinson continued to perform as Chung Ling Soo until 1918, when he was killed on stage during a "bullet catch" trick gone wrong.

∧ Ching Ling Foo's signature trick was to make a water-filled bowl weighing nearly 100 pounds (45 kg) suddenly appear onstage.

EMBRACING MODERNITY

Magic's Fabled Golden Age

On the stages of Europe and the United States, the 1880s to the 1920s was a period of innovation and glory that became known as the golden age of magic. Magic tricks tapped into a scientific and technological era, when real life was made more magical with innovations like electricity, automobiles, telephones, and radio. Magicians created elaborate—and often fake—backstories to boost their allure and sell tickets. (Launching this trend was French magician Jean-Eugène Robert-Houdin, who claimed to have fallen ill while traveling alone and been nursed back to health by an Italian magician, who then bequeathed him with a career's worth of secrets.)

As more and more magicians stepped into the spotlight, they promised over-the-top spectacles to eager audiences. Tricks became grander and more audacious: assistants cut in half, large animals vanishing from the stage, and performers disappearing from the end of a hangman's noose. Many of these tricks involved state-of-the-art constructions that used lighting,

---

ADELAIDE HERRMANN

In the 1870s, Adelaide Scarsez (1853–1932) was in the audience at London's iconic Egyptian Hall, enjoying a magic show featuring Alexander Herrmann, one of the world's most famous magicians. As the story goes, he borrowed Adelaide's ring, lit it on fire, and made it reappear around the neck of a dove. Whether or not the trick had been intended as a romantic gesture, they were soon married, and Adelaide would go on to assist in Alexander's show for two decades. Left penniless and in debt after his sudden death, Adelaide decided to take the show over herself. The self-dubbed "queen of magic" toured as one of the rare female stars in the field. She did daring tricks, including a bullet catch, and performed for nearly the rest of her life, showcasing beautifully staged dances, illusions, and costumes.

Cabinet card photograph of Adelaide Herrmann, circa 1880

In the late 19th century, London's Egyptian Hall theater was a mecca for stage magicians, including English performer David Devant (1868–1941).

IT WOULDN'T BE LONG BEFORE MAGIC REACHED ITS NEXT BIG STAGE: UNDER THE SHIMMERING NEON LIGHTS OF LAS VEGAS.

∧ In 1941, Gloria Dea performed Las Vegas's first magic act at the El Rancho Hotel.

paint, and clever concealments to pull off the impossible. As magicians' setups grew, so did performance venues. In London, the lavish Egyptian Hall began as a curiosities museum and became a hub of magic, showcasing the world's most famous performers.

Theater had long been reserved for the upper classes, but as industrialization boomed and American cities were flooded with a new class of workers with disposable income, savvy business owners recognized their potential as audiences. In an increasingly diverse country like America, magic was entertainment that required little education—or even language skill—to enjoy. As a result, people of all types flocked to see magicians.

In the United States, a series of magicians ruled the emerging vaudeville circuits.

Debonair, mischievous Alexander Herrmann (1844–1896) "caught" a bullet between his teeth. The devil-whispering Harry Kellar (1849–1922) "levitated" humans and tables with the wave of a hand. Kellar's handpicked successor, Howard Thurston (1869–1936), the "king of the cards," stunned audiences with sleight of hand and grand illusion alike, touring the States with an enormous production called *The Wonder Show of the Universe*. Carter the Great (1874–1936) delivered a pulpy, theatrical show as "the world's weird wonderful wizard."

With the decline of vaudeville and the rise of Hollywood in the 1920s, the golden age of magic would wind to a close. But the magic world was just beginning to welcome its most intimate style yet. Dai Vernon (1894–1992), also known as The Professor, fooled even Harry Houdini (see page 318)—something the stuntman claimed couldn't be done—with a routine that continuously surfaced Houdini's signed card to the top of a deck. Vernon revolutionized the art form with his style of close-up card magic, which magicians still perform today.

Meanwhile, magicians adapted to newer performance venues, from nightclubs to television. Early experiments in TV broadcasting proved that magic's thrill and awe could translate through the screen. In 1956, Indian magician P. C. Sorcar (1913–

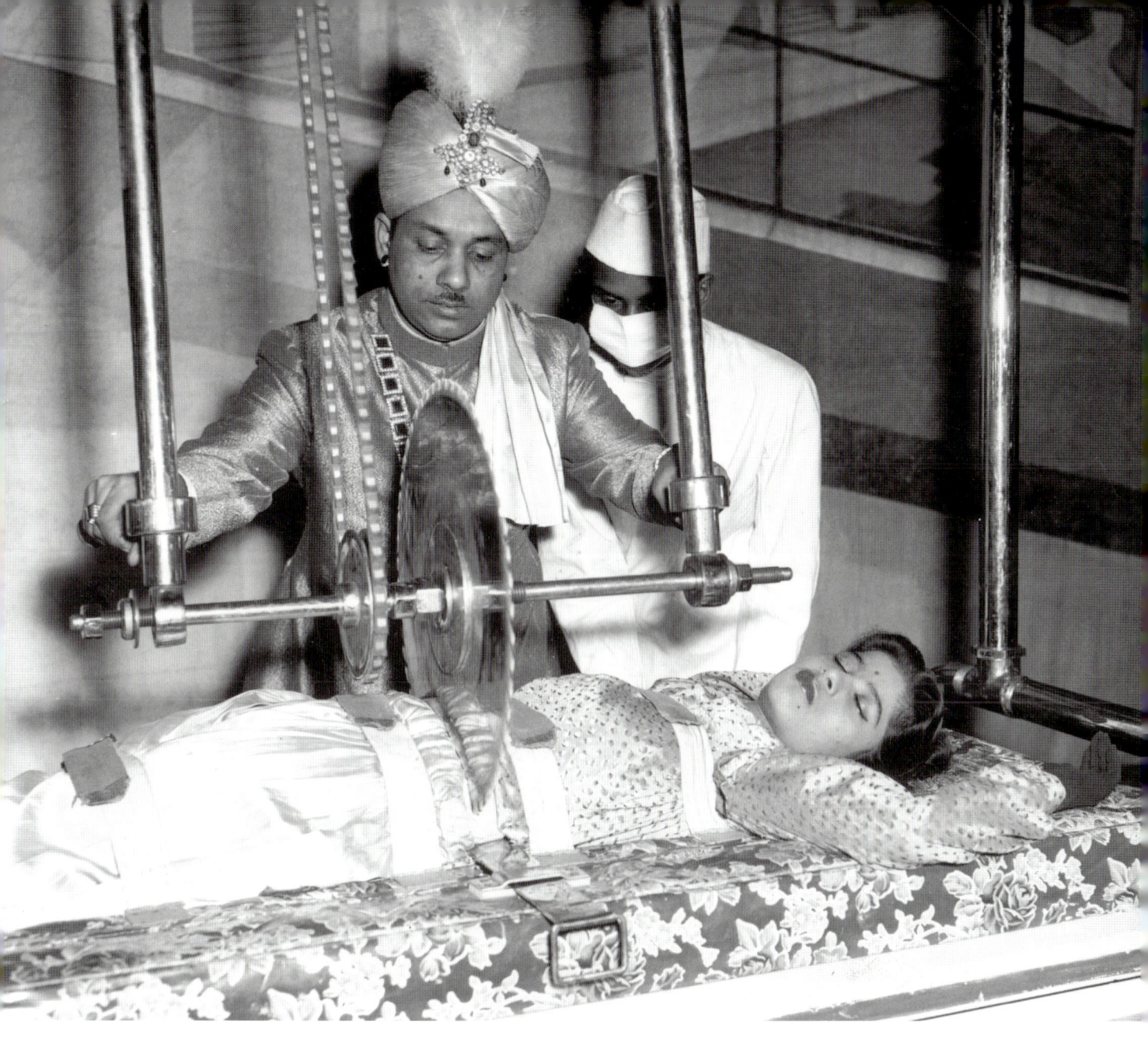

1971) sent British television audiences into a panic after a particularly convincing live performance of sawing a girl in half. From 1960 to 1965, American magician Mark Wilson (1929–2021) anchored the hit TV show *The Magic Land of Allakazam,* paving the way for the many magic TV specials that would follow (see page 331).

And it wouldn't be long before magic reached its next big stage: under the shimmering neon lights of Las Vegas. In 1941, a young woman named Gloria Dea took the stage at the El Rancho Hotel as the first magician to perform in Las Vegas, starting a tradition that would define the style and scope of performance magic. The scene reached its zenith in the 1980s and 1990s, with illusionists like David Copperfield, Lance Burton, and the duo Siegfried & Roy selling out theaters with lavish mega-productions. Today, acts like Penn & Teller and Mac King continue to make Vegas and its flashy style of showmanship synonymous with American magic.

∧ In 1956, Indian magician P. C. Sorcar and his assistant, Dipty Dey, astounded British audiences with their version of the sawing illusion.

MASTER ESCAPIST

Harry Houdini's Astonishing Feats

He's the most famous magician to ever live, but few realize that Harry Houdini (1874–1926) began life as Ehrich Weiss, a rabbi's son from Budapest. After moving to America as a young child, he was soon performing in his neighborhood circus as "Ehrich, the Prince of the Air." Before long, he was touring circuses and vaudeville circuits around the States as Houdini, a name inspired by the French father of modern magic, Jean-Eugène Robert-Houdin (see page 311). After years of minimal success,

Houdini and his wife, Bess, began experimenting with an escape routine that involved handcuffs and locked trunks. In 1899, a vaudeville producer spotted them, and Houdini was catapulted to the biggest stages of the day. The next year he set off for England and Europe, where he would publicize his shows by visiting local police stations and breaking out of their jail cells and handcuffs.

Soon, Houdini was known around the world as the "king of handcuffs." Confined by shackles, ropes, and manacles, he'd be

HOUDINI'S ESCAPES

It was Houdini's crowning achievement: a metal-lined wooden tank with a glass front. With his feet locked into the lid, he'd be lowered into the water-filled contraption headfirst. After a padlock was attached, a curtain was drawn, and two minutes later, Houdini would emerge, out of breath but alive. Houdini's legendary Chinese Water Torture Cell—an upgrade from his signature Milk Can Escape, in which he was locked in an oversize milk can filled with water—became his most famous routine. Even today, many of his most famous stunts are still a mystery: Houdini almost never applied for patents for his inventions for fear they would be stolen. What remains today is only speculation and magic.

Harry Houdini performing his famous Milk Can Escape trick in 1908

Houdini became one of the world's most famous performers by pledging to escape from any restraint.

As Houdini's fame grew, his stunts became more daring, like this 1914 escape from a crate lowered into New York Harbor.

© HOUDINI.
1914.

HOUDINI'S COMMITMENT TO BOLD, DARING STUNTS MAKES MANY REMEMBER HIM AS THE WORLD'S GREATEST MAGICIAN.

Dietz
N.Y.

locked inside a box and placed in an extreme situation—underwater, upside down, underground, hanging from impossible heights—from which he'd promptly escape. Over time, he evaded the world's most secure handcuffs; a famed Washington, D.C., jail; and an airtight bronze coffin.

Houdini's talent for escape was matched only by his knack for self-promotion. The era loved a daredevil, and Houdini was the ultimate American success story. He was an early adopter of corporate sponsorships—for example, inviting beer companies to manufacture the barrels he'd escape from for cross-promotional opportunities—and used the press to plant stories, good and bad, about his act. Often, Houdini's performances drew public derision from those who wanted to challenge him, although today it's thought that he himself planted many of those challengers to drum up attention.

As Houdini's fame grew, so did his bold public stunts. In 1908, he offered a $1,000 reward to anyone who could build a device that could successfully restrain him. (It appears no one ever claimed the prize.) A decade later, Houdini made an elephant disappear as he slowly turned the massive cabinet it stood in onstage at New York's Hippodrome Theater. With the dawn of cinema, Houdini also dabbled in movies, appearing in several stunt-filled films. But he never became a screen star.

Houdini's fame amplified his crusade against the spiritualist mediums popular in the late 19th and early 20th centuries (see page 260). His efforts would inspire generations of magicians to speak out against frauds and con artists, including religious figures claiming to channel spirits or possess mind-reading powers.

His stunts were not without real risk, and Houdini was often injured during his routines, once even rupturing his kidney when a longshoreman tied him up too tightly. But seemingly nothing could pierce his image of impermeability. Though Houdini was never considered as masterful in the art of technical magic as some of his contemporaries, his commitment to bold, daring stunts makes many remember him as the world's greatest magician.

Houdini's death on Halloween of 1926 was just as mysterious as his lifetime of tricks. His death is attributed to complications from appendicitis, which likely traced to a lecture at McGill University weeks earlier, where a student had challenged Houdini's claim that he could withstand punches and hit him forcibly in the stomach. But no autopsy was performed, and rumors of his cause of death have continued to swirl. Some even speculate that enemies in the Spiritualism movement planned his assassination.

Although he never believed the spiritualists' claims, Houdini did promise his wife, Bess, that he'd communicate a secret code to her from the beyond if he could. For a decade, Bess attended séances hoping for a signal from him, but his voice had been silenced by the grave.

THE MAGICIAN'S BAG OF TRICKS

To create impossible moments of wonder in the minds of their spectators, magicians combine talents of storytelling and misdirection with an extraordinarily dexterous use of a wide variety of props. And through the centuries, they have engineered ingenious devices that catapulted the art form to new heights.

Though magicians continue to incorporate new technologies and keep up with the ever shifting zeitgeist, magic is in many ways a deeply conservative art form. Magicians take advantage of innate biases in our abilities to pay attention and remember—and as long as these biases don't change, magic's basic principles of deception won't either. Likewise, magic's most classic props remain effective precisely because of their mundanity: A coin is a coin, a card is a card. Though materials and stylings may have changed, today's sleight-of-hand artists and illusionists would recognize the tools of the trade used by the street performers and conjurers of long ago.

NOT WHAT IT APPEARS >
Many early 20th-century Western magicians sought to exoticize themselves by appearing as Asian conjurers. This Asian-style vase, in which confetti or bran transformed into a dove, belonged to Dutch magician Theo Bamberg (1875–1963), better known as Okito.

< POWER PACKET
In this early 1900s card trick sold in England, a fan of four eights appears to magically transform into four twos, four red cards, and four black cards before returning to its original order.

NOW YOU SEE IT >
Many stage routines use small boxes such as this one to lock away a borrowed ring or coin—only for the borrowed object to vanish from the box and reappear elsewhere.

∧ THE TIES THAT BIND
A subgroup of magicians called escapologists specialize in freeing themselves from restraints. None has shined brighter than Harry Houdini, who owned this particular straitjacket.

< WHAT A MIX-UP

Wine and water are poured from two separate glasses into a decanter. After the glassware is briefly covered, the glasses are refilled—and the decanter is magically empty again.

∨ OUT WITH A BANG

When fired, this pistol can make a handkerchief draped over it vanish—a classic beat in many stage magic routines.

∧ KEG YOU BELIEVE IT?

For centuries, magicians have performed tricks in which an "inexhaustible" bottle produces many drinks on command. In this version by Charles Carter (1874–1936), an empty barrel is capped on both ends with paper—but when a spigot is placed on one end, beer flows forth.

< DRESSED TO IMPRESS

Used to perform many different tricks including making items appear, vanish, and reappear, the top hat was a mainstay of 19th- and 20th-century magic.

∨ BALLS & MAGIC

Modern equipment for the ancient sleight-of-hand trick is often made of metal—or, in the case of this 1920s set, finely turned wood.

BYE-BYE BIRDIE >

Magicians have long used doves in their tricks. When 20th-century magician Dell O'Dell placed a dove into the cabinet at right, the bird would vanish and reappear in the box below.

< HEARING VOICES

In the early 20th century, magicians both criticized and aped the style of spiritualists. This 1920s "spirit trumpet" supposedly amplified the voices of the departed during séances.

FALLING FOR FANTASY

Magic on the Page

The origins of the modern fantasy literature genre span centuries, with roots burrowed deep into mythology, folklore, and medieval romances such as the stories of King Arthur (see page 156), as well as the folktales turned fairy tales of the 18th and 19th centuries (see page 206).

Such sources inspired forerunners of modern fantasy in the late 1800s and early 1900s, beginning with Lewis Carroll's *Alice's Adventures in Wonderland* (1865), L. Frank Baum's *The Wonderful Wizard of Oz* (1900), and J. M. Barrie's *Peter and Wendy* (1904 play, 1911 novel). Edith Nesbit (1858–1924), author of 60 books including the time-travel novel *The Story of the Amulet* (1906), is widely credited with kick-starting children's fantasy during this period, placing her characters in incredible, often magical, circumstances.

Fantasy was changed forever by two Oxford professors. Literary scholar and lay theologian C. S. Lewis (1898–1963) published *The Chronicles of Narnia,* a series of seven fantasy novels, between 1950 and 1956. The books recount the Pevensie children's adventures in Narnia, a magical realm pitched in battles between good and evil and home to all manner of talking animals and magical beings. A convert to Christianity in 1931, Lewis often wove Christian themes into his stories; Narnia's talking lion, Aslan, is meant to be a Christlike figure.

Lewis's friend and colleague J. R. R. Tolkien (1872–1973) was a philologist who studied Old English literature and loved to invent languages. Inspired by medieval stories and ancient legends, Tolkien spent decades imagining the history, mythology,

< In Tomi Adeyemi's *Children of Blood and Bone* (part of the Legacy of Orïsha trilogy), the protagonist fights to restore magic to her people.

Alice's Adventures in Wonderland features one surreal scene after the next: in this case, a royal guard consisting of a pack of cards.

and cultures of "Middle-earth," a version of ancient Earth. *The Hobbit* was published in 1934, followed by the three-volume epic novel *The Lord of the Rings* (1954–1955). Tolkien set the standard, if not the template, for high fantasy: In a richly imagined world populated by many magical races, a ragtag group tries to defeat a powerful dark lord.

The Lord of the Rings' release in paperback triggered a surge of interest in fantasy, which authors responded to with a flurry of imaginative stories. The work of Ursula K. Le Guin (1929–2018), including *A Wizard of Earthsea* (1968) and *The Left Hand of Darkness* (1969), brought anthropological levels of rigor to world-building while also exploring issues of race and gender. Starting with *Dragonflight* (1968), Anne McCaffrey's Dragonriders of Pern series combined science fiction (human colonization of far-off planets) with classic fantasy imagery (fire-breathing dragons).

The 1990s brought a revival of Tolkienesque fantasy, as well as new riffs on the genre. The Wheel of Time series (1990–2013), created by James Oliver Rigney, Jr. (aka Robert Jordan, 1948–2007), won acclaim for its detailed world-building. In *A Game of Thrones* (1996), author

MAGICAL REALISM

Beyond fantasy, other forms of literature make use of magic. In the magical realism genre, associated strongly with Latin American literature, surreal events happening in our real world illuminate the emotional truth of our reality by stretching the bounds of what can occur within it. In Gabriel García Márquez's *One Hundred Years of Solitude* (1967), one character is inexplicably followed by a retinue of yellow butterflies. In Toni Morrison's *Beloved* (1987), a formerly enslaved Black woman fixates on a young woman who seems to be a reincarnation of her dead baby girl, whom she had killed to spare her from slavery. Other notable authors in this genre include Jorge Luis Borges, Isabel Allende, Laura Esquivel, Haruki Murakami, and Salman Rushdie.

Yellow butterflies are a recurring symbol of love, hope, and peace in *One Hundred Years of Solitude*.

George R. R. Martin began his Song of Ice and Fire series, with gritty political realism playing out against a history of magic. In the His Dark Materials trilogy (1995–2000), Philip Pullman responds to the Christian themes of Lewis's Narnia works with a coming-of-age story that culminates with a war on God. This decade also saw J. K. Rowling's first Harry Potter books; the world's best-selling series of all time is rich with references to ancient and medieval magic.

Fantasy remains alive and well today. N. K. Jemisin's Broken Earth trilogy (2015–2017) seamlessly combines magic and geology. Brandon Sanderson has set many novels in a vast fantasy universe known as the Cosmere. Inspired by both Harry Potter and the mythos of West Africa's Yoruba people, Nigerian-American novelist Tomi Adeyemi's Legacy of Orïsha trilogy (2018–2024) explores class and race in a magical, precolonial Yorubaland. And thanks in part to her collection *Where the Wild Ladies Are* (2020), which puts a feminist twist on traditional Japanese folktales, Aoko Matsuda has established herself as a master of the fantasy short story.

∧ C. S. Lewis's *The Chronicles of Narnia* have captivated generations through books and other media, such as this 2005 movie adaptation of *The Lion, the Witch and the Wardrobe*.

TRICKS ON FILM

Magic Moves to the Screen

For a brief moment, the history of cinema and magic melded together seamlessly. At the dawn of the moving picture, magicians and illusionists shaped the techniques, styles, and plots that would become enshrined in modern filmmaking. As audiences were first introduced to film in the 1890s, French magician and inventor Georges Méliès ushered in the heyday of the "trick film": revolutionary shorts that showcased the types of illusions he'd employed in his stage act. Across the Channel, well-known magician Félicien Trewey was screening the first moving pictures seen publicly in Britain.

Magicians, accustomed to using magic lantern projectors and visual special effects in live theater, were natural stars and filmmakers. Magicians turned filmmakers like Gaston Velle and Orson Welles pulled inspiration from their initial careers to indelibly transform cinema. Velle's often fantastical films featured complex characters and unusual-for-the-time editing techniques like close-ups and perspective changes. Welles revolutionized filmmaking with techniques like nonlinear storytelling and the use of sound for transitions. Magic and film remain intrinsically linked today, with magicians often being commissioned to design special effects.

Magicians put themselves center stage

IN LEGEND

THE HAUNTED HOUSE

In 1896, Georges Méliès made a short film called "Le Manoir du Diable" ("The House of the Devil"). The three-minute short about a devil inhabiting a medieval castle is considered the first horror film. The first feature film set in a haunted house was 1927's *The Cat and the Canary*, and in 1944 *The Uninvited* followed a brother and sister who moved into a spirit-inhabited home. The haunted-house subgenre, which would take off from there, included films like *House on Haunted Hill* (1959), *House* (made in Japan in 1977), *The Amityville Horror* (1979), and *Poltergeist* (1982). These films tap into an innate human desire to push the limits of fear—a product of evolution that tests our ability to tackle new challenges and adapt to surprises.

American actor and director Orson Welles, here in a still from *Citizen Kane* (1941), was an avid magician who performed for U.S. military personnel during World War II.

in early films, but as the movie industry evolved, witches, ghosts, and other supernatural beings emerged from folktales and novels to become box-office hits. Witches and the Salem witch trials formed the basis for many popular movie plots, and *Nosferatu* (1922) and *Dracula* (1931) spooked audiences with chilling on-screen depic-

tions of vampires' bloodsucking powers.

It would be three more decades before witches had a glow-up, thanks to the hit TV show *Bewitched*. Airing from 1964 until 1972, it featured Samantha, a beautiful young housewife who just happened to have magic powers. "It's not the broomsticks I mind so much," says one of Saman-

In *Nosferatu* (1922), German actor Max Schreck gave one of cinema's most enduring—and unnerving—horror performances as the vampire Count Orlok.

THE GOOD WITCH

When *The Wizard of Oz* made its cinematic debut in 1939, one sparkling figure enchanted audiences, floating on screen in a billowing pink dress and silver crown. Witches in fairy tales and literature had generally been dark, sinister figures, but Glinda the Good Witch was the antithesis of a villainous "old hag." She was likely the first witch to be depicted as purely "good" in a major movie, and the "good witch" soon became a Hollywood staple. Others would follow Glinda's shimmering footsteps to join the coven of powerful good counterparts, from *Bewitched*'s Samantha to the Harry Potter series' Hermione Granger. Glinda's creator, L. Frank Baum, drew inspiration from his own mother, a 19th-century feminist and suffragist named Matilda Joslyn Gage, who theorized that a woman accused of witchcraft was a "profoundest thinker" who had been persecuted by the church to temper the threat of her intellect.

Billie Burke as Glinda the Good Witch in *The Wizard of Oz* (1939)

tha's aunts in an early episode, "it's the way they make us look … those ugly, horrid warts and those long, crooked noses." According to the show, the "normal" witch was a regular-looking person with magical powers who might be living among us undetected.

That trend continued with the 1986 film *The Worst Witch*. Based on the series of children's novels by Jill Murphy, it features a regular-looking girl who struggles to fit in at a school of magic. These early productions are believed to have provided inspiration for J. K. Rowling as she crafted the universe of Harry Potter (see page 327), where witches are indistinguishable from "Muggles" at first glance.

The rise of the witch in Hollywood is sometimes thought to be connected to the spread of Wicca as a global religion in the mid to late 20th century. In the 1990s, hit TV shows starring young female witches included *Sabrina the Teenage Witch, Buffy the Vampire Slayer,* and *Charmed.* The shows' themes of gender empowerment, with portrayals of witches as strong female characters who undermine or parody the patriarchal order, appealed to the era's feminist sensibilities.

But it's not just witches who've received the Hollywood treatment. In the Star Wars films, the magical Force gives Jedis their power. Demonic possessions haunted films like *The Exorcist.* In modern cinema and television, werewolves, vampires, teen witches, Wicca covens, and Santeria priestesses all have had their share of time on the big screen.

Of course, it all comes back to magicians, who began regularly appearing on television in the 1950s (see page 317). In the 1970s, TV specials featuring the likes of Doug Henning and David Copperfield became wildly popular; these productions grew more ambitious in the 1980s as Copperfield made his name with high-profile stunts such as "flying" over the Grand Canyon, "walking through" the Great Wall of China, and "vanishing" the Statue of Liberty. By the turn of the 21st century, the TV specials of David Blaine made magic cool again as he performed "street magic" live on camera for regular people on the sidewalks of New York.

SHAZAM!
Magic in Comics, Manga & Anime

Magic has coursed through comics since the art form came of age in the early 20th century. Four years before Superman's debut, the first ever comic superhero was 1934's Mandrake the Magician, a crime-fighting illusionist whose name hearkens back to a magical herb (see page 283). Mandrake profoundly influenced the costumed crime-fighters who followed. Mr. Mystic, created in 1940, wielded magical powers unlocked by an arcane Tibetan forehead tattoo, followed in 1963 by the Marvel character Doctor Strange, a "Sorcerer Supreme" who gained his powers through training in the mystic arts in the Himalaya. The tuxedo-clad Zatara, created in 1939, could compel anyone or anything to do his bidding if he spoke backward. Zatara's magician daughter, Zatanna, created in 1964, remains a popular DC Comics superhero.

Other comic heroes drew power from ancient deities and magical practices.

∧ The comic book character Captain Marvel (aka Shazam) inspired a 12-part film serial in 1941.

GRANT MORRISON

Scottish comic book writer and screenwriter Grant Morrison (1960–) is best known for their work on comics such as *Batman, The Invisibles, Doom Patrol,* and *New X-Men.* Morrison has been a practicing magician since they were 19, when they saw a demon appear while trying out the procedures of Aleister Crowley (see page 185). They focus on chaos magic, a stripped-down and highly individualized form inspired by the works of English occultist Austin Osman Spare (1886–1956).

In chaos magic, magicians create sigils that represent specific desires or intentions. These sigils are charged with power during focused moments of gnosis—a quieting of the conscious mind achieved via meditation, sex, drug use, or other methods. Morrison described their personal system of chaos magic, Pop Magic!, in a chapter of a 2008 book of the same name.

Captain Marvel (aka Shazam), created in 1939, is a teenage boy who meets a 3,000-year-old wizard and gains the power to transform into a superhero by shouting "SHAZAM!" The incantation grants the boy the wisdom of Solomon, the strength of Hercules, the stamina of Atlas, the power of Zeus, the courage of Achilles, and the speed of Mercury.

In 1962, Archie Comics debuted the character Sabrina the Teenage Witch, a "half-witch" who lives with her two witch aunts and tries to reconcile her mortal and magical lives. Sabrina got her own stand-alone title in 1971 and has since spawned many successful adaptations, including a popular 1990s sitcom and a 2018 Netflix show.

Some comics even incorporate principles from modern magical traditions. The comic book series *Promethea,* written by practicing magician Alan Moore between 1999 and 2005, explores the power of the human imagination through references to tarot, kabbalah, and other esoteric practices. *The Invisibles,* published from 1994 to 2000, was described by its magician author Grant Morrison (see sidebar) as a "hypersigil" meant to function as both art and a working of Morrison's magic.

Japanese manga (comics) and anime (animation) commonly deal in magical narratives. Since the 1960s, the fantasy subgenre of *mahō shōjo* (magical girl) has featured stories of everyday schoolgirls who can transform into powerful magicians and heroines, starting with 1966's *Mahōtsukai Sarī* (*Sally the Witch*), inspired in part by *Bewitched* (see page 330). In the 1990s, the genre was buoyed by the global phenomenon *Bishōjo Senshi Sērā Mūn* (*Sailor Moon*).

Both anime and manga make ample use of magical otherworlds. In the subgenre known as *isekai,* characters inexplicably find themselves in alternate realities and must complete a grand quest to return to their former lives. In some works, such as Rumiko Takahashi's manga *Inuyasha,* the main character is transported to another time period; in others, such as Yuu Watase's manga series *Fushigi Yûgi (The Mysterious Play),* characters are transported into a book.

∧ The *Sailor Moon* anime franchise remains a globally influential example of the *mahō shōjo* (magical girl) fantasy subgenre.

STAIRWAY TO HEAVEN

Rock-and-Roll & the Occult

In 1967, the Beatles released the psychedelic rock–styled album *Sgt. Pepper's Lonely Hearts Club Band,* with cover art featuring a collage of famous figures from history. Staring out from the back row was the infamous wide-eyed gaze of Aleister Crowley, the 20th century's most notorious occult figure (see page 185). Crowley, who wore his moniker of "the world's wickedest man" proudly, preached self-interest and indulgences. His tagline "Do what thou wilt" resonated with the post–World War II counterculture.

As the world's biggest rock stars worshipped Indian gurus, quoted mythology, and read about the universe's unexplained mysteries, their fans followed enthusiastically. Young people running away from religion found rock-and-roll, and the music was no longer just fun or romantic; it was spiritual, transcendent, and dark. The Rolling Stones threaded satanic themes and black magic through their songs and albums, and rumors flew that they were dabbling in witchcraft.

Led Zeppelin guitarist Jimmy Page purchased Crowley's former home and had "Do what thou wilt" etched into the vinyl of the *Led Zeppelin III* album (1970). Astrology, mythical creatures, and demonic figures were all part of the band's repertoire. Page told reporters he believed in the supernatural and had attended séances. "I do not worship the Devil," he said to *Rolling Stone* in 1976. "But magic does intrigue me."

Throughout the 1970s, magical conspiracy theories would find a life of their own as fans scoured songs for hidden meanings. Some claimed "backmasked" secret messages could be revealed by playing songs in reverse, including purported satanic messages in Led Zeppelin's "Stairway to Heaven." These ideas helped turn rock into a cultural revolution. The genre had long been mainstream, but with magic it became edgy and different—even dangerous.

< American guitarist Jimi Hendrix toyed with occult beliefs, alluding to them in his song "Voodoo Chile" and once describing witchcraft as a "form of exploration and imagination."

That danger came to a head in the late 1960s when cult leader Charles Manson directed his followers to commit murder, claiming that subliminal messages in the Beatles' *White Album* urged a violent revolution. Fear of these dark undercurrents reached a fever pitch in the 1980s with the "satanic panic," which saw both media and law enforcement issuing baseless warnings about occult organizations involved in devil worship and ritualistic child sexual abuse.

Aleister Crowley, long dead, continued to draw the interest of rock stars, including David Bowie, who sang in 1971's "Quick-sand," "I'm closer to the Golden Dawn / Immersed in Crowley's uniform / Of imagery." A statue of Beethoven that some believed was Crowley appeared on a Doors' album cover, and Ozzy Osbourne wrote a song called "Mr. Crowley." His heavy-metal band, Black Sabbath, is thought to have taken its cues from an American rock band called Coven, which leaned heavily into black magic themes and may have originated the "sign of the horns" hand gesture.

It was—as folk singer Donovan crooned in his 1966 hit of the same name—the "season of the witch."

∧ By including famed occultist Aleister Crowley (top row, second from left) in the album art for *Sgt. Pepper's Lonely Hearts Club Band,* the Beatles sparked endless conspiracy theories.

PLAYING GAMES

Bards, Thieves & Paladins

The 1970s saw the emergence of a new, mystical game: one where players donned the roles of adventurers and fought their way through epic quests set within worlds of magic, mystery, and mayhem. This game, known as Dungeons & Dragons (D&D), forever changed the world of role-playing games (RPGs)—and introduced generations to a new mode of magical storytelling.

D&D was the brainchild of war-game enthusiasts Gary Gygax and Dave Arneson, who sought to expand their recreational activities beyond reconstructions of famous historical battles. They built a combat and storytelling system inspired by works of high and heroic fantasy, notably those of J. R. R. Tolkien (see page 324) and Robert E. Howard, who created Conan the Barbarian and pioneered the heroic fantasy subgenre. The first version of D&D was released in 1974; the property is now on its fifth edition.

PROFILE

MAGIC: THE GATHERING

One of the world's most popular modern card games, Magic: The Gathering combines brilliantly varied gameplay with deep magical lore. Players are styled as powerful wizards known as "planeswalkers" who battle one another in two-player duels. Each player has a deck of 60 or more cards that represent spells the player can cast to hurt the other player or bend the game's rules in a dizzying number of ways. Victory goes to the player who reduces the other player's "life total" from 20 to zero. Created by mathematician Richard Garfield, Magic: The Gathering was first released by game publishers Wizards of the Coast in 1993. There are now more than 28,000 unique Magic cards, each with different rule texts and effects. Well over 20 billion cards have been printed in all.

Text on the cards in Magic: The Gathering modifies gameplay rules on the fly.

In a D&D campaign, which often plays out over many individual sessions, players take on the roles of magical characters with diverse strengths and weaknesses, ranging from brute strength to spell-casting aptitude. The group of players must cooperatively complete various missions, guided and thwarted in equal measure by the puller of the plot's many strings: the campaign's Dungeon Master, who presides over each session. Attacks and interactions depend on a combination of the characters' traits and the outcomes of dice rolls.

D&D grew in popularity among teens in the late 1970s and 1980s, and it soon found itself the subject of public controversy, as Christian organizations baselessly accused the game of spreading satanic influence and causing a string of murders and suicides. This blowback is now regarded as a moral panic, an offshoot of the broader "satanic panic" (see page 335).

Today, millions play D&D in person, and the game's settings and mechanics have inspired many RPG video games. Since 1998, the video game series *Baldur's Gate* has been set within the Forgotten Realms, a high-fantasy world created by Ed Greenwood that has been a default D&D setting since the 1980s. Since 1994, *The Elder Scrolls* series of action RPGs has taken players to the magical continent of Tamriel, a world rife with swords, sorcery, and mythical creatures. *World of Warcraft,* first released in 2004, still courts millions of monthly users who form guilds to complete cooperative quests.

At its core, D&D has always been about live, collaborative storytelling. Fifty years on, that storytelling is on display in "actual-play" broadcasts of D&D campaigns played by improvisational actors. Shows such as *Critical Role* and *Dimension 20* reach audiences of millions and have expanded to include everything from animated TV series to live sessions in New York City's Madison Square Garden and London's Wembley Arena.

∧ Role-playing games have inspired many "cosplayers" to dress as their favorite characters, such as *World of Warcraft* character Sylvanas Windrunner.

#WITCHTOK TRENDING

Witchcraft in the Digital Age

Wicca has long been seen as a solitary practice, and the internet quickly became its most accessible temple. On platforms like YouTube, TikTok, and Reddit, witches converge to share spells, history, and community, while new witches find mentors and resources. Thanks to social media, "baby witches"—those just starting to explore an interest in witchcraft—may identify with an endless variety of styles, from kitchen witch (someone who incorporates magic into cooking) to sea witch (one with a strong connection to water and the ocean). For every field of interest, podcasts, apps, and witch news services deliver the latest information.

On TikTok, the #WitchTok hashtag is attached to videos with tens of billions of views and counting. Tags such as #spirituality and #crystals guide users into dozens of avenues to suit different needs. "Manifesting" influencers provide spells for things like getting someone to text you back, while creators of spell jars offer guides to mixing the perfect brew to reach any goal.

PROFILE

GREEN WITCH MOVEMENT

Wiccan beliefs are deeply connected to nature, but green witches take this connection a step further. Like other variants of Wicca (see page 292), this movement practices rituals, spells, and sabbats in its own way. With beliefs rooted in the power of the earth, similar to those of the Druids (see page 154), green witch rituals revolve around flowers, herbs, and other plants, and their tools come from natural found objects. To connect with the spirit world, they commune with animal or plant guides. Most important to green witches are the historical ways plants have been used for healing (see page 282). Often they grow and harvest their own herbs, like purifying white sage and the natural antidepressant Saint-John's-Wort, for use in potions and spells.

Bundles of sage and crystals are potent ingredients in the Wiccan toolbox.

Why has witchcraft struck a chord in the digital age? Academic research is sparse, but perhaps young people who have been dealt an uncertain future seek to bring order to the chaos by clinging to a type of optimism that may not be entirely rational. In other words: If the typical ways of pursuing goals aren't working out, perhaps a spell or an altar can change the game.

The desire to use witchcraft as a way to create change in a world where the individual has little control is as old as time. For decades, Wiccans have harnessed magic as a tool for political and social resistance. In 1968, a group called the Women's International Terrorist Conspiracy from Hell (WITCH) used witchcraft to rail against politics, sexism, and capitalism. Nearly 300 years after the Salem witch trials, self-proclaimed witches gathered on Wall Street in 1968 and performed a zap—a mixture of witchcraft and protest—to erase the power of money and gold. They pioneered the concept of a large-scale hex, hexing President Richard Nixon after he launched an invasion of Cambodia. More recently, witches have used social media sites like X to arrange hexes on powerful entities like the Supreme Court, U.S. police forces, Wall Street, and President Donald Trump.

Proponents argue that social media has brought pagan and Wiccan beliefs to a wider, more diverse audience, and that it has allowed witches of all varieties to network and see themselves represented. But not all adherents find the internet a helpful tool; some consider it a passing trend that allows anyone to call themselves a witch, or a platform that promotes consumerism. Others worry that witchcraft has gotten too mainstream, diluting its power. But it seems both sides can agree on one thing: Witchcraft has never been more popular.

∧ Wiccans have a long history of social protest; here, a group gathers at the 2017 March for Science.

ENCHANTING TRAVEL

Magic, it seems, is everywhere. So how can we see it out in the world? In our modern age, the concept of magic ranges from profound spiritual beliefs and ritual practices to performances of one of humanity's most mysterious and misunderstood art forms.

Many destinations around the globe lay claim to a "magical" heritage, and each of these spots will educate, entertain, and enrich the lives of the magically curious.

1 LOS ANGELES, CA, U.S.A.
The City of Angels is home to the members-only Magic Castle, a private club and the world's most prestigious magic performance venue.

2 LAS VEGAS, NV, U.S.A.
Sin City is a global mecca for performance magic, especially grand stage illusions, and home to the International Museum and Library of the Conjuring Arts. (p. 317)

3 NEW ORLEANS, LA, U.S.A.
Long associated with vodou, the Big Easy has been a major center of modern magic and witchcraft and hosts the annual Hex Fest.

4 COLON, MI, U.S.A.
The "Magic Capital of the World," this small Michigan town of 1,200 has four magic theaters and Lakeside Cemetery, where more than 45 magicians are buried.

5 LILY DALE, NY, U.S.A.
This hamlet is the largest home of the Spiritualist movement, with thousands of visitors coming through annually to attend lectures and consult with mediums.

6 SALEM, MA, U.S.A.
The setting of an infamous series of witch trials in 1692 and 1693, "Witch City" is a major tourism attraction for all things witchcraft. (p. 169)

7 MEXICO CITY, MEXICO
Home of the Mercado Sonora, a city-run traditional market where vendors sell supplies for mystical practices and Indigenous Mexican religions. Wares range from incense to handicrafts and sacrificial animals.

8 CATEMACO, MEXICO
This small town, host to an annual magic conference, gained a reputation as the "witchcraft capital of Mexico" in the 1970s after celebrated local sorcerer Gonzalo Aguirre began organizing Black Masses there.

9 LA PAZ, BOLIVIA
The Bolivian capital is home to the Mercado de las Brujas (Witches' Market), where shoppers can stock up on supplies for rituals of Bolivia's Indigenous Aymara peoples—including offerings to Pachamama, the goddess of the earth.

10 STONEHENGE, WILTSHIRE, ENGLAND, U.K.

A monument to the spiritual beliefs of ancient British peoples, the site is a focal point for modern paganism.

11 BASINGSTOKE, ENGLAND, U.K.

For more than 20 years, the organizers of Witchfest have staged a multiday festival featuring talks, workshops, live music, and a mead-slinging bar.

12 LONDON, ENGLAND, U.K.

Some of 20th-century occultism's biggest names passed through the city's magic bookshops, including Watkins Books and the Atlantis Bookshop.

13 PARIS, FRANCE

The birthplace of modern stage magic, the French capital is home to the longest continuously operated magic store in the world: Mayette Magie Moderne, in the city's Latin Quarter.

14 TURIN, ITALY

Piazza Statuto—formerly a Roman necropolis and Turin's gallows—is the city's "black heart," with a central monument dedicated to workers who died building the Fréjus tunnel connecting Italy and France.

15 BERLIN, GERMANY

Magicum is a one-of-a-kind museum with some 450 exhibits on all aspects of magic and mysticism through the ages.

16 BLÅ JUNGFRUN, SWEDEN

Since the 16th century, local folklore has maintained that witches gathered on this island on Maundy Thursday to worship the devil. You can also explore a mysterious rock labyrinth here.

17 DELPHI, GREECE

The center of the ancient Greek world is now a UNESCO World Heritage site, with long-running archaeological excavations revealing the sanctuary's hidden past.

18 LOMÉ, TOGO

The Togolese capital is home to the Akodessewa Fetish Market, the world's largest supply source for vodou rituals. Goods include a large variety of dried or otherwise preserved animal carcasses.

19 GIZA, EGYPT

The Pyramids at Giza are monuments to the mighty Egyptian pharaohs who built them and meccas for occultists and New Age spiritualists who see them as sources of great spiritual energy. (p. 38)

20 BADODIYA, INDIA

Every Diwali, villagers fill the streets of this small village with magic tricks and impossible-looking displays of precariously balanced motorbikes.

21 MAYONG, INDIA

For centuries, this city and the surrounding region, home to many practicing witch doctors today, have been held as the "Land of Black Magic."

22 BUSAN, SOUTH KOREA

South Korea is a global superpower in the modern art of magic. The annual Busan International Magic Festival is one of the largest gatherings of its kind in Asia.

23 TOKYO, JAPAN

The Japanese capital hosts a one-of-a-kind expression of the magical arts: small, intimate magic bars, where world-class magicians perform tricks over cocktails.

CONTRIBUTORS

PATRICIA S. DANIELS is a writer and editor with a particular interest in science and history. She has written or co-authored dozens of books and special-edition magazines for National Geographic, Macmillan, Time Incorporated, Encyclopedia Britannica, and other publishers. Among her titles are *National Geographic Mind, The New Solar System,* and *The Body: A Complete User's Guide.* Pat lives in Pennsylvania with her college-professor husband and two pudgy cats.

MICHAEL GRESHKO, an amateur magician since middle school, was nearly kicked out of a driver's education class over a card trick (the instructor branded him a "warlock"). Now a journalist, Greshko has written for publications including the *New York Times,* the *Washington Post, Science, Scientific American,* and *National Geographic,* where he worked as a staff science writer for seven years and co-authored the *National Geographic Stargazer's Atlas.* In 2023, he

and Nina Strochlic received a National Arts & Entertainment Journalism Award for their coverage of magic. Michael lives in Washington, D.C., with wife Jaclyn, son Andrew, and dog Luna.

Growing up in Oregon, **NINA STROCHLIC** dressed as Harry Houdini for a fourth-grade career day and dreamed of becoming a professional psychic. Instead, she became a journalist and has reported from 23 countries as a former staff writer for *National Geographic* magazine. She previously worked at *Newsweek* and the Daily Beast and has been a fellow with the International Women's Media Foundation and the Alicia Patterson Foundation. Her writing has been featured in anthologies and adapted into podcasts, television episodes, and social media campaigns. She co-founded the Milaya Project, a nonprofit working with South Sudanese refugees in Uganda. She lives in Brooklyn. ▪

EXPERT CONSULTANT

CHRIS GOSDEN has been at the University of Oxford for the last 30 years, first as a curator-lecturer at the Pitt Rivers Museum and then as a professor of European archaeology, a role he retired from in 2023. Gosden has carried out archaeological fieldwork in Papua New Guinea, Borneo, Turkmenistan, and Britain, among other places. He has led research projects on the history of the English landscape (published by Oxford University Press in 2021 as *English Landscapes and Identities*) and on Celtic art in both Brit-

ain and Europe, including Eurasian links. His most recent work is *The History of Magic* (Penguin, 2020). His current project is tentatively titled *Humans: The First Seven Million Years.* He is a trustee of the British Museum, a member of the Board of Visitors of the Ashmolean Museum, and a fellow of a number of learned societies, including the British Academy and the Society of Antiquaries. His major current research project focuses on horsepower, with fieldwork in Mongolia and China. ▪

Top: Persian winged sun disk; Bottom: Tlingit amulet of whale and raptor

ILLUSTRATIONS CREDITS

Shutterstock; 119 (UP), Vaclav Zilvar/Adobe Stock; 119 (CTR LE), svarshik/Adobe Stock; 119 (CTR), Ashmolean Museum/Bridgeman Images; 119 (LO LE), adi92/Shutterstock; 119 (LO RT), The Metropolitan Museum of Art; 120, Saint Louis Art Museum/Bridgeman Images; 121, Nicolas Jallot/Gamma-Rapho/Getty Images; 122, Bridgeman Images; 123, Bridgeman Images; 124 (ALL), Bridgeman Images; 125, Charles Walker Collection/Alamy Stock Photo; 126–127 (all major arcana), josemanuel 246/Adobe Stock; 127 (UP RT), manuta/Adobe Stock; 128, Ullstein Bild Dtl./Getty Images; 129, General Photographic Agency/Moviepix/Getty Images; 130, Sergey Kamshylin/Adobe Stock; 131, John Margolies/LOC; 132, Eric Risberg/AP Photo; 133, photology1971/Adobe Stock.

CHAPTER FOUR: MAGI, WITCHES & OCCULT SOCIETIES

134–135, Guildhall Library & Art Gallery/Heritage Images/Hulton Archive/Getty Images; 136, Minneapolis Institute of Art; 137, Newberry Library/Bridgeman Images; 138, Gideon Hartman/Hebrew University/Getty Images News; 139, British Library Archive/Bridgeman Images; 140, NPL-DeA Picture Library/Bridgeman Images; 141, The Metropolitan Museum of Art; 142, kasbah/Adobe Stock; 143, The Metropolitan Museum of Art; 144, Art Institute Chicago; 145, incamera stock/Alamy Stock Photo; 146, NPL-DeA Picture Library/Bridgeman Images; 147, Birmingham Museums and Art Gallery/Bridgeman Images; 148, steve estvanik/Shutterstock; 149, CM Dixon/Print Collector/Hulton Archive/Getty Images; 150, Luisa Ricciarini/Bridgeman Images; 151, Gali Tibbon/AFP/Getty Images; 152, Logic Images/Alamy Stock Photo; 153, Ghigo Roli/Bridgeman Images; 154, The Metropolitan Museum of Art; 155, CSG CIC Glasgow Museums Collection/Bridgeman Images; 156, British Library Archive/Bridgeman Images; 157, Ann Ronan Pictures/Print Collector/Getty Images; 158, The Metropolitan Museum of Art; 159, The Metropolitan Museum of Art; 160, NPL-DeA Picture Library/Bridgeman Images; 161, Jenne Gustafsson/TT via AP; 162 (UP RT), Boltin Picture Library/Bridgeman Images; 162 (CTR LE), Kate Smith/iStock/Getty Images; 162 (CTR), Historic Images/Alamy Stock Photo; 162 (CTR RT), Sabena Jane Blackbird/Alamy Stock Photo; 162 (LO LE), Bridgeman Images; 162 (LO CTR), The Print Collector/Alamy Stock Photo; 162 (LO RT), Thomas Roslund/Adobe Stock; 163 (UP RT), Ashmolean Museum/Bridgeman Images; 163 (stones), New Africa/Adobe Stock; 165, Fine Art Images/Bridgeman Images; 166, Bridgeman Images; 167, British Library Archive/Bridgeman Images; 168, New York Historical Society/Bridgeman Images; 169, sunnychicka/Adobe Stock; 172, Werner Forman/Universal Images Group/Getty Images; 173, Universal Art Archive/Alamy Stock Photo; 174, Werner Forman/Universal Images Group/Getty Images; 175, G. Dagli Orti/NPL-DeA Picture Library/Bridgeman Images; 176, British Library Archive/Bridgeman Images; 177, The Metropolitan Museum of Art; 179, National Gallery of Art; 180, Archives Charmet/Bridgeman Images; 181, Museum of Freemasonry, Reproduced by permission of the Grand Lodge of England/Bridgeman Images; 182, Florilegius/Bridgeman Images; 183, Everett Collection/Bridgeman Images; 184, Charles Walker Collection/Alamy Stock Photo; 185, Bridgeman Images.

CHAPTER FIVE: SPELLS, TOOLS & RITUALS

186–187, Wellcome Collection; 188, The Metropolitan Museum of Art; 189, Archives Charmet/Bridgeman Images; 190–191, The Metropolitan Museum of Art; 192 (CTR LE), The Metropolitan Museum of Art; 192 (LO LE), SSPL/UIG/Bridgeman Images; 192 (CTR), The Metropolitan

Museum of Art; 192 (LO CTR), The Metropolitan Museum of Art; 192 (RT), World History Archive/Alamy Stock Photo; 193 (UP LE), The Metropolitan Museum of Art; 193 (UP CTR), Jenny Tonkin/Adobe Stock; 193 (UP RT), Walters Art Museum; 193 (CTR LE), Walters Art Museum; 193 (CTR), Walters Art Museum; 193 (CTR RT), The Metropolitan Museum of Art; 193 (LO LE), The Metropolitan Museum of Art; 193 (LO CTR), The Metropolitan Museum of Art; 194, The Metropolitan Museum of Art; 195, The Metropolitan Museum of Art; 196 (UP LE), Ekaterina/Adobe Stock; 196 (UP CTR), The Metropolitan Museum of Art; 196 (UP RT), Natural History Museum, London/Bridgeman Images; 196 (CTR), Natural History Museum, London/Bridgeman Images; 196 (CTR RT), Africa Studio/Adobe Stock; 196 (LO LE), The Metropolitan Museum of Art; 196 (LO CTR), The Metropolitan Museum of Art; 196 (LO RT), NickKnight/Shutterstock; 197 (UP LE), Henri Koskinen/Adobe Stock; 197 (UP RT), The Metropolitan Museum of Art; 197 (CTR LE), Björn Wylezich/Adobe Stock; 197 (CTR UP), The Metropolitan Museum of Art; 197 (CTR RT), Björn Wylezich/Adobe Stock; 197 (CTR LO), photoobject/Adobe Stock; 197 (LO LE), Sebastian/Adobe Stock; 197 (LO RT), The Metropolitan Museum of Art; 198, The Metropolitan Museum of Art; 199, Walters Art Museum; 200, Bridgeman Images; 201, Art Institute Chicago; 203, The Metropolitan Museum of Art; 204, G. Dagli Orti/NPL-DeA Picture Library/Bridgeman Images; 205, Chronicle/Alamy Stock Photo; 206, Patrice Cartier/Bridgeman Images; 207, Paul Williams/imageBROKER RF/Getty Images; 208, British Library Archive/Bridgeman Images; 209, The Stapleton Collection/Bridgeman Images; 210, Wellcome Collection; 211 (UP), British Library Archive/Bridgeman Images; 211 (LO), Charles Walker Collection/Alamy Stock Photo; 213, Veneranda Biblioteca Ambrosiana/Mondadori Portfolio/Bridgeman Images; 214 (LE), Universal History Archive/Shutterstock; 214 (UP), Luisa Ricciarini/Bridgeman Images; 214–215 (LO), Album/Alamy Stock Photo; 215 (UP LE), Album/Alamy Stock Photo; 215 (UP RT), Universal History Archive/Shutterstock; 216, Christie's Images/Bridgeman Images; 217, Hulton Fine Art Collection/Getty Images; 218, Wellcome Collection; 219, Christie's Images/Bridgeman Images; 220, Heritage Image Partnership Ltd/Alamy Stock Photo; 221, The Holbarn Archive/Bridgeman Images; 222, Corbis Historical/Getty Images; 223, British Library Archive/Bridgeman Images; 224 (UP RT), Giancarlo Costa/Bridgeman Images; 224 (LE), SSPL/UIG/Bridgeman Images; 224 (LO CTR), F2G/Shutterstock; 224 (CTR RT), The Metropolitan Museum of Art; 224 (LO RT), SSPL/UIG/Bridgeman Images; 225 (UP LE, BOTH), The Metropolitan Museum of Art; 225 (UP RT), SSPL/UIG/Bridgeman Images; 225 (CTR), SSPL/UIG/Bridgeman Images; 225 (LO LE), SSPL/Science Museum/Getty Images; 225 (CTR RT), Militarist/Shutterstock; 225 (LO), SSPL/UIG/Bridgeman Images; 226, xiaoliangge/Adobe Stock; 227, Nick Servian/Bridgeman Images; 228, alexey_arz/Adobe Stock.

CHAPTER SIX: GHOSTS & THE WORLD OF THE DEAD

230–231, Bianca/Adobe Stock; 232, The Metropolitan Museum of Art; 233, Wellcome Collection; 234, Natural History Museum, London/Bridgeman Images; 235, Kenneth Garrett/GEO Image Collection/Bridgeman Images; 236, The Metropolitan Museum of Art; 237, The Metropolitan Museum of Art; 238, Vladimir Melnik/Adobe Stock; 239 (BOTH), The Metropolitan Museum of Art; 240 (ALL), The Metropolitan Museum of Art; 241 (UP LE), Bonhams, London, UK/Bridgeman Images; 241 (CTR LE), The Metropolitan Museum of Art; 241 (CTR RT), The Metropolitan Museum of Art; 241 (UP RT), The Metropolitan Museum of Art; 241 (LO LE), The Metropolitan Museum of Art; 241 (LO

CTR), Art Institute Chicago; 241 (LO LE), Walters Art Museum; 243, The Stapleton Collection/Bridgeman Images; 244, Bonhams, London, UK/Bridgeman Images; 245, Duncan Andison/Adobe Stock; 246, British Library Archive/Bridgeman Images; 247, PVDE/Bridgeman Images; 248, Shutterstock; 249, The Holbarn Archive/Bridgeman Images; 250, FilmPublicityArchive/United Archives/Hulton Archive/Getty Images; 251 (LO), Luisa Ricciarini/Bridgeman Images; 251 (UP), Carl/Adobe Stock; 252, Mauritius Images GmbH/Alamy Stock Photo; 253, Estate of Gerald Bloncourt/Bridgeman Images; 254, GraphicaArtis/Bridgeman Images; 255, The Metropolitan Museum of Art; 256, Volgi archive/Alamy Stock Photo; 257, The Metropolitan Museum of Art; 258, Fine Art Images/Bridgeman Images; 259, Fine Art Images/Bridgeman Images; 260, fergregory/Adobe Stock; 261, British Library Archive/Bridgeman Images; 262, British Library Archive/Bridgeman Images; 264 (LE INSET), Fototeca Gilardi/Bridgeman Images; 264 (UP), Colin Waters/Alamy Stock Photo; 264 (LO CTR), Bridgeman Images; 264 (LO RT), Bridgeman Images; 265 (UP LE BOTH), Historia/Shutterstock; 265 (RT BOTH), Charles Walker Collection/Alamy Stock Photo; 265 (LO LE), Peter Newark American Pictures/Bridgeman Images; 266, Neil Setchfield/Alamy Stock Photo; 267, Dondi Tawatao/Getty Images; 268 (UP LE), The Metropolitan Museum of Art; 268 (LO LE), Universal History Archive/Shutterstock; 268 (CTR), The Metropolitan Museum of Art; 268 (UP RT), The Metropolitan Museum of Art; 268 (LO CTR), Art Institute Chicago; 268 (LO RT), The Metropolitan Museum of Art; 269 (UP LE), Bridgeman Images; 269 (UP RT), Art Institute Chicago; 269 (CTR LE), The Metropolitan Museum of Art; 269 (CTR UP) The Metropolitan Museum of Art; 269 (CTR), The Metropolitan Museum of Art; 269 (LO CTR BOTH), Cleveland Museum of Art; 269 (LO RT), Tarker/Bridgeman Images.

CHAPTER SEVEN: HEALING, DREAMS & THE MIND
270–271, Sylvain Sonnet/The Image Bank RF/Getty Images; 272, Dmytro/Adobe Stock; 273, Bridgeman Images; 274, The Metropolitan Museum of Art; 275, Natural History Museum, London/Bridgeman Images; 276, Archives Charmet/Bridgeman Images; 277, The Metropolitan Museum of Art; 278, Pictures from History/Bridgeman Images; 279, Pierce Archive LLC/Buyenlarge/Getty Images; 280, Fine Art Images/Bridgeman Images; 281, Pictures from History/Bridgeman Images; 282 (UP RT), Soho A Studio/Adobe Stock; 282 (UP CTR RT), spline_x/Adobe Stock; 282 (CTR LE), shansh23/Shutterstock; 282 (CTR LO), Ruckszio/Adobe Stock; 282 (CTR RT), emberiza/Adobe Stock; 282 (LO LE), Gleti/Adobe Stock; 282 (LO RT), Amphawan/Adobe Stock; 283 (UP LE), volff/Adobe Stock; 283 (UP RT), Andris Tkachenko/Adobe Stock; 283 (UP CTR LE), Levon/Adobe Stock; 283 (UP CTR), photohampster/Adobe Stock; 283 (CTR LE), kolesnikovserg/Adobe Stock; 283 (CTR), vainillaychile/Adobe Stock; 283 (CTR RT), Scisetti Alfio/Adobe Stock; 283 (LO LE), Dionisvera/Adobe Stock; 283 (LO RT), zcy/Adobe Stock; 284, National Library of Medicine; 285, Stefano Bianchetti/Bridgeman Images; 286, Cleveland Museum of Art; 287, Blank Archives/Hulton Archive/Getty Images; 288, nikonka1/Shutterstock; 289, Andrew Matthews/PA Images/Getty Images; 290, Andre Coelho/Getty Images; 291, Snowbelle/Adobe Stock; 292, ANL/Shutterstock; 293, Werner Forman/Universal Images Group/Getty Images; 294, TopFoto/Bridgeman Images; 295, Louise OLIGNY/Gamma-Rapho/Getty Images; 296, sallydexter/Adobe Stock; 297, The Maas Gallery, London/Bridgeman Images; 298, World History Archive/Alamy Stock Photo; 299, biondo3rd/Adobe Stock; 300, Mondadori Portfolio/Electa/Claudio Franzini/Bridgeman Images; 301, mofles/iStock/Getty

Images; 302, Dublin City Gallery the Hugh Lane/Bridgeman Images; 304, The Metropolitan Museum of Art; 305, Fototeca Gilardi/Bridgeman Images.

CHAPTER EIGHT: MAGIC IN POPULAR CULTURE
306–307, Wayne Anderson/Bridgeman Images; 308, Potter and Potter Auctions/Gado/Getty Images; 309, Library of Congress; 310, British Library Archive/Bridgeman Images; 311, Martin Bergsma/Adobe Stock; 312, Library of Congress; 313, The Picture Art Collection/Alamy Stock Photo; 314, Potter and Potter Auctions/Gado/Getty Images; 315, British Library Archive/Bridgeman Images; 316, The Advertising Archives/Bridgeman Images; 317, Terry Fincher/Keystone/Getty Images; 318, Library of Congress; 319, Library of Congress; 320, Library of Congress; 322 (LE), Christie's Images/Bridgeman Images; 322 (UP), Lotus_studio/Shutterstock; 322 (UP RT), Potter and Potter Auctions/Gado/Getty Images; 322 (CTR LO), Marc Tielemans/Alamy Stock Photo; 322 (LO RT), Potter and Potter Auctions/Gado/Getty Images; 323 (UP LE), Potter and Potter Auctions/Gado/Getty Images; 323 (UP RT), Potter and Potter Auctions/Gado/Getty Images; 323 (UP CTR), Potter and Potter Auctions/Gado/Getty Images; 323 (CTR LE) The Metropolitan Museum of Art; 323 (LO LE), Potter and Potter Auctions/Gado/Getty Images; 323 (LO CTR LE), Potter and Potter Auctions/Gado/Getty Images; 323 (LO CTR, LO RT), Potter and Potter Auctions/Gado/Getty Images; 324, Look and Learn/Bridgeman Images; 325, Bridgeman Images; 326, Tanya Sid/Shutterstock; 327, Walt Disney Pictures/Walden Media/Kobal/Shutterstock; 329, Moviestore/Shutterstock; 330, HA/THA/Shutterstock; 331, Mgm/Kobal/Shutterstock; 332, Snap/Shutterstock; 333, Netflix/THA/Shutterstock; 334, Mark and Colleen Hayward/Redferns/Getty Images; 335, Vinyls/Alamy Stock Photo; 336 (ALL), Simon/Adobe Stock; 339, Karen Wong/Alamy Stock Photo.

342 (UP), Kambiz Pourghanad/Shutterstock; 342 (LO), The Metropolitan Museum of Art; 345, Minneapolis Institute of Art.

> An Igbo figure of water spirit Mami Wata

fertility, reproduction and, 274–77

Hindu, 278–79, 286

history of, 13, 272

humors and, 280

magi, witches, and shamans' role in, 139, 140, 143–44, 158–59, 169, 175, 182–83, 281, 284–85

medieval medicine for, 280–83

meditation and, 273, 279, 287, 298, 301, 305

New Age, 286–87, 290, 305

pagan and neo-pagan, 288–91, 295

places of power for, 20, 24

plants for, 281–83, 284–85, 287, 301, 338

spells, tools, and rituals for, 188, 191, 194–97, 206, 218, 272, 274–76, 278–83, 287–91

Wiccan, 295, 338. *See also* Wicca

Hecate, 146

hei-tiki pendant, **192**

Heka, 240–**41**

henbane, **282**

Hendriks, Anneken, 170

Henettawy, coffin of, **255**

Henning, Doug, 331

Henry IV, 221

Henry VI, 221

herbal medicine, 281–**83, 284**–85, 287, 301, **338**

Herbert, George, 254

Hermes Trismegistus, 220

Hermetic Order of the Golden Dawn, 122, **125, 184**–85, 255

hermit (tarot card), **126**

Herodotus, 69, 143

Heron-Allen, Edward, 133

Herrmann, Adelaide, **314**

Herrmann, Alexander, 314, 316

Hesiod, 72, 75

Hess, Rudolf, 129

hierophant (tarot card), **126**

high priestess (tarot card), **127**

Hilazon Tachtit funerary artifacts, **138**

Hinduism, 184, 193, **278–79,** 286, 301

Hippocrates, 280

His Dark Materials trilogy (Pullman), 327

Hitchcock, Ethan Allen, 222

Hitler, Adolf, 128–29

Hobbit, The (Tolkien), 326

Hockett, Mary, 89

Homer, 31, 98, 146, 190, 283

hoodoo, **182–83**

Hopewell Ceremonial Earthworks, 20, **48–49**

Hopkins, Matthew, 89, 169

Horne, Janet, 178

Horned God, 292–93

horoscopes, 112, 117, 130, 175–76

horses, **109**

Hortus Sanitatus, 76

Horus, **240**

Houdini, Harry, **15,** 263–**65,** 308, 313, 316, **318–21,** 322

hourglasses, **224**

House, 328

House on Haunted Hill, 328

Howard, Robert E., 336

huacas, 52–53

Huei Teocalli, 55

Huitzilopochtli, 20, 51, 54–55

Humāyūn, 175–76

humors, 280

Hurston, Zora Neale, **183**

Hyakki, Komatsuya, 144

Hy-Brasil, 42

hydria, **98**

Hyppolite, Hector, 253

I

Ibn Sina (aka Avicenna), 280

I Ching, **107**

Iliad, The (Homer), 31, 98, 283

Illuminati, 181

immortality, 144–45, 218–**19,** 278

Inca empire, 20, 52–53

incantation bowls, **194**

incense, **300**

India

divination in, 133

healing and health in, 277–79, 287

magic in popular culture in, **312,** 316–17, 341

mythical creatures in, 79

occult movements in, 184

places of power in, **27**

spells, tools, and rituals in, 192, 204, 218

witch hunts/trials in, 169, **171**

Indigenous Australians. *See* Aboriginal Australians

Indigenous North Americans

astrology of, **137**

healing and health among, 282, 287, 301

magi, witches, and shaman of, 139, 182–83

mythical creatures of, 66, 84–87, 93

places of power for, 14, 20, 48–55

spells, tools, and rituals of, 192

Iniskim Umaapi medicine wheel, 20, 52

Injalak Hill, 21, **24–25**

inscriptions, 194–**95,** 196, 198–99, **216**

inuhariko, **193**

Inuyasha, 333

Invisibles, The, 333

Ireland, 154, 156, 242–**45.** *See also* Celts; Druids

Isidore of Seville, 79

Isis, 148–**49,** 240–**41, 295**

Islam, 110–13, 210, 220

islands, legendary, 42–47, 145

Isle of Demons, 44

Israel, 234

Italy. *See also* Roman empire

astrology and zodiac in, 119

ghosts and the dead in, 254

healing and health in, 276, 281–82

magic in popular culture in, 341

mythical creatures in, 70, 73

spells, tools, and rituals in, 191, 202

tarot cards in, 122, 124–26

Itzamnaaj, 214

Ix Chel, 214, 215

J

Jābir ibn Hayyān ("Geber"), **220–21**

jack-o'-lanterns, **245**

Jahāngīr, 174

jalap root, **182**

Jamaica, 120

James VI (later James I), 172, 175, 176

Jammeh, Yahya, 169

Japan

divination in, 13, 104, 106–7

ghosts and the dead in, 256, 305

healing and health in, 301

magic in popular culture in, 328, 333, 341

mythical creatures in, 82–83

places of power in, 21, 56–57

spells, tools, and rituals in, 193, **199**

jasper, **197**

Jemisin, N. K., 327

Jesus Christ, **143,** 152–**53,** 202–3

jinn/jinni (genies), **10, 204, 256**

Johnson, Robert, 206

John the Baptist, 201

Joyeuse, 199

Judaism, **13,** 122, 126, 128, **150–52,** 210. *See also* kabbalah

judgment (tarot card), **127**

jugglers, 312–13

juju, 158

Jung, Carl, 133, **305**

justice (tarot card), **127**

K

kabbalah, 122, 126, 181, 184

Kamal-ol-Molk, 95

kappa, 83

Penn & Teller, 317
pentacle/pentagram star, **296**
Pepper, John Henry, 310
Pepper's ghosts, **310**
perfume/perfume containers, **7, 274**
Perrault, Charles, 206
Persian simurgh, **61**
Peru, 170. *See also* Inca empire
Peter and Wendy (Barrie), **324**
Peters, Helen, 263
Petit Albert, 212
petroglyphs, 20, 26–27, 85
Petronilla de Meath, 164
Pettigrew, Thomas, 255
peyote, **282**
Philip II, 269
Philippines, 266–**67**
philosopher's stone, **218,** 221, 222, 283
Picatrix, **14,** 112
pigs, **109**
Pisano, Andrea, 150
Pisces, **118**
Pishra de-Rabbi Hanina ben Dosa, 150
placebo effect, 285, 286, 298
places of power, 16–57
    birth of magic and, 18
    cave and rock art in, 21, 22–27
    figurines in, 18, 24, 28, 31, 38, 48, 56
    Indigenous North American, 14, 20, 48–55
    legendary islands as, 42–47, 145
    map of key, 20–21
    natural spaces as, 52, 56–57
    pyramids as, 21, 38–41, 54–55
    standing stones as, 21, 32–37
    temples as, 16–17, 20–21, 28–31
plague charms, 191
plants, medicinal, 281–**83, 284**–85, 287, 301, **338**
plastromancy, **13,** 104–**05**
Plato, 44, 143
Pliny the Elder, 13, 60, 79, 103, 133, 154, 229, 286
Pliny the Younger, 256
Po Chü-i, 218
Polidori, John, 249, 259
Poltergeist, 328
popular culture, magic in, 306–41
    in comics, anime and manga, 332–33
    dragons as, 306–07
    films of, 321, 326–27, 328–31. *See also* films
    games for, 336–37
    golden age of magic for, 314–17
    history of, 11, 14–15, 308
    Houdini performing, 15, 263–65, 308, 313, 316, 318–21, 322

jugglers and conjurers performing, 312–13
    literary fantasy as, 324–27
    magi and witches as, 294, 296–97, 330–31, 338–39
    magic tricks as, 14, 308–23
    map of, 340–41
    props for, 322–23
    rock-and-roll and, 334–35
    tarot cards as, 125
    televised, 294, 316–17, 330–31, 337
    theater and stage for, 15, 310–21
    vampires as, 251
    Wiccan, 294, 331, 338–39
Posada, José Guadalupe, 266
Potter, Richard, 311
power. *See* objects of power; places of power
Priscus, 199
Promethea, 333
Properties of Animals, The, **80**
Prophéties, Les (Nostredame), **14, 117**
Psellus, Michael, 176
Ptah, **241**
Ptolemy, Claudius, 110, 130
Pueblo settlements, 20, **50–51**
Pulcher, Publius Claudius, 103
Pullman, Philip, 327
pyramids, **12–13,** 21, **38–41,** 54–55, 341
pyromancy, 104
Pythagoras, 149

Q

Qin Shi Huangdi, 218
qitou, **269**
Quetzalcoatl, **66**
Quigley, Joan, **132**–33

R

rabbits, **109**
rain, ritual for, 215
Rainbow Serpent, 66
Ramo Samee, 312
rapid eye movement (REM) sleep, 302
Rasputin (formerly Grigori Novykh), **175**
rats, **89, 108**
rattlesnakes, **85,** 88
ravens, 84, 86–**87, 101,** 103
Reagan, Nancy and Ronald, 132–33
Re-Atum, 240
Red Lady of Paviland, 234
Rees, William Dewi, 302
relics, **200–203, 269**
religion, 11–15. *See also* temples and places of worship; specific religions
Remus, 103

reproduction, **274–77**
retorts, **225**
Revelation (biblical), painting of, 179
Revelation: The Birth of a New Age (Spangler), 15
Richardson, Mark Wyman, **265**
Rigney, James Oliver, Jr., 326
rituals. *See* spells, tools, and rituals
Rivera, Diego, 266
River Witham sword, 198–99
Robert-Houdin, Jean-Eugène, 14, 311, 314, 318
Robertson, Étienne-Gaspard, 311
Robinson, William Ellsworth ("Chung Ling Soo"), 313
rock-and-roll, 334–**35**
rock art. *See also* gemstones; standing stones
    ancient, 26–27
    cave art as, 21, 22–25
    history of, 12
    magi, witches, and shaman and, 22, 24, 139
    petroglyphs as, 20, 26–27, 85
    runes on, **161–63**
Rök stone, **161**
role-playing games, 336–**37**
Rolling Stones, The, **334**
Roman empire
    divination in, 101–03, **102**
    Druids observed by, 154
    ghosts and the dead in, 256
    healing and health in, 274, 280–82
    magi and witches in, **146–49,** 172
    magic tricks in, 310
    mythical creatures in, 13, 68, 72–75, 76, 79
    spells, tools, and rituals in, 194, **196,** 216, 274
    standing stones in, 35
Romulus, 103
Romuva, 291
Roosevelt, Franklin Delano, 191
roosters, **96, 109**
rope trick, **312**
rosemary, **283**
Rosy Cross, **125**
Rothwell, Richard, 259
Rowling, J. K., 222, 327, 331
royal magi, **172–77.** *See also* court priests
rubies, 194, **196**
Rudolf II, 114, 221–22
runes, **161–63**
Russell, George William, 303
Russia, 175, 189, 199, 258, 275

S

Since 1888, the National Geographic Society has funded more than 14,000 research, conservation, education, and storytelling projects around the world. National Geographic Partners distributes a portion of the funds it receives from your purchase to National Geographic Society to support programs including the conservation of animals and their habitats.

National Geographic Partners, LLC
1145 17th Street NW
Washington, DC 20036-4688 USA

Get closer to National Geographic Explorers and photographers, and connect with our global community. Join us today at nationalgeographic.org/joinus

For rights or permissions inquiries, please contact National Geographic Books Subsidiary Rights: bookrights@natgeo.com

Produced by WonderLab Group

Thank you to those who lent their talents to these pages: executive editor Hilary Black; creative director Elisa Gibson; editorial project manager Ashley Leath; senior photo editor Meredith Wilcox; senior cartographer Michael Horner; production editor Becca Saltzman; editorial assistant Margo Rosenbaum; writers Patricia S. Daniels, Michael Greshko, and Nina Strochlic; adviser Chris Gosden; and the team at WonderLab Group, LLC.

At WonderLab: editor Maya Myers; photo editor Annette Kiesow; designer Dawn Ripple McFadin; map editor Mike Boruta; researchers Betsy Levine and Eva Dasher; copy editor Jane Sunderland; proofreaders McKenzie Baker and Pamela Juarez; and indexer Christine Hoskin.

ISBN: 978-1-4262-2401-0
ISBN (special edition): 978-1-4262-2510-9

Printed in South Korea

25/QPSK/1